Farai Chigavazira

The Regulation of Agricultural Subsidies in the World Trade Organization Framework

A Developing Country Perspective

Anchor Academic
Publishing

Chigavazira, Farai: The Regulation of Agricultural Subsidies in the World Trade Organization Framework. A Developing Country Perspective, Hamburg, Anchor Academic Publishing 2016

Buch-ISBN: 978-3-96067-059-9
PDF-eBook-ISBN: 978-3-96067-559-4
Druck/Herstellung: Anchor Academic Publishing, Hamburg, 2016

Bibliografische Information der Deutschen Nationalbibliothek:
Die Deutsche Nationalbibliothek verzeichnet diese Publikation in der Deutschen Nationalbibliografie; detaillierte bibliografische Daten sind im Internet über http://dnb.d-nb.de abrufbar.

Bibliographical Information of the German National Library:
The German National Library lists this publication in the German National Bibliography. Detailed bibliographic data can be found at: http://dnb.d-nb.de

Hermannstal 119k, 22119 Hamburg
http://www.diplomica-verlag.de, Hamburg 2016
Printed in Germany

ABSTRACT

The Agreement on Agriculture (AoA) was adopted to eliminate the illegitimate use of trade-distorting agricultural subsidies and thereby reduce and avoid the negative effects subsidies have on global agricultural trade. However, the AoA has been fashioned in a way that is enabling developed countries to continue high levels of protectionism through subsidization, whilst many developing countries are facing severe and often damaging competition from imports artificially cheapened through subsidies.

The regulation of subsidies in the World Trade Organisation (WTO) has been a highly sensitive issue. This is mainly due to the fear of compromising food security especially by developed countries. Developing countries have suffered negatively from the subsidy programmes of developed countries who continue to subsidize their agricultural sector. This position of the developing countries in the global trade system which has been described as weak, has drawn criticism that the WTO as it currently operates does not protect the interests of the weak developing nations, but rather strengthens the interests of the strong developed nations.

The green box provisions which are specifically designed to regulate payments that are considered trade neutral or minimally trade distorting has grossly been manipulated by developed countries at the mercy of the AoA. Developed countries continue to provide trade distorting subsidies under the guise of green box support. This is defeating the aims and objectives of the AoA.

The study examines the regulation of WTO agricultural subsidies from the developing countries' belvedere. It looks at the problems WTO member states face with trade distorting subsidies, but focuses more on the impact these have on developing states. It scrutinizes the AoA's provisions regulating subsidies with a view to identify any loopholes or shortcomings which undermine the interests and aspirations of developing countries. This is behind the background that some of the provisions of the AoA are lenient towards the needs of developed countries at the expense of developing countries.

DEDICATION

This work is dedicated to Jehovah the Lord God Almighty. I wouldn’t have made it without him.

ACKNOWLEDGEMENTS

This study is a fulfillment of a dream that has been close to my heart and which I have always hoped to achieve. Its achievement would not have been possible without the Lord, God Almighty. I feel very privileged to have had this opportunity.

Writing this dissertation has been a larger task than I had initially anticipated. I owe much to many who contributed to this work. I am particularly indebted to Professor Osode who supported and encouraged me from the beginning and commented on all chapters. This dissertation would never have been finished without his untiring help and capable assistance.

I am similarly indebted to Goven Mbeki Research and Development Centre (GMRDC) for the financial and academic support. I am equally grateful to all members of staff at the University of Fort Hare Nelson Mandela School of Law who assisted me with the research.

My special thanks to my mother Dorothy Chigavazira for giving me the motivation and support to write and complete this piece of work.

Finally I would like to express my gratitude to the Chigavazira family, Machiwana family, Nyatsanza family and all my dear friends and colleagues for being there for me when I needed them and for their unwavering support.

TABLE OF CONTENTS

LIST OF ABBREVIATIONS/ACRONYMS

AB - Appellate Body

AD – Agreement on Antidumping

AoA - Agreement on Agriculture

AU - African Union

CBI – Caribbean Basin Initiative

CVA – Customs Valuation Agreement

DDA – Doha Development Agenda

DSU- Understanding on Rules and Procedures for the Settlement of Disputes

EC - European Community

EU - European Union

FICCI – Federation of Indian Chambers of Commerce and Industry

FTA – Free Trade Agreement

GATS - General Agreement on Trade in Services

GATT - General Agreement on Tariffs and Trade

GSP – Generalized System of Preferences

LDCs – Least Developed Countries

MFN – Most Favored Nation

MTNs – Multilateral Trade Negotiations

NAM – US National Association of Manufacturers

NAMA – Non-Agricultural Market Access

NORAD – Norwegian Agency for Development Cooperation

NTBs – Non Tariff Barriers

PRS – Price Rating System

SCM - Agreement on Subsidies and Countervailing Measures

SDT- Special and Differential Treatment

SSM – Special Safeguard Mechanisms

STEs – State Owned Enterprises

TBT - Technical Barriers to Trade

TPA – Trade Promotion Authority

TRIPS – Agreement on Trade Related Aspects of Intellectual Property Rights

UNCTAD – United Nations Conference on Trade and Development

US - United States

USD – United States Dollar

USTR – United States Trade Representatives

WTO – World Trade Organization

CHAPTER 1

Introduction and Overview of the Study

1 1 BACKGROUND OF AGRICULTURAL SUBSIDIES IN THE WTO

A subsidy in the World Trade Organization (WTO) context may be defined as a financial contribution by a government or a public body, which confers a benefit.[1] Agricultural Subsidies under the WTO legal framework are mainly regulated by three separate agreements. These are the General Agreement on Tariffs and Trade (GATT), the Agreement on Subsidies and Countervailing Measures (SCM) and the Agreement on Agriculture (AoA). Ongoing disputes over subsidies that violate existing WTO rules have led to the largest amount of authorized retaliation in GATT/WTO history.[2] They present more complex issues for policy makers than other instruments subject to GATT/WTO rules[3] because they are used by different countries in pursuit of a variety of objectives.[4] Even though some of the objectives are fully legitimate, this does not make them legal in the WTO legal framework. Subsidies can distort free trade as they are capable of flooding foreign markets with cheap or dumped products and also restrict market access.[5]

The AoA contains a comprehensive outline of rules on agricultural subsidies. On April 14, 1994, trade ministers from more than 100 countries met in Marrakesh, Morocco, and signed "The Final Act embodying the results of the Uruguay Round of Multilateral Negotiations".[6] Prior to the Uruguay Round, agricultural commodities were largely exempted from the application of GATT requirements.[7] In developing countries, the agricultural sector was taxed in order to earn badly

[1] Van Den Bossche *The Law and Policy of the World Trade Organization* (2013) at 560 para 3. A more detailed definition of the concept is found in Article 1.1 of the Subsidies and Countervailing Measures Agreement (SCM) in which the presents of a subsidy is deemed to exist where there is a financial contribution by a government or any public body within the territory of a Member. The SCM agreement further lists examples of when a subsidy is deemed to exist. These include a government practice which involves a direct transfer of funds (e.g. grants, loans, and equity infusion), potential direct transfers of funds or liabilities (e.g. loan guarantees); when government revenue that is otherwise due is foregone or not collected (e.g. fiscal incentives such as tax credits) among others.

[2] Bagwell "Subsidy Agreements" http://www.nber.org/papers/w10292.pdf?new_window=1 (accessed on 27/04/14).

[3] See WTO World Trade Report Subsidies Trade 2006 available at http://www.wto.org/english/res_e/booksp_e/anrep_e/wtr06-2a_e.pdf (accessed on 27/04/14).

[4] In most cases the objectives are fully legitimate and necessary. For example most countries introduce agricultural subsidies to ensure food security and employment security.

[5] WTO "World Trade Report Subsidies and the WTO" 2006 http://www.wto.org/E23B7EF9-82CD-4A8C-8A8D-AD1C1530D902/FinalDownload/DownloadId-04A744801BAC228AE8C05294EA164779/E23B7EF9-82CD-4A8C-8A8D-AD1C1530D902/english/res_e/booksp_e/anrep_e/wtr06-2f_e.pdf . (Accessed on 29/04/14 at 21:19).

[6] WTO "A Summary of the Final Act of the Uruguay Round" at http://www.wto.org/english/docs_e/legal_e/ursum_wp.htm (accessed on 22/04/14).

[7] Gonzalez "Institutionalizing Inequality: The WTO Agreement on Agriculture, Food Security, and Developing Countries" 2002 *Columbia Journal of Environmental Law* 433-489.

needed revenue whilst developed countries utilized a variety of instruments to enhance agricultural production, including export subsidies, import tariffs, import quotas, and other non-tariff barriers.[8] Under the pre-Uruguay Round GATT, agricultural policy in developed countries was characterized by high levels of protectionism and by a transfer of income from urban consumers and tax payers to the agricultural sector.[9] These policies enhanced agricultural production for both domestic and international markets.[10]

In contrast to the trend of agricultural policy in developed countries towards favouring agricultural producers at the expense of urban consumers, agricultural policy in developing countries under the pre-Uruguay Round was characterized by a transfer of income from rural areas to urban areas.[11] Policies that conveyed income from farmers to consumers included taxes on agricultural exports, subsidies on agricultural imports, and the payment to farmers of less than world market prices by state purchasing agencies.[12] In general, developing countries lacked the necessary financial resources to subsidize agriculture[13] and frequently viewed agriculture as less important than industry in the competition for limited government funds and as an important source of revenue for industrialization.[14] The effect of agricultural subsidies employed in developed countries was devastating to free trade and largely prejudiced the developing world.[15]

This led to the proposal of the WTO AoA which was shaped by the intense rivalry between the United States (US) and the European Union (EU) for world agricultural markets.[16] Developing

---

[8] Bilal "Agriculture in a Globalizing World Economy, in Negotiating The Future Of Agricultural Policies; Agricultural Trade And The Millennium WTO Round" as referenced by Gonzalez "Institutionalizing Inequality: The WTO Agreement on Agriculture, Food Security, and Developing Countries" 2002 *Columbia Journal of Environmental Law* 434-489.

[9] Stewart *The GATT Uruguay Round: A Negotiating History 1986-1992* (1993) 120-150.

[10] *Ibid.*

[11] Gonzalez 2002 at 435-489.

[12] Hathaway "Agricultural Liberalization and the Uruguay Round, in The Uruguay Round and the Developing Countries" http://elibrary.worldbank.org/78881611-3465-4346-A23C-5075449F48F1/FinalDownload/DownloadId-F82C89A4285339E02F5C4871F365B28C/78881611-3465-4346-A23C-5075449F48F1/doi/pdf/10.1596/0-8213-3469-7 (accessed on 27/04/14).

[13] *Ibid.*

[14] See Gonzalez 2012 at 444 para 2. Also see Bilal "The Political Economy of Agricultural Policies and Negotiations" 2000 *Kluwer Law International* at 1-13.

[15] See Steward 1993 at 120-150 stating developing countries were responsible for a significant share of global food production, and relied on agriculture as a major source of export earnings. Consequently, they were harmed by tariff and non-tariff barriers that excluded their exports from developed country markets and by subsidies that undermined the competitiveness of developing country exports in world markets.

[16] Schoenbaum "Agricultural Trade Wars: A Threat to the GATT and Global Free Trade" 1993 *GATT and Trade Liberalization in Agriculture* at 93.

countries were almost entirely left out of the negotiating process. The negotiations occurred in the background of robust competition between the United States and the European Union to expand their respective shares of world agricultural markets.[17] The EU had transformed itself from a net food importer to a net food exporter, and was rapidly gaining market share by dumping surplus production on world markets through a combination of domestic price support measures and export subsidies adopted pursuant to its Common Agricultural Policy.[18]

United States on the other hand made agricultural reform a high priority in GATT negotiations because it faced budgetary pressure to reduce agricultural subsidies and it was looking forward to protecting its domestic producers by curbing EU subsidies.[19] This led the EU and the US to be the major players in agricultural negotiations. It is therefore possible that developing countries might have been left out of the negotiations and the AoA addressed the concerns of developed countries and failed to fully address the problems faced by developing countries. It is also likely that the AoA created a biased world agricultural policy which favoured those who were at the centre stage of negotiating and drafting it.[20] The reduction of export subsidies which became the critical issue in the negotiations and the final agreement incorporating agriculture into the multilateral trade regime was a result of compromises between the US and the EU.[21]

The intended objectives of the AoA is to liberalize agricultural trade in three significant respects. First, the Agreement expands market access by requiring the conversion of all Non-Tariff Barriers (NTBs) to tariffs (tariffication) and the binding and reduction of these tariffs.[22] Second, the agreement requires the reduction of both the volume of and expenditures on subsidized exports.[23] Third, the Agreement requires the reduction of trade-distorting domestic subsidies.[24] The Agreement also provides for the negotiation of further agricultural reforms, beginning in early

[17] O'Brien "Subsidy Regulation and State Transformation in North America, The GATT and the EU" 1997 132 carefully describes the conflict between the U.S. and the E.U. over world export markets.
[18] *Ibid.*
[19] See Schoenbaum 1993 at 93-94.
[20] Clapp "Developing Countries and the WTO Agriculture Negotiations" 2006 available at https://www.cigionline.org/sites/default/files/Developing%20Countries%20and%20the%20WTO%20Agriculture%20Negotiations.pdf (accessed on 19/03/14).
[21] *Ibid.*
[22] McNiel "Agricultural Trade Symposium: Furthering the Reforms of Agricultural Policies in the Millennium Round" 2000 *Global Trade* at 41-61. The tariff reduction and other market access obligations are spelled out in individual country schedules rather than in the body of the Agreement. See Agreement on Agriculture article 4.
[23] AoA Part V article 8.
[24] AoA Part IV article 6.

2000, and exempts both domestic subsidies and export subsidies from certain provisions of the GATT 1994 and the SCM agreement until 2003.[25]

However, concerns have been raised that the AoA has been fashioned in a way that is enabling developed countries to continue high levels of protectionism through subsidization, whilst many developing countries are facing severe and often damaging competition, from imports artificially cheapened through subsidies.[26] This problem is supposedly defeating the aims of the Agreement on Agriculture. Agricultural subsides are imposing heavy burdens on developing countries even though they are sometimes legitimately used.[27] This is certainly not surprising as there have been distressing calls about the failure of the world trading system to deliver visible benefits of international trade to the majority of developing countries and address the gap between these nations and developed countries.[28] This position of the developing countries in the global trade system which has been described as weak, has drawn criticism that the WTO as it currently operates does not protect the interests of the weak developing nations, but rather strengthens the interests of the strong developed nations.[29]

In principle the AoA should not lead to adverse effects on developing countries but it should rather facilitate global trade and serve as a means to discipline agricultural subsidies.[30] It is against this background that the AoA must be assessed to find out whether its regulatory framework, interpretation and implementation advance the interests of developing countries. It is possible that the interests of developing countries may be frustrated because of the gaps or loopholes that the regulatory framework of this Agreement might have.

This study therefore seeks to examine the AoA, to establish whether the agreement has really managed to discipline export subsidies and trade distorting domestic subsidies in the agricultural

---

[25] Part VII article 13 of the AoA

[26] Martin. "The WTO Agriculture Agreement: Features, Effects, Negotiations, and What is at Stake?" www.twn.org.

[27] Van Den Bossche 2013 560-561.

[28] Staiger *What can Developing Countries Achieve in the WTO? A Book Review of Jawara and Kwa Behind the Scenes at the WTO* (2005) generally.

[29] *Ibid.*

[30] United Nations Conference on Trade and Development: Trade and Environment Review 2013 http://unctad.org/FEFD153439264A48FB8/FinalDownload/DownloadIdC19482F4764CD1C1A554F820A5B82BEC/FEFD1536-7542-4887-8EEE-439264A48FB8/en/PublicationsLibrary/ditcted2012d3_en.pdf (Accessed on 07/05/14).

sector. It will focus on (i) Domestic Support Commitments,[31] (ii) Export Subsidy Commitments,[32] (iii) Special and Differential Treatment,[33] (iv) Due Restraint,[34] and (v) Continuation of the Reform Process.[35] It will further examine the shortcomings encountered in negotiating and drafting the AoA as well as some of the loopholes in the AoA and it will also highlight the consequences thereof. The ultimate aim of the study is to assess the weaknesses of the WTO agricultural subsidies regulation framework from a developing countries perspective. Emphasis will be on the AoA since it primarily aims to regulate agricultural trade.

1 2 RESEARCH PROBLEM

The use of agricultural subsidies in developed countries has clearly weakened the agricultural sector in most developing countries.[36] It has proved difficult for developing countries to integrate into the world trading system because of subsidizing policies adopted by developed countries[37] that have led to devastating effects on developing countries' agricultural sector. Developing countries are excessively burdened by the implementation of the related requirements of the AoA and as a result fail to derive visible benefits from the Agreement. Both developed and developing countries are required by the AoA to reduce agricultural subsidies but evidence shows that most developed countries are still massively subsidising agriculture whilst developing countries are reducing subsidies.[38] Agricultural subsidies in developed countries have therefore been regarded as a significant barrier to developing country's exports on the global markets.[39]

The AoA is supposed to open up the world agricultural market for all countries by fairly reducing the use of subsidies by all member states. However, regardless of the commitments made to place the special needs of developing countries at the core of the international trading system, developing countries are still lagging behind. The regulatory framework of the WTO AoA, its application and implementation should provide an effective means by which agricultural subsidies are not used

---

[31] Part IV article 6 of AoA
[32] Part V article 8 of AoA
[33] Article 15 of AoA
[34] Article 13 of the AoA
[35] Article 20 of the AoA
[36] Mousseau "Inequity in International Agricultural Trade: The Marginalization of Developing Countries and Their Small Farmers" http://www.oaklandinstitute.org/node/2299 (Accessed on 24/04/14).
[37] This largely applies to United States and the European Union countries.
[38] Gonzalez. "Institutionalizing Inequality: The WTO Agreement on Agriculture, Food Security, and Developing Countries" 2002 *Columbia Journal of Environmental Law* 450-489.
[39] Martin. "The WTO Agriculture Agreement: Features, Effects, Negotiations, and What is at Stake?" www.twn.org (Accessed on 15/04/14).

unfairly or in a prejudicial manner. It should advance market access as well as reduce trade distorting subsidies whilst ensuring better living standards for the developing member countries. A pertinent question therefore is: whether the AoA can be said to be effective in the pursuit of that objective?

In short, the research problem to be addressed is whether the WTO AoA is facilitating the interests and meeting developmental needs of developing countries through the proposed reduction of subsidies? The study thus looks at the nature and content of the WTO regulatory framework especially the AoA which was designed to facilitate free agricultural trade. It further interrogates whether the AoA is assimilating developing states into global trade, and benefiting developing countries? Hence the study investigates the shortcomings/gaps and loopholes of the relevant AoA provisions and the impact these might be having on developing states.

1 3 RESEARCH AIMS/OBJECTIVES

It is the objective of this study to examine the regulation of WTO agricultural subsidies from the developing countries' belvedere. It looks at the problems WTO member states face with trade distorting subsidies, but focuses more on the impact these have on developing states. It seeks to scrutinize the AoA's provisions regulating subsidies, with a view to identifying any loopholes or shortcomings which might undermine the interests and aspirations of developing countries.

Furthermore, it will explore the challenges faced by the WTO member states, in particular developing countries, in implementing the AoA and how these are linked to the nature of its regulatory framework and the after effects of its implementation. In addition it seeks to establish whether there are benefits developing countries can gain from compliance with the Agreement.

1 4 SIGNIFICANCE OF THE STUDY

The reduction of subsidies in developed countries can lead to socio-economic development[40] in developing countries through increased market access.[41] This however depends on the ability of developing countries to participate in global trade and the willingness of developed countries to

---

[40] Raghavan "Agriculture: Liberalization needs to address socio-economic effects" http://www.twnside.org.sg/title/socio-cn.htm (accessed on 10-05-14).

[41] *Ibid.* Most developing countries are still have agro based economies. Their fiscus largely depends on agricultural exports. If developing countries reduce subsidies, they will open the market for imports which will in turn benefit developing countries. Examples of countries like these are Zambia and Malawi among others.

open up their markets. Subsidy policies in developed countries are clearly affecting developing countries through a massive reduction of exports, increase of imports and dumping of agricultural products in developing states.[42] Developing country exporters seeking access to foreign markets will have to compete with local producers who are massively supported by illegal subsidies thereby creating unfair competition. It is therefore important that the AoA pays appropriate attention to developing countries' special circumstances, in order to allow them to gain noticeable benefits from the Agreement.

This study is significant because it examines whether the AoA was fashioned in way to protect and uplift developing countries. It investigates the possibility of loopholes and gaps in the AoA which could have possible adverse impacts on the developing countries. It is therefore important that it be established whether the AoA effectively accommodates the special circumstances of developing countries; if not then why it is not capable or failing to do so? It is crucial for developing country members to know the nature and content of the global trading system's regulatory framework capable of accommodating their developmental needs or interests. This study should make a valuable contribution to that effort.

1 5 RESEARCH QUESTIONS

The study seeks to raise questions on how the WTO regulatory framework has dealt with trade distorting agricultural subsidies from a developing country perspective. It will explore the legal constraints behind the failure of developing countries to fully engage in global agricultural trade and maximise the opportunities created by the AoA. Thus it pursues the following questions:

1. What are the problematic aspects of the nature and content of the AoA and other WTO regulations related to agricultural subsidies?
2. What are the problems of implementing the AoA in developing countries?
3. How are the developing countries' interests and special circumstances accommodated in the AoA.
4. Whether the AoA has gaps which might result in the undermining of developing countries' interests?

[42] Diao "The Impact of Agricultural Trade Policies on Developing Countries" 2003 http://www.ifpri.org/FEFD1536-7542-4887-8EEE-439264A48FB8/FinalDownload (Accessed on 08-05-14).

1 6 LITERATURE REVIEW

A substantial amount of literature has been written about the negative impact of developed countries' agricultural subsidies on most developing countries. The scope of literature identifies the challenges faced by developing nations to integrate into the world agricultural trading system because of a significant amount of subsidies provided to farmers in developed countries. The literature also highlights the problems developing countries have with the current implementation of the AoA and how these are linked to the gaps in the regulatory framework of the Agreement. The literature also covers how some provisions of the AoA are open for possible abuse by developed countries and other protectionists.

Young and Wilmer[43] assess the 2005 land mark case in which the WTO found in favour of Brazil in its complaint against US cotton subsidies, the first case pressed by a developing country against a developed country's agricultural policy. The writers further look at West African cotton-producing nations' proposal for compensation for damages caused by US cotton subsidies in the WTO agricultural negotiations. The paper examines the two cases from a world system perspective in an effort to evaluate whether the relative power of semi-peripheral states compared to peripheral states can account for Brazil's potential for success in utilizing the legal rules of the WTO to curb hegemonic domination of the WTO by the US.

Cardwell and Rodgers [44] examine the EU law of the Common Agricultural Policy against the background of the domestic support reduction commitments contained in the 1994 Uruguay Round Agreement on Agriculture. They question the extent to which the single farm payment scheme fulfils the requirements for 'green box' exemption from such commitments. Options for the re-negotiation of the Agreement on Agriculture are discussed, including measures to improve the justiciability of its terms and to exclude discriminatory and trade-distorting domestic support which have an impact on the developing countries.

An article written Economist[45] discusses the World Trade Organization's summit discussions in Doha, Qatar. It exposes the talks about cutting tariffs and agricultural subsidies, in addition to

[43] Young "WTO Challenges to Core Country Agricultural Policies: A World Systems View" 2006 *Conference Papers International Studies Association* 1.

[44] Cardwell "Reforming the WTO Legal Order for Agricultural Trade: Issues for European Rural Policy in the Doha Round" 2006 *International & Comparative Law Quarterly* at 805-838.

[45] Economist "The Doha round...and round...and round." 2008. http://www.economist.com/node/1184859 (Accessed 9/04/14).

liberalising agricultural trade services which began in 2001. It however, expresses that no consensus has been achieved as of the 2008 summit. The writer submits that Uruguay Round results on sub subsidies affected these discussions, and that developing countries argue that proposed regulations favour developed countries.

Lee-David[46] examines the factors that are believed to be instrumental in the trade imbalance between the European Union and the developing world in the agricultural sector. The study focuses on the main reason for the existence of this imbalance which is the continued use of export subsidies by the European Union. The discussion attempts to highlight the inadequacies which exist in the current trade relationship between the European Union and developing nations, in particular South Africa, with regard to agricultural produce.

Bhala[47] exposes why developed countries stand accused of selfish adherence to domestic support and export subsidies that impoverish farmers in developing countries. Developing countries are blamed for self-inflicted wounds, caused by stubborn adherence to protectionist policies, covering both agricultural and industrial sectors. He argues that agricultural subsidy cuts, as well as increased market access, are politically impossible for developed countries to concede without reciprocal access from developing countries, not only on farm products, but also in non-agricultural markets and service sectors.

Matthews[48] explains the four themes in the developing countries' position in WTO agricultural trade negotiations as follows. (i) They are seeking meaningful improvements in market access for their agricultural exports. (ii) They have highlighted the asymmetry of current WTO obligations under the Uruguay Round Agreement on Agriculture, and are seeking greater equality of outcomes in the new round. (iii) Meaningful concessions on special and differential treatment will be necessary to satisfy the interests of both exporters and importers, especially on the scope to be allowed for tariff protection of domestic food production. (iv) Innovative and reliable guarantees

[46] Carolissen "An analysis of the impact of the European Union's policy of export subsidies has on South Africa's Agricultural sector".

[47] Bhala "Empathizing with France and Pakistan on Agricultural Subsidy Issues in the Doha Round" 2007 *Vanderbilt Journal of Transnational Law* 949-985.

[48] Matthews "Developing Countries' Position in WTO Agricultural Trade Negotiations, Development Policy Review" 2001 at 75-90.

will need to be provided to the least developed food importers to protect them against the risk of world price volatility.

Jensen[49] exposes how the on-going Doha Development Round under the World Trade Organization (WTO) has its main focus on development. This is due to the widespread disappointment with the results from the former Uruguay Round Agreements. Developing countries have not reaped the benefits of free trade. For this current Round to be a success, developing countries have to be more integrated into the multilateral trading system. One of the means of integrating them is Special and Differential Treatment (SDT). SDT is a deviation from the basic principle of Most Favoured Nation, positing that developing countries can have more flexibility than others. The writers investigate the positions on SDT taken by WTO members. The analysis gives some insights into the negotiations. First, it reveals the fact that the positions of WTO members are relatively close to each other. This could indicate that countries in fact agree that sensitive areas are maintained will not be affected. Second, being able to sustain a certain level of tariff rates attracts most interest from developing countries. Third, higher income developing countries want to retain their right to support domestic producers. Finally, the writer identify the July Package right in the middle of the positions which indicate a future agreement.

1 7 RESEARCH METHODOLOGY

The research methodology to be used in this study is the qualitative research method. This will be done through library research, use of internet sources and case law. The WTO's AoA will be the main primary source of regulatory information. Other primary sources to be consulted are the GATT and the SCM agreement.

The secondary sources will consist of research papers, reports, journals, articles and books. The research papers and journals that explore the relevant provisions for this study will be examined. The research will employ scholarly works which scrutinize the possible gaps in the AoA regulatory framework. To enrich the analysis, academic work which supports the regulatory framework of the agreement will also be used.

---

[49] Jensen "Special and differential treatment in the WTO agricultural negotiations: Analysis and Policy Recommendation" 2005 at 87-98.

Case law from the WTO will be used as the main source from which the interpretations and applications of the relevant AoA, GATT and SCM provisions will be drawn.

1 8 OUTLINE OF CHAPTERS

This study will be divided into six chapters.

Chapter one deals with the general overview of the study. It outlines the aims objectives, problem statement, rationale and limitations of the research and the methodology.

Chapter two discusses the historical and socio-economic background of agricultural subsidies regulation on a global level. It looks into its negotiating history and also establishes the historical origins of the AoA and of subsidies.

Chapter three discusses the key elements of the AoA. It then isolates the most problematic provisions for developing countries. It explores the relevant provisions for possible deficiencies or gaps.

Chapter four explores the WTO agricultural subsidies disputes mainly dealing with trade distorting export and domestic subsidies. It analyses whether the interpretations adopted by the DSB accommodate the developmental needs of developing states.

Chapter five exhumes what is taking place in Doha Development Round. It examines the demands of both developed countries and developing countries and attempts to highlight the problems affecting the negotiations.

Chapter six of the study presents the conclusions and the findings of the study on whether the WTO AoA adequately caters for the devolopmental needs of developing countries. Recommendations for developing countries will also be made in this chapter.

1 9 DELINEATION OF THE RESEARCH

The major limitation in this research is that it does not seek to evaluate the entire AoA regulatory framework. Instead it focuses on some of the most relevant and problematic provisions of the Agreement. The provisions which were designed to keep out protectionism and ensure participation of developing countries will be particularly scrutinised. The study will only look at trade distorting subsidies which consequently have an impact on developing countries. It will not cover the entire SCM agreement since it will specifically focus on agricultural subsidies.

The study will mainly focus on (i) Domestic Support Commitments, (ii) Export Subsidy Commitments, (iii) Special and Differential Treatment, (iv) Due Restraint, and (v) Continuation of the Reform Process. It will proceed further to highlight the shortcomings encountered in negotiating and drafting the AoA as well as some of the loopholes in the AoA and it will also indicate the consequences thereof.

1 10 REFERENCING STYLE

The referencing style used is that of Speculum Juris, an accredited journal which is published by the Nelson R Mandela School of Law, University of Fort Hare. The study will therefore not have any intellectual property implications in terms of copyright law as all works used will be acknowledged.

1 11 POSSIBLE ETHICAL IMPLICATIONS OF THE RESEARCH

The study at hand will not involve any ethical implications, as questionnaires or interviews will not form part of this research. The research will be qualitative and proper referencing will be employed to acknowledge sources used.

CHAPTER 2

Historical Background and Impact on Developing Countries

2 1 INTRODUCTION

Prior to the inception of the World Trade Organisation (WTO) Agreement on Agriculture (AoA), there was no single treaty or convention that regulated agricultural subsidies.[50] The General Agreement on Tariffs and Trade (GATT) had a few provisions on the regulation of agricultural trade, but the provisions were vague and subject to manipulation.[51] Interpretation of these provisions was quite problematic. Countries employed trade distorting subsidies which were devastating on free trade.[52] Most of the agricultural policies of developed countries, as well as developing countries, were protectionist and most countries were unwilling to open up their agricultural markets due to the political sensitivity of agricultural markets.[53] Most of the justifications of agricultural protectionism had to do with food security.[54] Hence negotiators of the present agricultural agreement were faced with the task of trying to strike a balance between liberalising the agricultural sector whilst ensuring food security.

This chapter explores the history of agricultural subsidies regulation from the 1947 GATT. The essence of this is to scout for the reasons behind the present agricultural subsidies regulation framework. The chapter addresses the question why the use of agricultural subsidies needed to be regulated. The chapter also exposes the negotiating process that led to the formation of the AoA. The purpose is to identify any possible flaws in the negotiating process. The last part of the chapter

---

[50] Fernando "The Cumulative Application of the Agreement on Agriculture and the Subsidies and Countervailing Measures Agreement: An Approach to Agricultural Subsidies Based on its Effects" 2007 *International Law Journal* page 209.

[51] Article XVI of the GATT basically provided that "any subsidies affecting exports to and imports from Members should be notified in writing. Members should recognise the deleterious impact of subsidies and avoid their general and specific use. In the case of primary products, it merely required that export subsidies shall not be applied "in a manner which results in that contracting party having more than an equitable share of world trade in that product, account being taken of the shares of the contracting parties in such trade in the product during a previous representative period, and any special factors which may have affected or be affecting such trade in the products".

[52] WTO "World Trade Report: Subsidies and the WTO". http://www.wto.org/E23B7EF9-82CD-4A8C-8A8D-AD1C1530D902/FinalDownload/DownloadId-04A744801BAC228AE8C05294EA164779/E23B7EF9-82CD-4A8C-8A8D-AD1C1530D902/english/res_e/booksp_e/anrep_e/wtr06-2f_e.pdf . (Accessed on 29/04/14 at 21:19).

[53] Matthews "The Agricultural Negotiations in the Uruguay Round and the Developing Countries" http://www.trocaire.org/sites/trocaire/files/resources/policy/1988-agriculture-developing-countries-uruguay-round.pdf. (Accessed on 27/04/14).

[54] Fernando 2007 at 209-210.

deals with the impact of subsidies on developing countries. The impact of subsidies is included in this study because it informs the law and helps to identify any possible loopholes in the law.

2 2 AN OVERVIEW OF AGRICULTURAL POLICIES PRIOR TO THE WTO

Prior to the WTO multilateral trade regime, agricultural trade was regulated by the GATT 1947.[55] The differences between the approach to agriculture and the approach to trade in manufactures in the GATT 1947 are fundamental in understanding the special role of agriculture in the GATT.[56] For this, it is vital to look into the agricultural policy background in major trading countries during that period. The United States (US), which was the main agricultural exporter at the time the GATT was introduced, had its Agricultural Adjustment Act of 1933 fully operational by 1947.[57] This Act permitted authorities to resort to tariffs and quantitative import controls and export subsidies where required in order to stabilize domestic producer prices.[58] The European Community (EC) did not exist then and its Common Agricultural Policy (CAP) did not come into full force until the early 1960s. A majority of other countries that have now become major traders were either recovering from war or were newly independent.

[55] With specific reference to subsidies, the GATT 1947 only had a section that required the contracting parties to report "any subsidy, including any form of income or price support, which operates directly or indirectly to increase exports of any product from, or to reduce imports of any product into its territory, to other parties". Thus, originally there was no prohibition on subsidies, domestic or export. This became what is now Article XVI: 1. Later, the prohibition against export subsidies on other than primary products was added as Article XVI: 4.

[56] Sharma "Multilateral Trade Negotiations on Agriculture: A Resource Manual I. Introduction and General Topics Agriculture in the GATT: A Historical Account". www.fao.org%2Fdocrep%2F003%2Fx7352e%2Fx7352e04.htm&ei=Yo3oU_KPDMye7AbXvYCwDQ&usg=AFQjCNFd-jvPB9lJ-RXUPE0Rb3Vzv-GSNQ&sig2=vAiJmvT-jNEwExn-Pe6uow&bvm=bv.72676100,d.ZWU . (Accessed on 11 August 2014).

[57] The goal of the Agricultural Adjustment Act was restoring farm purchasing power of agricultural commodities or the fair exchange value of a commodity based upon price relative to the pre-war 1909-14 level, and it was to be accomplished through the use, by the Secretary of Agriculture, of a number of methods. These included the authorization (1) to secure voluntary reduction of the acreage in basic crops through agreements with producers and use of direct payments for participation in acreage control programs; (2) to regulate marketing through voluntary agreements with processors, associations or producers, and other handlers of agricultural commodities or products; (3) to license processors, associations of producers, and others handling agricultural commodities to eliminate unfair practices or charges; (4) to determine the necessity for and the rate or processing taxes; and (5) to use the proceeds of taxes and appropriate funds for the cost of adjustment operations, for the expansion of markets, and for the removal or agricultural surpluses.

[58] The policy had a negative impact on trade since it imposed massive tariffs on trade as well as export subsidies in order to stabilize the domestic economy. This crippled free trade.

Domestic political and social pressures were also important factors behind some contracting parties seeking exemptions for agriculture.[59] In richer countries, agriculture was in decline as industry expanded rapidly.[60] The resulting difficulties in maintaining farm incomes and populations emerged as a politically sensitive issue.[61] Agriculture was seen as a unique sector of the economy which could not be treated like other sectors.[62] Sharma[63] states that, given this environment, not only did agriculture receive "special treatment" in the GATT, but this treatment appeared to have been tailored, to fit the US farm programmes then in existence.

The GATT 1947 contained several important differences with respect to the rules that applied to agricultural primary products as opposed to industrial products. It permitted countries to use export subsidies on agricultural primary products whilst export subsidies on industrial products were prohibited.[64] Article XI: 2(c) of the GATT allowed countries to resort to import restrictions for instance, import quotas under certain conditions, notably when these restrictions were necessary to enforce measures to effectively limit domestic production. This exception was also conditional on the maintenance of a minimum proportion of imports relative to domestic production.[65]

However, in practice many non-tariff border restrictions were used by members to reduce imports without any effective counterpart limitations on domestic production and without maintaining minimum import access.[66] In some cases this was achieved through the use of measures not specifically provided for under Article XI.[67] In other cases it reflected exceptions and country-specific derogations such as grandfather clauses, waivers and protocols of accession.[68] In still other

---

[59] Sharma "Multilateral Trade Negotiations on Agriculture: A Resource Manual I. Introduction and General Topics - Agriculture in the GATT: A Historical Account" http://www.fao.org/docrep/003/x7352e/x7352e04.htm (Accessed on 23/04/14).

[60] Dale *Agriculture and the GATT: Rewriting the Rules* (1997).

[61] *Ibid.*

[62] *Ibid.*

[63] Sharma "Multilateral Trade Negotiations on Agriculture: A Resource Manual I. Introduction and General Topics - Agriculture in the GATT: A Historical Account" http://www.fao.org/docrep/003/x7352e/x7352e04.htm.

[64] The only conditions were stated in Article XVI: 3 of GATT which stated that agricultural export subsidies should not be used to capture more than an "equitable share" of world exports of the product concerned.

[65] Sharma.

[66] WTO "The WTO Agreements Series 3: Agriculture". http://www.wto.org/FDA5F5E0-CA85-4273-9BDF-11A5AE9317C6/FinalDownload/DownloadId-D7801155E7BB232A41142B27CA043082/FDA5F5E0-CA85-4273-9BDF 11A5AE9317C6/english/res_e/booksp_e/agrmntseries3_ag_e.pdf . (Accessed on 26-05-14).

[67] *Ibid.*

[68] *Ibid.*

cases non-tariff import restrictions were maintained without any apparent justification.[69] The result of all this was a proliferation of impediments to agricultural trade, including by means of import bans, quotas setting the maximum level of imports, variable import levies, minimum import prices and non-tariff measures maintained by state trading enterprises.[70] This caused a massive restriction on trade thereby distorting the free trade principle which underpinned multilateral trade.[71]

The protection of domestic markets was partly the result of domestic measures originally introduced following the collapse of commodity prices in the 1930s great depression.[72] Additionally, after the Second World War many governments were concerned primarily with increasing domestic agricultural production so as to feed their growing populations.[73] With this objective in mind and in order to maintain a certain balance between the development of rural and urban incomes, many countries, particularly in the developed world, resorted to market price support and farm prices were administratively raised.[74] Import access barriers ensured that domestic production could continue to be sold.[75]

In response to these measures and as a result of productivity gains, self-sufficiency rates rapidly increased. In a number of cases, expanding domestic production of certain agricultural products not only replaced imports completely but resulted in structural surpluses.[76] Export subsidies were progressively used to dump surpluses on the developing world market, thus depressing global market prices.[77] On the other hand, low food price policies in favour of urban consumers and certain other domestic measures implemented in developed countries, reduced in a number of

---

[69] WTO "The WTO Agreements Series 3: Agriculture". http://www.wto.org/FDA5F5E0-CA85-4273-9BDF-11A5AE9317C6/FinalDownload/DownloadId-D7801155E7BB232A41142B27CA043082/FDA5F5E0-CA85-4273-9BDF 11A5AE9317C6/english/res_e/booksp_e/agrmntseries3_ag_e.pdf . (Accessed on 26-05-14).
[70] WTO "The WTO Agreements Series 3: Agriculture". http://www.wto.org/FDA5F5E0-CA85-4273-9BDF-11A5AE9317C6/FinalDownload/DownloadId-D7801155E7BB232A41142B27CA043082/FDA5F5E0-CA85-4273-9BDF 11A5AE9317C6/english/res_e/booksp_e/agrmntseries3_ag_e.pdf (Accessed on 26-05-14).
[71] *Ibid.*
[72] Marchildon *The Impact of the Great Depression on the Global Wheat Trade* (2010) 15-23. It is worth noting some of the domestic policies and the socio economic environment that prevailed prior to the coming in force of the GATT. The depression had a strong impact on the on the GATT specifically on agriculture because of food security measures that were implemented by states. After the Second World War new states were formed and there was a rapid increase in population. The states had to come with measures to protect the domestic agricultural industry.
[73] See Bailey "From the Corn Laws to Free Trade: Interest, Ideas and Institutions in Historical Perspective" 2006.
[74] *Ibid.*
[75] *Ibid.*
[76] WTO "The WTO Agreements Series 3: Agriculture" 2003 *World Trade Organization Documents* generally.
[77] *Ibid.*

developing countries the incentive for farmers to increase or even maintain their agricultural production levels.[78] It can be clearly noted that the GATT 1947's regulatory system was weak and it did not adequately protect the developing world from the negative effects of agricultural subsidies. It is submitted that the developed countries continued to distort free trade by heavily subsidizing their domestic farmers and dumping their surplus on developing countries.[79]

2 3 AGRICULTURAL TRADE UNDER THE GATT[80]

One of the reasons attributed to the failure in agricultural trade liberalisation during the GATT period is that special rules applied to agriculture.[81] Most of the GATT rules were intended to set down how governments may intervene to protect domestic markets and industries.[82] Once these rules were agreed, governments were expected to bring their policies/practices in line with them. However, for agriculture, the process was exactly the opposite. The GATT rules were written to fit the agricultural programmes then in existence, especially in the United States.[83] Even though special treatment for agriculture was clear particularly on subsidies and quantitative restrictions, it is submitted that this was not beneficial to developing countries as it further tightened the screws of protectionism in developed countries.[84]

Subsidies under the GATT were regulated by Article XVI. It specifically prohibited export subsidies on all products other than primary products. In the case of primary products, it merely required that export subsidies shall not be applied "in a manner which results in that contracting party having more than an equitable share of world trade in that product, account being taken of the shares of the contracting parties in such trade in the product during a previous representative period, and any special factors which may have affected or be affecting such trade in the products". The vagueness of this injunction was obvious, as it gave plenty of latitude to exporters to use such

---

[78] WTO "The WTO Agreements Series 3: Agriculture" 2003 *World Trade Organization Documents* generally.

[79] More on this will be fully discussed in Chapter 3. It is argued that developing countries lacked the resources to fully benefit from the SDT provisions hence the gap between the agricultural sector of developing and developed countries continued to widen.

[80] The following work is largely dependent of Allan Matthews's work. Acknowledgement is therefore given to all his work as well as other writers who have also made incredible contributions to this topic.

[81] Matthews "The Agricultural Negotiations in the Uruguay Round and the Developing Countries" http://www.trocaire.org/sites/trocaire/files/resources/policy/1988-agriculture-developing-countries-uruguay-round.pdf (Accessed on 27/04/14).

[82] *Ibid.*

[83] Hathaway *Agriculture and the GATT: Rewriting the Rules* (1987).

[84] *Ibid.*

subsidies.[85] There were attempts was to tighten up this provision in the negotiations on the Subsidies Code during the Tokyo Round , but it went in vain.[86] More importantly, there were no prohibitions in the GATT against domestic subsidies.[87] It merely imposed an obligation to report such subsidies if they were likely to affect trade.

The GATT rules relating to quantitative restrictions on trade were another area where agriculture received special treatment, as set out in Article XI.[88] These rules permitted countries to impose quotas on imports of agricultural or fishery products, provided domestic commodity programmes to limit domestic production were also put in place.[89] Although this formulation of the rules was written to fit the US agricultural programmes existing at the time, the US later found that it could not live with it.[90] In 1955 it insisted upon and received a temporary waiver which allowed it to impose import restrictions without the necessity for similar domestic restrictions.[91] The US sugar and dairy programmes were under this waiver until the Uruguay Round. It is quite ironic that US was leading the campaign for freer agricultural trade when it was largely at its insistence that the special rules for agriculture were put adopted in the first place.[92] The EC controlled imports not through quantitative restrictions but through a variable levy which, in practice, may have been even more restrictive. Technically, the status of the variable levy under the GATT was never determined.[93]

From the beginning, agriculture was accorded special treatment in the GATT.[94] The reason for this differential treatment can be attributed to the specific nature of agricultural protection.[95] Protection for industry[96] is intended to provide a margin of support for domestic industry against lower-cost

---

[85] Matthews 1988.
[86] *Ibid.*
[87] Matthews 1988.
[88] Trebilcock *The Regulation of International Trade* (2005).
[89] *Ibid.*
[90] Matthews "The Agricultural Negotiations in the Uruguay Round and the Developing Countries" 1988. http://www.trocaire.org/sites/trocaire/files/resources/policy/1988-agriculture-developing-countries-uruguay-round.pdf (Accessed on 27/04/14 at 13:17).
[91] *Ibid.*
[92] *Ibid.*
[93] *Ibid.*
[94] Healy "The Implications of the Uruguay Round Agreement on Agriculture for Developing Countries". www.fao.org/docrep/004/w7814e/w7814e00.htm (Accessed on 28/07/14).
[95] *Ibid.*
[96] This applies to secondary and tertiary industries.

competition from abroad.[97] Agricultural protection, however, functioned primarily in support of domestic price support policies intended to redistribute income to agriculture.[98] Agricultural trade barriers can be reduced only if there is a willingness to reduce domestic farm prices and to put in place farm income support measures which do not distort trade.[99] It is the interaction of agricultural trade policy and the use of commodity price policy to support farm incomes which makes the removal of agricultural trade barriers so difficult.[100]

A difference that existed between industrial and agricultural protection is that tariffs were the predominant form of protection for the industrial sector.[101] On the other hand quantitative restrictions and various other forms of non-tariff barriers were used in the agricultural sector.[102] Tariffs are easily measured, and comparisons of the degree of tariff protection on commodities and countries easily made.[103] Countries can relatively easily weigh up the gains and losses from particular tariff-cutting proposals, and thus multilateral tariff reduction negotiations can be conducted in a transparent way.[104] In the case of non-tariff barriers, their protective effect is much more difficult to assess, and the wide variety of measures in use makes it much more difficult for countries to evaluate and monitor proposals for their removal.[105]

2 3 1 Initial Negotiating Positions on Agricultural Trade

During the negotiating stage, participating countries were called to deposit their proposals on how the agricultural negotiations should proceed.[106] The negotiations were mainly centred between the United States and the European Community, which accounted for the bulk of world agricultural exports of temperate zone commodities.[107] Both countries had different views on how the

---

[97] Healy *The Implications of the Uruguay Round Agreement on Agriculture for Developing Countries: A Training* (1998).
[98] Matthews 1988.
[99] Healy 1988 Manual Food & Agriculture Org.
[100] *Ibid.*
[101] Zietz *The Growth of Agricultural Protection* http://www.nber.org/chapters/c8073 (accessed on 30-06-14).
[102] Matthews "The Agricultural Negotiations in the Uruguay Round and the Developing Countries" Trocaire Development Review 1988. http://www.trocaire.org/sites/trocaire/files/resources/policy/1988-agriculture-developing-countries-uruguay-round.pdf (Accessed on 27/04/14).
[103] *Ibid.*
[104] *Ibid.*
[105] Edward "The political economy of Non-Tariff Barriers : A cross national analysis" http%3A%2F%2Ffaculty.georgetown.edu%2Fmlb66%2FIO.pdf&ei=iTLWU7OeA_LQ7Abp_YCwDw&usg=AFQjCNGpiwrWUYSjoRTyq2H0A-3M4FLO9w&sig2=817BOm_2fbgeKF6fRbuVzA&bvm=bv.71778758,d.ZWU. (Accessed on 24/03/14).
[106] Matthews 1988.
[107] Matthews 1988.

negotiations should proceed and what their eventual outcome would be.[108] Once common ground reached between these two US and EU and, to a lesser extent, with Japan would become the accepted outcome.[109] However, other countries, especially the developing world were struggling to make their voices heard partly because of the economic and political prowess of the US and the EU.

While countries were concerned and affected by the state of world agricultural markets, there were different views of how to address the fundamental problem of overcapacity in the agricultural sector, whether by lower agricultural support or by taking steps to blunt its consequences for world markets.[110] Japan, the Nordic countries and some EC members favoured the managed approach to world markets, which aimed at regulating world trade so as to limit the extent of the distortions introduced by domestic subsidy programmes.[111] Quantitative controls would be used to restrict production, and market access for other exporting countries would be dealt with through bilateral or multilateral access agreements for specific quantities of specific commodities.[112] This would mean that member countries would have domestic intervention programmes which implied restrictions on international trade.[113]

Another suggested approach, was the alternative approach which strived for an agreement on the elimination of all import restrictions and production subsidies which would affect international trade and open up agricultural trade to market forces.[114] This approach would utilise some overall measure of protection, such as aggregate Producer Subsidy Equivalent (PSE), agree to limit it and then gradually reduce it over time.[115] This was proposed by the United States, which was supported

[108] *Ibid.*
[109] *Ibid.* These countries dominated international lobby groups who protected their interest. Developing countries were left out because of the significant contributions to agricultural trade made by the US and the EU.
[110] Franklin "Rich Man's Farming: The Crisis in Agriculture" 1988.
[111] Matthews "The Agricultural Negotiations in the Uruguay Round and the Developing Countries" 1988. http://www.trocaire.org/sites/trocaire/files/resources/policy/1988-agriculture-developing-countries-uruguay-round.pdf .
[112] Matthews 1988.
[113] *Ibid.*
[114] *Ibid.*
[115] Stefan "Is the Concept of the Producer Support Estimate in need of Revision?" http://www.oecd.org%2Fdataoecd%2F6%2F49%2F35091989.pdf&ei=f2DXU6q_CYb17AaMloHYAw&usg=AFQjCNGiCpY0lec5JNgilJojcIZiZTbmrw&sig2=92xsK8gSPWsuaIPcOkAg-w&bvm=bv.71778758,d.ZWU (Accessed on 04 July 2014). Stefan also states that the level of protection provided to an industry by tariffs is traditionally measured by indicators such as the nominal and effective rates of protection. Because of the complexity of agricultural support mechanisms, in which tariff protection is just one and not necessarily the most important component, there has been an attempt to define more comprehensive measures of support in the case of agriculture. In 1987 the OECD

by the Cairns group of agricultural exporting countries, whose membership included both developed and developing countries (Philippines, Argentina, Australia, Colombia Canada, Chile, Hungary, Uruguay, Indonesia, Malaysia, New Zealand, Thailand and Brazil).[116]

The US also lobbied for a complete removal of all import barriers and agricultural subsidies over a ten-year period, but with the exceptions of income subsidies unrelated to production and *bona fide* food aid and food assistance programmes.[117] They proposed a two-stage negotiating process. In the first stage, it was suggested that the level of support provided by each country would be measured.[118] In the second stage, 'implementation plans' would be agreed for each country setting out how it intends to move from its present support level to complete elimination over the ten-year period.[119] These plans would be bound in GATT and subject to appropriate monitoring.[120] It is argued that the US proposal would take agricultural trade to a position where it would be far more liberal than even industrial trade.[121] However, politically, the domestic agricultural income and agricultural price stability implications of this approach would make it unattractive to many governments.[122] It was not even clear whether the US, which is the sturdiest proponent of this approach, could in fact carry such a proposal through Congress during that period.[123]

2 3 2 Implications of Agricultural Trade Liberalisation for Developing Countries

Much of the developing countries' interest in agricultural trade liberalisation was created by the effects of the agricultural subsidising policies of the developed countries.[124] Policies of agricultural protection affected developing countries primarily through their impact on the level, pattern and stability of world prices.[125] However, due to the close interrelationship between agricultural products in both production and consumption, the impact of trade liberalisation on commodity

---

introduced two measures, the Producer Subsidy Equivalent (PSE) and the Consumer Subsidy Equivalent (CSE), which in those years became the *de facto* standard for the measurement of agricultural support levels.

[116] Matthews "The Agricultural Negotiations in the Uruguay Round and the Developing Countries" 1988. http://www.trocaire.org/sites/trocaire/files/resources/policy/1988-agriculture-developing-countries-uruguay-round.pdf . (Accessed on 29/07/14)

[117] *Ibid.*

[118] *Ibid.*

[119] *Ibid.*

[120] *Ibid.*

[121] Valdes "Agriculture in the Uruguay Round: Interests of developing countries" 1987 *World Bank Economic Review* at 571-593.

[122] Valdes 573-593.

[123] Valdes *ibid.*

[124] Matthews, "The Common Agricultural Policy and the Less Developed Countries" 1985.

[125] Matthews 1985.

prices was not always obvious.[126] It was generally expected that agricultural trade liberalisation will lead to an increase in world market prices because total agricultural production would be smaller than before.[127] But there were exceptions to this. A clear example of this was the high protection given to cereals in the EC which created a demand among animal feed compounders for imported cereal substitutes, at low or zero duties.[128] In this case, agricultural trade liberalisation would eliminate this trade, and exporters would suffer as a result.[129]

Furthermore, the effects of liberalizing the cereals livestock sector as a whole was even more complex.[130] Negotiators were afraid that lower support to cereals producers would lead to the rise of world cereal prices because fewer cereals would be grown.[131] If livestock production was to be reduced because its support was lowered, this would have the indirect effect of reducing the demand for cereals for animal feed.[132] A lesson that can be derived from this is that the interdependencies between agricultural commodities should not be neglected when assessing the impact of trade liberalisation.[133]

If the consequences of lowered protection for markets other than the market immediately affected were ignored, then the impact on particular developing countries would depend solely on whether the developing countries concerned were importers or exporters of the commodity in question.[134] Higher world market prices as a result of agricultural trade liberalisation by industrial countries implied more expensive imports for food importing countries, and it was anticipated that they would suffer in terms of trade loss.[135] However, higher world market prices would benefit

---

[126] Matthews *ibid.*
[127] Matthews "The Agricultural Negotiations in the Uruguay Round and the Developing Countries" 1988. http://www.trocaire.org/sites/trocaire/files/resources/policy/1988-agriculture-developing-countries-uruguay-round.pdf. (Accessed on 29/07/14).
[128] *Ibid.*
[129] *Ibid.*
[130] *Ibid.*
[131] *Ibid.*
[132] *Ibid.*
[133] Williams "Rethinking Agricultural Development: The Caribbean Challenge". http://www.ccmfuwi.org%2Ffiles%2Fpublications%2Fconference%2F1004.pdf&ei=3zDaU6_3HbOv7AbR1ID4Aw&usg=AFQjCNFJsOHkULqZXu7TMiCm0_u0u0B4qA&sig2=bymEg24pAeb1RE2ldUgvA&bvm=bv.72185853,d.ZGU&cad=rjt . (Accessed on 25/06/14).
[134] Matthews "The Agricultural Negotiations in the Uruguay Round and the Developing Countries" 1988. http://www.trocaire.org/sites/trocaire/files/resources/policy/1988-agriculture-developing-countries-uruguay-round.pdf . (Accessed on 29/07/14).
[135] Matthews 1988.

agricultural exporters, who were expected to experience a consistent trade gain.[136] The welfare consequences of these terms of trade bearing in developing countries were expected to be influenced, in addition, by the extent to which countries would permit their domestic prices to respond to the rise in world prices, by their flexibility in shifting resources between production sectors, and by the structure of production and consumption of the commodity, among other factors.[137]

2 3 3 Developing Countries' Interests in the Agricultural Trade Negotiations

During the Uruguay Round all countries at least agreed or rather believed that there was a problem in global agricultural markets and that trade liberalisation was the only available solution.[138] However, for most developing countries, the major question was whether they should participate in this undertaking by opening up their own agricultural markets to world market trends.[139] For Least Developed Countries (LDCs)[140], strict compliance with the outcome of the negotiations was not necessarily required.[141] When the Uruguay Round started, as was the case with previous GATT negotiations, developed countries agreed that special and differential treatment should be provided for developing countries, and that the LDCs would not be required "to make contributions which are inconsistent with their individual development, trade and financial needs".[142] In the past this was interpreted to allow LDCs to maintain tariff barriers against imports as part of their development strategies.[143] This of course was of great interest to developing countries as they argued on similar grounds, that they should not be restricted in their use of whatever agricultural

---

136 *Ibid.*

137 *Ibid.*

138 WTO "Participation of developing countries in World Trade: Overview of major trends and underlying factors". http%3A%2F%2Fwww.wto.org%2Fenglish%2Ftratop_e%2Fdevel_e%2Fw15.htm&ei=oZDoU4fbJbKv7Aar-YHwDQ&usg=AFQjCNE_v0e5TNcoujjBNeai2a51I5oO0g&sig2=dtjZ9sCd68VEUBqrQtnVXw&bvm=bv.72676100,d.ZGU . (Accessed on 08/07/14).

139 World Savvy "International Trade Policy" http://www.google.co.za/url?sa=t&rct=j&q=&esrc=s&source=web&cd=1&cad=rja&uact=8&ved=0CBsQFjAA&url=http%3A%2F%2Fworldsavvy.org%2Fmonitor%2Findex.php%3Foption%3Dcom_content%26view%3Darticle%26id%3D345%3Ainternational-trade-policy%26catid%3D143%3Atools%26Itemid%3D544&ei=3pHoU6qgJOSu7Abn3oGYAQ&usg=AFQjCNESix1UO_Zlhwi0ZS91qzPE008AbA&sig2=VFt9qRvr0mwxkEEjtiz9bg&bvm=bv.72676100,d.ZGU (accessed on 13/07/14).

140 For the purposes of this research, LDC hereafter will referred to as developing countries. However, where certain aspects are unique to them, they will be referred to as LDC.

141 World Savvy.

142 WTO "Framing Development at the GATT and WTO: Development at the World Trade Organization" 2014.

143 Matthews, "The Agricultural Negotiations in the Uruguay Round and the Developing Countries" 1988. http://www.trocaire.org/sites/trocaire/files/resources/policy/1988-agriculture-developing-countries-uruguay-round.pdf . (Accessed on 29/07/14).

policies they deemed necessary to pursue food security, rural development and their economic development objectives.[144]

Agricultural policies in most developing countries were far from homogeneous.[145] The major difference was seen on export crops in which domestic policies of most developing nations often resulted in negative protection.[146] Among some of the rapidly industrialising, middle income developing countries, there was evidence of positive agricultural protection.[147] Government intervention, whether positive or negative, invariably imposed costs on developing countries. A study done by the World Bank in 1986 estimated that liberalisation by developing countries themselves, of their own agricultural policies could benefit them by around $18 billion.[148] The study revealed that, these gains would come about because resources would be used more productively, consumers would be better off and developing countries would make better use of scarce foreign exchange.[149] Some commentators argued that the benefits from negative protection of developing countries' agriculture were worth these costs, as witnessed by many developing countries which had embarked on reforms of their agricultural pricing policies in those days.[150] What posed difficulties during the Uruguay Round negotiations, were the concerns of developing nations that provided positive protection to their agricultural sectors.[151] The major contention was whether they should dismantle this protection as part of a global move towards liberalisation.[152]

The arguments in favour of positive agricultural protection, especially in those middle-income developing countries which were in a position to envisage transfers from the urban to the rural

---

144 Matthews 1988.
145 Tangermann, "OECD Area Agricultural Policies and the Interests of Developing Countries Organization for Economic Co-operation and Development". https://www.google.co.za/?gfe_rd=cr&ei=n5DoU8WcMKTd8gfl1YHYDg&gws_rd=ssl (Accessed on 04/08/14).
146 Matthews 1988.
147 *Ibid.*
148 *Ibid.*
149 Anderson "Public and Private Roles in Agricultural Development Proceedings of the Twelfth Agricultural Sector Symposium". https://www.tcd.ie%2FEconomics%2Fstaff%2Famtthews%2FFoodCourse%2FCourseMaterials%2FReadings%2FTangermann_DCs.doc&ei=q5joU92jKrDn7Aa4r4DQDQ&usg=AFQjCNGe6UU6dbLLF0CxKqCnD8BEC5jotg&sig2=oWZJT91TZmitotOylRrDRQ&bvm=bv.72676100,d.ZGU.
150 *Ibid.*
151 Michalopoulos "Trade and Development In the GATT and WTO: The Role of Special And Differential Treatment for Developing Countries". http://www.wto.org%2Fenglish%2Ftratop_e%2Fdevel_e%2Fsem01_e%2Fcosta_e.doc&ei=M6DoU8OaEYfy7AagtIGYDQ&usg=AFQjCNGoLfpsu3Ly4q-6GW9Mb8wFBn5TiA&sig2=h7CPgu2Z15y11he4zfcUNA&bvm=bv.72676100,d.ZGU (Accessed on 02/08/14).
152 *Ibid.*

sector, included arguments of food security, the maintenance of rural populations and the redistribution of income towards a low-income sector.[153] The weight of the evidence on the costs and distributional consequences of agricultural protection strongly suggested that these developing countries, in their own interests, would find it beneficial to at least place a ceiling on the amount of support provided as a prelude to its ultimate dismantling, possibly over a longer time span than that agreed for developed country policies.[154]

Another vexing question during the Uruguay Round was the question of reciprocity.[155] As discussed above, the industrial countries had accepted that developing countries could benefit from tariff reductions on the most-favoured-nation principle in the past, without requiring that these countries extend reciprocal concessions in return.[156] Indeed, under the General System of Preferences, developing countries were entitled to more favourable treatment for much industrial trade on a unilateral basis.[157] However, it is argued that this 'privilege' was not good for developing countries during the negotiation process as it marginalised them and reduced their ability to argue for concessions in areas of particular interest to them.[158]

In the light of the increasing export success of a number of the middle-income developing countries, the industrial countries were keen to introduce the notion of 'graduation' in the Uruguay round which entailed that the more successful among the developing countries would no longer be exempt from the GATT rules and should become subject to the same disciplines as apply to them.[159] This would imply differentiating the rights and obligations of smaller, low-income developing countries from those of the larger, middle-income developing countries.[160]

---

[153] Matthews 1988.
[154] *Ibid.*
[155] Capling "Australia and the Global Trade System: From Havana to Seattle". http://books.google.co.za/books/about/Australia_and_the_Global_Trade_System.html?id=GHHa5pN2KAkC . (accessed on 27/07/14 at 10:30 am)
[156] Matthews *ibid.*
[157] Michalopoulos "Trade and Development in the GATT and WTO: The Role of Special and Differential Treatment for Developing Countries". http://www.wto.org%2Fenglish%2Ftratop_e%2Fdevel_e%2Fsem01_e%2Fcosta_e.doc&ei=M6DoU8OaEYfy7AagtIGYDQ&usg=AFQjCNGoLfpsu3Ly4q-6GW9Mb8wFBn5TiA&sig2=h7CPgu2Z15y11he4zfcUNA&bvm=bv.72676100,d.ZGU (Accessed on 02/08/14).
[158] Matthews *ibid.*
[159] Matthews 1988 *Ibid.*
[160] *Ibid.*

It is argued that LDCs faced a similar danger of marginalisation in the context of the agricultural trade negotiations.[161] As pointed out by Valdes, there is a possibility that the three big powers, the US, EC and Japan striked a deal among themselves before starting negotiations with the developing countries.[162] He believed that to become influential the developing countries had to offer some incentive to the major powers to take their interests into account.[163] This argument would seem to be particularly important for the middle income developing countries associated with the Cairns group.[164] These countries had a particular interest in more liberal market arrangements for beef and sugar, for example, which had a lower priority for the developed country negotiators.[165]

Reciprocity and graduation were two areas where these middle-income developing countries had bargaining chips.[166] The reduction in positive agricultural protection and industrial tariffs[167] were two areas which these developing countries traded to gain concessions in agricultural areas of particular interest to them.[168] The lower-income developing countries, which had little to gain from increases in world food prices, could nonetheless support this move on the grounds that it would mean the available preferences in industrial trade would not be reserved exclusively for them.[169] If this argument about negotiating strategy was accepted, then a corollary was that developing countries would not oppose the preference of some industrial countries to hive off the agricultural negotiations into a separate, self-contained box, because this would limit the developing countries' ability to offer concessions on graduation and reciprocity.[170]

In terms of the two competing philosophies of how to deal with this crisis, developing countries were expected to side with countries like Japan, the Nordic economies and some EC members which would prefer to manage world trade in ways which were consistent with maintaining high

---

[161] Valdes "Agriculture in the Uruguay Round: Interests of developing countries" 1987 *The World Bank Economic Review* 575-593.
[162] Valdes 1987 at 575-590.
[163] *Ibid.*
[164] Matthews 1988.
[165] *Ibid.*
[166] *Ibid.*
[167] Tariffs were often instituted in support of import substitution industrialisation strategies but increasingly continued because of the power of vested interests.
[168] Tangermann "Multilateral negotiations on farm- support levels" 1987 World Economy 265-279.
[169] Matthews *ibid.*
[170] Matthews *Ibid.*

levels of domestic price support.[171] Such an approach would have to be based on a series of international commodity agreements which would specify the minimum import obligations of importers and the maximum export quantities of exporters.[172] Developing countries were strong supporters of commodity agreements in the 1970s and were expected to favour this approach in the 1980s.[173] The previous experience with commodity agreements, however, did not hold much hope for the long-term success of this approach to managing world trade.[174] The lack of enthusiasm for the Integrated Programme for Commodities, even among developing countries, and the lessons from the collapse of the International Tin Agreement in 1986, suggested that developing countries were increasingly aware of the limitations of this approach.[175] Developing countries were therefore better advised to support the negotiating approach which would seek to use a single measure of support and to reduce it over time.[176]

For food importing developing countries, whose balance of payments was already in a critical condition because of high debt repayments and low commodity prices, the prospect of higher world food prices could not be viewed with composure.[177] Within the Uruguay Round negotiations Jamaica had articulated the fears of this group (developing countries) without, however, making any specific proposals to alleviate any adverse consequences which such countries could face.[178] Two possibilities were to be considered. The then existing IMF Compensatory Financing Facility, was designed in part to assist food importing countries faced with an unexpected rise in cereal prices.[179] The restrictive conditions of access to this facility, together with inadequacies in the rules for calculating foreign exchange shortfalls, made it less useful than it could be for this purpose, and developing countries lobbied for the agreement of the industrial countries for reform of this facility within the context of a GATT agreement.[180] Alternatively, provision could be made for a

---

171 Valdes 1987 at 577-593.

172 Valdes "Agriculture in the Uruguay Round: Interests of developing countries" 1987 *The World Bank Economic Review* 577-593.

173 Matthews 1988.

174 *Ibid.*

175 *Ibid.*

176 *Ibid.*

177 Tangermann "Multilateral negotiations on farm- support levels" 1987 *World Economy* at 265-279.

178 *Ibid.*

179 Tangermann "Multilateral negotiations on farm- support levels" 1987 *World Economy* at 265-279.

180 *Ibid.*

special fund which could be used to increase food aid shipments or to cap the rise in cereal prices over a specified period, at least for the developing countries.[181]

2 4 TOKYO ROUND: AGRICULTURAL NEGOTIATIONS

In an effort to address the flaws in the 1947 GATT, the Tokyo Round was launched on the 14th of September 1975 at a Ministerial meeting in Tokyo. The ministerial declaration setting out the ambit for the negotiations foresaw work aimed at reducing or eliminating non-tariff measures, negotiations in agriculture, taking into account the special characteristics and problems in this sector, *inter alia*. The Tokyo Round negotiations were dominated by events within the United States, the European Economic community (EEC), Japan and the relations between them. [182]

The developing countries were much more involved in the negotiating process as compared to the Kennedy round which was largely dominated by the developing world.[183] This was a time of heightened developing country expectations in that it coincided with preparations for the New International Economic Order initiative. However, even though the necessary preparatory work was done between 1973 and early 1977, there were no real developments in the negotiations until the new United States administration had formulated its policies and appointed its negotiating team.[184] This already showed an imbalance in the negotiations because the US had to place its house in order first for the negotiations to take place. Negotiations only began in July 1977 following a meeting between the US and the EEC, which levelled out some of their major differences on policy and procedure.[185]

---

[181] Matthews 1988.

[182] The EEC and US had some of the worst protectionist policies that massively distorted trade and Japan had achieved its transformation into a first-rate trading power and had become the subject of protectionist pressures in many economies. See World Trade Review "Tokyo Round 1973 to 1979". http://worldtradereview.com/webpage.asp?wID=438 (accessed on 31-05-2014).

[183] However, the interests of developing countries were not served. For instance it was the aim of EC negotiators, for example, to achieve the best possible settlement for the European Community in the fields of non-tariff barriers, industrial tariffs and agriculture which would safeguard European interests and improve Community export. 'We want the outcome to be satisfactory for the European Community,' said the chief negotiator, Wilhelm Haferkamp, which is the world's greatest importer and exporter. No one has a greater interest than ourselves in a satisfactory outcome. See Kakabadse "The Tokyo Round and After". http://www.jstor.org/stable/pdfplus/40395495.pdf?acceptTC=true.

[184] World Trade Review "Tokyo Round 1973 to 1979". http://worldtradereview.com/webpage.asp?wID=438 (accessed on 31-05-2014).

[185] World Trade Review "Tokyo Round 1973 to 1979". http://worldtradereview.com/webpage.asp?wID=438 (accessed on 31-05-2014).

In July 1978 a large group of developed countries was able to put forward a "Framework of Understanding" which set out the principal elements they considered necessary for a balanced outcome to the negotiations.[186] The developing countries objected to this on substantive and procedural grounds. They objected particularly to what they saw as an attempt to leave them at the periphery of the negotiations.[187] The package nevertheless was an important factor in maintaining momentum in the negotiations which were supposed to end by 15 December 1978. The concerns of developing countries were not taken into cognisance by the developing world. It is submitted that the developed world played a bullying role by deliberately leaving out the concerns of developing countries.

A major obstacle which turned up in the form of a provision of the United States Trade Act stopped the negotiations from ending in 1978.[188] The provision permitted the President to waive a requirement that countervailing duties be imposed on subsidized imports over the four year period ending on 3 January 1979.[189] The implication of this was that, if the existing waiver lapsed, countervailing duties would become automatic.[190] The US congress appeared reluctant to renew the waiver, but it did so once the EEC declared that it could not conclude the negotiations unless the United States first solved its internal problems.[191] The Tokyo round in the end was a fight between the US and the EEC. The Tokyo Round negotiations ended formally on 12 April 1979 after the US had decided to sort out its internal protectionist policies.

After several years of negotiating, little progress was made on systemic issues in the trade of agricultural products. There was an agreement that, negotiations should be continued after the round, on the development of a Multilateral Agricultural Framework aimed at avoiding continuing political and commercial confrontations in this highly sensitive sector.[192] In reality this was nothing more than a device enabling the conclusion of the round as a whole and, as many expected,

---

[186] *Ibid.*
[187] *Ibid.*
[188] World Trade Review "Tokyo Round 1973 to 1979". http://worldtradereview.com/webpage.asp?wID=438 (accessed on 31-05-2014).
[189] *Ibid.*
[190] Kakabadse "The Tokyo Round and After" 1981 The World Today 305. http://www.jstor.org/action/showArticleImage?image=images%2Fpages%2Fdtc.65.tif.gif&suffix=40395495 . (Accessed on 27-05-14).
[191] *Ibid.*
[192] Kakabadse "The Tokyo Round and After 1981 The World Today" 305. http://www.jstor.org/action/showArticleImage?image=images%2Fpages%2Fdtc.65.tif.gif&suffix=40395495 . (Accessed on 27-05-14).

it did not lead anywhere once negotiations resumed.[193] Hence, the Tokyo Round did little to address the problem of trade distorting agricultural subsidies.[194] It rather left the issue hanging, perhaps because of its highly sensitive political nature.[195]

The Tokyo round can however be credited for rebuilding confidence in the multilateral framework of rules and procedures which would subject trade policies to a system of on-going examination and consultation. The consultative framework in agricultural trade offered the possibility of scrutinizing the trade limiting effects of domestic agricultural policies and of encouraging governmental justification of objectives and measures with the view of gradually lowering levels of agricultural support and reducing conflict.[196]

2 5 URUGUAY ROUND: AGRICULTURAL NEGOTIATIONS

When the Tokyo Round under GATT finally concluded in 1979 after nearly six years of negotiations, the general feeling among many exhausted negotiators was "never again".[197] But less than three years, the US raised the idea of a new round which sought the liberalization of world agricultural trade and multilateral rules for investment and trade in services.[198] Furthermore, American Multinational Enterprises (MNEs), especially the pharmaceutical industry, were demanding stronger measures against the infringement of several intellectual property rights.[199] The US administration also saw a new round as a way to counter protectionist pressures that were stimulated by the large US trade deficit and increasing job losses.[200]

The other developed countries had differing views as to the desirability and necessity of starting a new multilateral trade round.[201] The EU was not particularly interested in supporting new

---

193 World Trade Review "Tokyo Round 1973 to 1979". http://worldtradereview.com/webpage.asp?wID=438 (accessed on 31-05-2014).
194 *Ibid.*
195 *Ibid.*
196 Kakabadse "The Tokyo Round and After 1981 The World Today". http://www.jstor.org/stable/pdfplus/40395495.pdf?acceptTC=true . (Accessed on 27-05-14).
197 Kleen "So alike and yet so different: A comparison of the Uruguay Round and the Doha Round" 2008. http://www.ecipe.org/media/publication_pdfs/so-alike-and-yet-so-different-a-comparison-of-the-uruguay-round-and-the-doha-round.pdf (Accessed on 28-05-14).
198 The Tokyo Round and earlier GATT rounds had failed to fully address the problems faced through international trade of agricultural products. Subsidies were still distorting global trade and the practice of granting agricultural subsidies by governments was still dominant in developing countries.
199 Kleen 2008.
200 *Ibid.*
201 Kleen "So alike and yet so different: A comparison of the Uruguay Round and the Doha Round" 2008. http://www.ecipe.org/media/publication_pdfs/so-alike-and-yet-so-different-a-comparison-of-the-uruguay-round-and-the-doha-round.pdf (Accessed on 28-05-14).

initiatives in the GATT.[202] Its stance was mainly defensive because of its interests in agriculture. Japan took the EU stance and hoped that nothing would happen.[203] The other active developed contracting parties in the GATT Australia, Canada, Sweden and Switzerland inclined towards the US position.[204]

The developing countries were deeply divided. A group of 10 hardliners, under the leadership of India and Brazil, fiercely opposed a new round, especially the inclusion of services, intellectual property and investments, which was central to the US's agenda.[205] However, most of the developing countries were prepared to enter into negotiations under certain conditions. Among the factors behind the less negative attitudes of these countries were an increasing awareness of the limitations of their earlier import substitution policies and, perhaps more importantly, the threat of possible unilateral actions against their exports in the US market.[206]

In 1983 the Director General of GATT, Arthur Dunkel, invited an independent group of businessmen, academicians and civil servants to study and report on problems facing the international trading system. Fritz Leutwiler, who was then head of the Swiss National Bank, chaired the group. Its report, *Trade policies for a better future*,[207] was published in 1985 and created the ground for a new round of multilateral trade negotiations. The Leutwiler report was remarkably predictive and included recommendations that were fulfilled in the final settlement of the Uruguay Round: clearer and fairer rules for agriculture, dismantlement of grey zone measures, the return of textile and clothing to normal GATT rules, surveillance of individual countries' trade policy, multilateral rules for trade in services and reinforcement of the dispute settlement procedures *inter alia*.[208]

---

[202] *Ibid.*

[203] *Ibid.*

[204] Kleen "So alike and yet so different: A comparison of the Uruguay Round and the Doha Round" 2008. http://www.ecipe.org/media/publication_pdfs/so-alike-and-yet-so-different-a-comparison-of-the-uruguay-round-and-the-doha-round.pdf (Accessed on 28-05-14).

[205] These countries are Argentina, Brazil, Cuba, Egypt, India, Nicaragua, Nigeria, Peru, Tanzania and Yugoslavia.

[206] WTO "World Trade report 2007 Six decades of multilateral cooperation: What have we learnt?" 2007 World Trade Organization Documents.

[207] GATT "Trade policies for a better future - proposals for action 'The Leutwiler Report'". 1985 General Agreement on Tariffs and Trade Documents.

[208] GATT "Trade policies for a better future - proposals for action 'The Leutwiler Report'". 1985 General Agreement on Tariffs and Trade Documents.

After an inconclusive ministerial meeting held under auspices the GATT in 1982, caused by a lot of infighting between the proponents and opponents of a new round, the contracting parties of the GATT in 1985 at least managed to set a date for a ministerial meeting in Punta Del Este, Uruguay, in September 1986, with the intention of launching the round. However, with reference to the substantive issues, the deadlock was almost total between the US and EU on the one hand and the hardliners on the other.[209] This deadlock prompted several outward looking developed and developing countries to join together in early summer 1986 just a few months before the Punta Del Este meeting and hammer out their own proposal for a Ministerial Declaration giving a mandate for the new round.[210]

The group of initially more than 40 developed and developing countries got the nickname "*Café au Lait*"[211] because it was chaired by the Colombian and Swiss ambassadors.[212] In a short space of time the US and the EU unofficially joined the discussions without formally associating themselves with the coalition.[213] The *Café au Lait* group also comprised most members of the 14 agriculture exporting developed and developing countries. The developing countries involved in the meeting in Punta Del Este, formed the Cairns Group at a meeting in Cairns, Australia, in August 1986.[214] The formation of this group increased pressure for prioritizing the agricultural sector issues in the agenda for the Uruguay round.[215] Before the ministerial meeting, the chairman for the ministerial received two comprehensive papers, one from India and Brazil and the other from the *Café au Lait* group.[216] After a couple of days of rancorous discussions, the Chairman decided to base the negotiations on the *Café au Lait* paper, which after only minor changes became the

[209] *Ibid.*

[210] Kleen "So alike and yet so different: A comparison of the Uruguay Round and the Doha Round" 2008. http://www.ecipe.org/media/publication_pdfs/so-alike-and-yet-so-different-a-comparison-of-the-uruguay-round-and-the-doha-round.pdf . (Accessed on 07/06/14).

[211] Narlikar "Fairness in international trade negotiations: Developing countries in the GATT and WTO" 2006 The World Economy 1005-1029. The English translation of this is, light brown colour of coffee with milk.

[212] Kleen 2008 *ibid.*

[213] Kleen 2008 *ibid.*

[214] The Cairns Group is an interest group of 19 agricultural exporting countries, composed of Argentina, Australia, Bolivia, Brazil, Canada, Chile, Colombia, Costa Rica, Guatemala, Indonesia, Malaysia, New Zealand, Pakistan, Paraguay, Peru, the Philippines, South Africa, Thailand, and Uruguay.

[215] Kleen 2008 *ibid.*

[216] GATT "Communication from the delegations of Colombia and Switzerland" 1986 General Agreement on Tariffs and Trade Documents.

Ministerial Declaration on the Uruguay Round.[217] Without the efforts of the *Café au Lait* coalition, the meeting would likely have ended in failure.[218]

2 5 1 Uruguay Round: Aims and Objectives

In the Uruguay Round (UR) the desire was to create "new" frameworks and rules for services, and eventually for intellectual property. Agriculture was of course one of the main subjects, but it could hardly be characterized as a new issue since several provisions in the GATT formally covered it. However, agricultural negotiations were quite sensitive and they dragged the negotiations.[219] The UR agricultural negotiations aimed at the development and implementation of a framework to address barriers and distortions to trade in three major policy domains, market access, and domestic support and export subsidies. One of the chief aims was to establish an overall framework for the re-instrumentation of agricultural support towards less trade distorting policies.[220]

Special and differential treatment (SDT) of developing countries manifested itself in different ways during the UR. It was not necessarily the aim of the UR but it was mentioned in the *Punta Del Este* Declaration although it did not high on the agenda. The outcome of the round led to a considerable narrowing of the kind of differential treatment which the developing countries had enjoyed earlier under the GATT.[221] Bringing agriculture, textiles and clothing under normal GATT rules put an end to the permanent *de facto* differentiation that for decades had worked against the developing countries.[222] The decision to affiliate all countries to all agreements as a result of the creation of the WTO was in a sense also a move to end another kind of differential treatment but in a way that hardly was anticipated by the "beneficiaries".[223] Both the Subsidies and the AoA reduced the degree of "informal SDT" that countries felt they had in order to carry out their

---

[217] Kleen 2008 *ibid.*

[218] Kleen "So alike and yet so different: A comparison of the Uruguay Round and the Doha Round". http://www.ecipe.org/media/publication_pdfs/so-alike-and-yet-so-different-a-comparison-of-the-uruguay-round-and-the-doha-round.pdf (Accessed on 10/06/14).

[219] This is possibly because these negotiations were politically sensitive as they threatened food security in countries that had hanging memories of the Second World War. It is argued that, no country was willing to open its markets and reduce subsidies in the agricultural sector if the proposed reduction would affect the country's food security.

[220] GATT "Trade policies for a better future - proposals for action 'The Leutwiler Report'". 1985 General Agreement on Tariffs and Trade Documents.

[221] *Ibid.*

[222] Kleen "Special and differential treatment of developing countries in the World Trade Organization" 2005 London: Overseas Development Institute.

[223] Kleen 2005 pg 14.

industrial policies.[224] This was a potential time bomb for developing countries as it would soon result in unfair treatment.[225]

2 5 2 Results of the Uruguay Round

The UR agricultural negotiations resulted in the adoption of the AoA. One of the main achievements of UR has been the development and implementation of a framework to address barriers and distortions to trade in three major policy domains namely market access, domestic support and export subsidies.[226] New and operationally effective rules were established and quantitative constraints were agreed upon for all three pillars.[227] In addition, the URAA provided an overall framework for the re-instrumentation of agricultural support towards less trade distorting policies. More importantly, the AoA provides the basis for further negotiations.[228]

The AoA was regarded a major step towards liberalising agricultural trade and it was the first multilateral agreement that specifically dealt with disciplining multilateral trade.[229] It marked an historic point in the reform of the agricultural trade system.[230] For the first time, member governments committed to reduce agricultural export subsidies and trade-distorting domestic support. They agreed to prohibit subsidies that exceed negotiated limits for specific products. And the commitments to reduce domestic support were a major innovation of the AoA and were quite unique to the agricultural sector. This at least was a dawn to multilateral agricultural trade.

2 6 THE IMPACT OF THE AOA ON DEVELOPING COUNTRIES

The main objective of the AoA is to establish a fair and market-oriented trading system in agriculture, to increase market access and reduce trade-distorting agricultural subsidies.[231] However it is argued that the agreement has not met these expectations. It has been described as

---

[224] Kleen 2005

[225] *Ibid.*

[226] Meléndez-Ortiz "The Future and the WTO: Confronting the Challenges" http://www.ictsd.org/downloads/2012/07/the-future-and-the-wto-confronting-the-challenges.pdf (Accessed on 04-11-14).

[227] Meléndez-Ortiz "The Future and the WTO: Confronting the Challenges" http://www.ictsd.org/downloads/2012/07/the-future-and-the-wto-confronting-the-challenges.pdf (Accessed on 04-11-14).

[228] *Ibid.*

[229] Prior to the URAA, agricultural trade rules were scattered in separate agreements. The GATT had provisions disciplining agricultural trade but they were unclear and ambiguous. The rules did not adequately address the concerns of developing countries.

[230] In the words of the GATT secretariat, the results of the negotiations were described as providing a framework for long term reform of agricultural trade and domestic policies over the years to come. News of the Uruguay Round December 1993.

[231] See the Preamble of the AoA.

flawed and highly iniquitous; and that instead of levelling the playing field in international trade in agriculture, it is strengthening the monopoly control of developed countries over global agricultural production and trade.[232] The agreement is not balanced and fair as it is mainly skewed in favour of developed countries' interests.[233] Its provisions on market access, domestic support and export subsidies basically enhance measures used by developed countries to protect their markets and agriculture.[234]

The concept of free trade which underpins the trade liberalization commitments in the AoA works against the development and food security needs of developing countries.[235] Under free trade, countries should produce only the goods which they can produce cheaply or on which they have comparative advantage and import those goods including the food crops which they produce domestically, from others who can produce them cheaper and more efficiently.[236] The implication of this is that developed countries, by virtue of their huge subsidies will end up dumping food products in developing markets.[237] Thus, developing countries end up becoming more dependent on artificially cheapened imports that continue to drain their limited foreign reserves, retard the growth of their agriculture and economies and weaken their capacity to feed their own population in the long-term.[238]

It is argued that the AoA mainly focuses on further opening the markets of developing countries whilst it continues protecting the subsidies and protectionist measures such as tariff peaks and

[232] Glipo "The WTO AoA: Impact on Farmers and Rural Women in Asia Asia-Pacific Network for Food Sovereignty". http://www.glow-boell.de/media/de/txt_rubrik_5/sus_arze_ruralwomen.pdf (Accessed on 29/06/14).

[233] Glipo "An Analysis of the WTO-AoA Review from the Perspective of Rural Women in Asia." 2003 *WTO Documents.*

[234] Glipo 2003.

[235] This is despite the commitments under the reform programme which should be made "in an equitable way among all Members, having regard to non-trade concerns, including food security and the need to protect the environment; having regard to the agreement that special and differential treatment for developing countries is an integral element of the negotiations, and taking into account the possible negative effects of the implementation of the reform programme on least-developed and net food-importing developing countries." As indicated in the preamble of the Agreement on Agriculture.

[236] Amadeo "Comparative Advantage" 2014. David Ricardo's Theory of Comparative Advantage states that that a country that is better at producing a particular good or service will become more successful by focusing and placing much emphasis on that industry. Ricardo developed the comparative advantage theory to curb trade restrictions on wheat that England has imposed. He stressed out that it is more beneficial for England to import lower-cost, higher-quality wheat from countries that had the favourable climate and soil conditions to grow it. England could get more value by exporting products that required skilled labour and machinery, and trading that for the wheat. This theory of comparative advantage became the rationale for free trade agreements.

[237] Suparmoko "The Impact of the WTO Agreement on Agriculture in the Rice Sector" 2002 WTO Documents.

[238] Glipo "An Analysis of the WTO AoA Review from the Perspective of Rural Women in Asia" 2003 *WTO Documents.*

other trade barriers used by developed countries.[239] Trade, which is a core principle of the WTO and which purportedly, directs the trade liberalization commitments of members has been rendered meaningless.[240] In fact, it has misled many developing countries to quickly open up their markets to dumped imports from developed countries in order to gain access to the latter's huge markets.[241] However the actions of developing countries are not "reciprocated" by equally aggressive steps in the developed world. Instead, developed countries continue to put higher tariff walls called tariff peaks and tariff escalation upon tariffication which is effectively discriminating against developing countries' exports.[242]

Additionally, the subsidies employed by developed countries to protect their agriculture, expand their production and gain monopoly control in the international market are accorded more protection with the exemptions introduced in the AoA's subsidy reduction.[243] The classification of subsidies into trade-distorting, which are subject to reduction discipline and non-trade distorting, which are not, permits the developed countries to shift their existing grossly huge subsidies into acceptable boxes or categories that are exempted from subsidy reduction. The exemptions applying to developing countries are often of not much use, considering the long-running negative economic position of many developing countries.[244] In the end, it can be argued that with such huge loopholes, the AoA clearly aids to legitimize and strengthen the trade-distorting practices of developed countries.[245]

It is also argued that the AoA is not fair because it prohibits developing countries from using the same tools that enabled developed countries to pursue their development and food security goals in the past decades.[246] Furthermore developed countries are allowed to retain and even expand their huge agricultural subsidies whilst developing countries are prohibited from increasing their

---

[239]Glipo "The WTO-AoA: Impact on Farmers and Rural Women in Asia" http://www.glow-boell.de/media/de/txt_rubrik_5/sus_arze_ruralwomen.pdf (accessed on 16-07-14).

[240] *Ibid.*

[241] *Ibid.*

[242] Glipo "The WTO-AoA: Impact on Farmers and Rural Women in Asia" http://www.glow-boell.de/media/de/txt_rubrik_5/sus_arze_ruralwomen.pdf (accessed on 16-07-14).

[243]Glipo "Agreement on Agriculture and Food Sovereignty Perspectives from Mesoamerica and Asia" 2003 Global issue Papers. http://www.boell.de/sites/default/files/assets/boell.de/images/download_de/internationalepolitik/gip3.pdf (Accessed on 16-07-14).

[244] Glipo "The WTO-AoA: Impact on Farmers and Rural Women in Asia" http://www.glow-boell.de/media/de/txt_rubrik_5/sus_arze_ruralwomen.pdf (accessed on 16-07-14).

[245] Glipo *Ibid.*

[246] Arze "An Analysis of the WTO-AoA Review from the Perspective of Rural Women in Asia" 2003 *WTO Documents.*

subsidies beyond the *de minimis* level.[247] Prospects are high that they will not be allowed to use any export subsidy in the future.[248] Many important provisions in the AoA allow developed countries to evade their trade liberalization obligation thus ensuring that their agriculture remain protected.[249]

The AoA increases the inequalities existing between the highly industrialized agriculture of developed countries and the predominantly subsistence and backward agriculture of developing countries.[250] In many developing countries, agriculture is dominated by small-scale producers ploughing very small plots of land, with very little access to capital and productive resources, and are continually indebted to landlords and moneylenders.[251] Because of their marginal position, the small-scale farmers are not in a position to compete with international markets especially of developed nations.[252] In the end, the small-scale and traditional farmers of the developing world lose out in a clearly unfair competition with the industrial farmers of developed countries.[253] It is exanimated that millions of small farmers are displaced and the livelihoods of the majority of agricultural producers in these countries are put to increasing risks.[254] This condition exacerbates the deepening income inequalities between and within nations.

The AoA and its inherent bias for commercial agriculture production devastate not only the livelihood of poor farmers but also the food security prospects of many developing countries.[255] The dismantling of protection and support to agriculture in developing countries creates not only gross disincentives against domestic food production, but wipes out its viability and sustainability.[256] Since the mid-90's developing countries have faced declining growth rates in food production output which is threatening their capacity to meet domestic food consumption

247 Arze 2003.

248 Arze 2003

249 For instance, The Due Restraint Clause under Article 13 protects those subsidies that have been exempted from reduction from being challenged. The Special Safeguard provision, which applies only to those products which have been tariffed have benefited mostly developed countries.

250 Khor "The WTO Agriculture Agreement: Features, Effects, Negotiations, and What is at Stake?" www.twn.org. (Accessed on 09/0614).

251 Glipo "Agreement on Agriculture and Food Sovereignty Perspectives from Mesoamerica and Asia" 2003 Global issue Papers. http://www.boell.de/sites/default/files/assets/boell.de/images/download_de/internationalepolitik/gip3.pdf (accessed on 16/07/14).

252 *Ibid.*

253 Glipo 2003.

254 Glipo *Ibid.*

255 Glipo "The WTO-AoA: Impact on Farmers and Rural Women in Asia" http://www.glow-boell.de/media/de/txt_rubrik_5/sus_arze_ruralwomen.pdf (accessed on 16-07-14).

256 *Ibid.*

requirements.[257] Since the implementation of the AoA in 1995, the capacity of developing countries to ensure their long-term food security has been increasingly eroded.[258] Two patterns that have direct impact on food security and agriculture in developing countries have clearly emerged.[259] They are discussed below.

2 6 1 Rise of Subsidies in Developed Countries

Even though the AoA was designed to discipline domestic support and export subsidies in developed countries, the years following the enforcement of the AoA ironically saw an unusual rise in these subsidies.[260] The AoA's classification of subsidies into trade distorting and non-trade distorting, caused the developed countries to shift their existing trade distorting subsidies into acceptable boxes that are exempted from reduction such as the green and blue boxes.[261] As a result of this, subsidies under the AMS (Amber Box) decreased, and there was a corresponding increase in subsidies under the Green and Blue Boxes.[262] In the US, for instance, Green Box subsidies amounted US$50 billion in 1998, compared to a total of $10 billion Amber Box subsidies.[263]

The enactment of the US Farm Bill in 2002 led to the provision of extra support amounting to US $ 180 billion for a period of ten years to its domestic producers.[264] The trend is also the same in the EU. Its Aggregate Measurement of Support (AMS)[265] under the amber box is being shifted to direct payments (blue box), which are supposedly less trade distorting as they are tied to production limiting programmes.[266] The current Common Agricultural Policy (CAP) reforms are in the course of further moving subsidies in the form of direct payments to decoupled payments, which basically

---

257 Glipo "The WTO-AoA: Impact on Farmers and Rural Women in Asia" http://www.glow-boell.de/media/de/txt_rubrik_5/sus_arze_ruralwomen.pdf (accessed on 16-07-14).

258 *Ibid.*

259 An example is the increasing agricultural subsidies in developed countries, despite the avowed goal of the AoA to curb trade-distorting subsidies. Another clear example is the massive flooding of artificially cheap food imports in developing countries' markets that continues to displace domestic food production.

260 Wise, "The Paradox of Agricultural Subsidies: Measurement Issues, Agricultural Dumping, and Policy Reform" 2004. http://ase.tufts.edu/gdae/pubs/wp/04-02agsubsidies.pdf. (Accessed on 15-07-14).

261 Khor.

262 *Ibid.*

263 Khor.

264 Glipo "An Analysis of the WTO AoA Review from the Perspective of Rural Women in Asia" 2003 WTO Documents.

265 According to Article 1 (a) of the AoA "Aggregate Measurement of Support" (AMS) means the annual level of support, expressed in monetary terms, provided for an agricultural product in favour of the producers of the basic agricultural product or non-product specific support provided in favour of agricultural producers in general, other than support provided under programmes that qualify as exempt from reduction under Annex 2 of AoA.

266 Glipo "The WTO-AoA: Impact on Farmers and Rural Women in Asia" http://www.glow-boell.de/media/de/txt_rubrik_5/sus_arze_ruralwomen.pdf (Accessed on 16-07-14).

is shifting again from the blue to the green boxes characterised as non-trade distorting.[267] The effect is, that AoA has normalised and legitimized the trade-distorting subsidies and dumping practices of developed countries by permitting the shifting of directly price-related subsidies to direct payments or decoupled payments that are protected and even allowed to increase under the AoA.[268]

Export subsidies of developed countries are continuing to rise because world prices continue to fall.[269] The effect of this is that developed countries subsidise exports in order to offset possible losses of domestic producers.[270] It is alleged that the EU continues to provide export subsidies while the US hides its export support under export credits and food aid.[271] In both the US and EU, domestic Support has increased for their farmers, despite the fact that most of the beneficiaries of these subsidies are the big producers and traders.[272] The US and EU continue to dump agricultural products in the world market, meaning that they are selling their products at less than the cost of production.[273] Their enormous subsidies in agriculture for both domestic farmers and exporters have led to dumping which continue to cause mayhem on farmers' livelihoods in developing countries.[274] A noted Indian food policy analyst, Devinder Sharma, pointed out "the gross injustice of this system when compared to the amount of subsidy a cow in Europe and America receives per day, is about US $ 2.70 per cow while the daily income of a small and marginal farmer in the Third World, is about less than half of this amount."[275]

---

[267] The Common Agricultural Policy is an agricultural policy that was introduced by the EU in 1962 to implement a system of agricultural subsidies and other programs related to agriculture. It was introduced when the founding members of the EC emerged from over a decade of severe food shortages during and after World War II. As part of building a common market, tariffs on agricultural products would have to be removed. However, due to the political clout of farmers, and the sensitivity of the issue, it would take many years before the CAP was fully implemented. Its reform is currently in the pipeline.

[268] *Ibid.*

[269] Food and Agriculture Organisation of the United Nations (FAO) "The State of Food Security in the World: How does international price volatility affect domestic economies and food security?" http://www.fao.org/95FD9558-E7CC4BD0A1FB2A58B82EAF13/FinalDownload/DownloadIdF0783CFD87D7DA65603F20B7BDE4489F/95FD9558-E7CC-4BD0-A1FB-2A58B82EAF13/docrep/014/i2330e/i2330e.pdf . (Accessed on 18-07-14).

[270] *Ibid.*

[271] Glipo 2003.

[272] *Ibid.*

[273] Green "Dumping on the Poor: The Common Agricultural Policy" 2002 CAFOD. http://www.iatp.org%2Ffiles%2FDumping_on_the_Poor_The_Common_Agricultural_Po.htm&ei=iPTIU6uuCuPF7AbBoYHoBQ&usg=AFQjCNGuBZYb2LFeisK9ki2V2NAzn7bynA&sig2=hjFpEXtTRS7fcIAr571eow&bvm=bv.71198958,d.bGQ&cad=rjt (Accessed on 15-07-18).

[274] Glipo "The WTO-AoA: Impact on Farmers and Rural Women in Asia" http://www.glow-boell.de/media/de/txt_rubrik_5/sus_arze_ruralwomen.pdf (Accessed on 16-07-14).

[275] Ahmad "India and China: Conflict, Competition, and Cooperation in The Age Of Globalization" 2008. http%3A%2F%2Fxa.yimg.com%2Fkq%2Fgroups%2F18630209%2F1685782545%2Fname%2Fglobalization.doc&

2 6 2 Increase of Food Imports in Developing Countries

Another disastrous consequence of the flawed AoA is the massive penetration of highly subsidized food imports into developing countries' domestic markets.[276] Thus, as a result of tariffication and the progressive reduction of tariffs stipulated in the AoA, developing countries now have very low tariffs with bound rates averaging 30-40%.[277] Such low rates cannot provide protection to domestic producers who are overburdened by depressed farm gate prices, increasing costs of production and lack of access to scarce capital and resources.[278] In Glipo's words "Food imports and sudden import surges have led to the displacement of small farmers and the erosion of food security in many developing countries."[279]

The Food and Agriculture Organization (FAO) conducted a study on the impact of the AoA on 14 developing countries in 2001 which revealed that the AoA's liberalization policy significantly increased food importation in these countries, with many registering sudden increases in the value of their food imports in the years following their accession to the AoA.[280] The food import bill doubled in major food producers and exporters such as Brazil and India and it also increased by 50-100% in countries like Bangladesh, Pakistan and Thailand.[281] As a result of the AoA, many agricultural product exporting countries in the 70's and 80's like the Philippine have been transformed into net food importers.[282] As there were no corresponding dramatic increases in developing countries' agricultural exports after their accession to the WTO, the massive food imports and import surges contributed to the huge trade deficits in agriculture they incurred during this period.[283] The study exhumed the general trend towards land concentration as small-scale farms were edged out in the competition.[284] This has led to displacement of small farmers and to food-insecure groups, further exacerbating hunger and food insecurity among rural households.[285]

---

ei=i_zIU4f4FnF7Aa5yYCQAg&usg=AFQjCNEPACQiFNmmFL4hRyjRe4Svx5euhw&sig2=r2224SiiIy0eeuIg_J1_0A&bvm=bv.71198958,d.bGQ . (Accessed on 18-07-14).

[276] Glipo "The WTO-AoA: Impact on Farmers and Rural Women in Asia" http://www.glow-boell.de/media/de/txt_rubrik_5/sus_arze_ruralwomen.pdf (accessed on 16-07-14).

[277] *Ibid.*

[278] *Ibid.*

[279] *Ibid.*

[280] FAO "Agriculture Trade and Food Security" 2001 *Food and Agriculture Organization.*

[281] *Ibid.*

[282] Glipo "The WTO-AoA: Impact on Farmers and Rural Women in Asia" http://www.glow-boell.de/media/de/txt_rubrik_5/sus_arze_ruralwomen.pdf (accessed on 16-07-14).

[283] *Ibid.*

[284] FAO 2001.

[285] *Ibid.*

Besides agricultural protectionism practised by developed countries, the AOA also promotes market liberalization in developing countries which has seriously damaged rural livelihoods and food security.[286] Agricultural subsidies granted in developing countries have been significantly reduced and in many cases withdrawn resulting in increased indebtedness of poor farmers.[287] In many developing countries, State procurement and public food distribution programs have been scaled down while in some countries, procurement centres that were tactically located in farming villages were shut down like in Pakistan.[288] These polices have left poor farmers at the mercy of traders and moneylenders who make huge profits from under-pricing farmers' produce and raising loan interests exorbitantly.[289] In many cases, government stopped buying from their own farmers and relied on cheap food imports to top up their stocks.[290]

It is also argued that the very same tools that developed countries used to achieve food security and food self-sufficiency such as import controls and higher tariffs are now being denied to developing countries as they are now considered trade barriers under the AoA.[291] According to Glipo, "Subsidies that could have provided support to subsistence and cash-strapped farmers are being withdrawn as these are also considered trade-distorting under the AoA. Indeed in a short span of time, AoA has actually succeeded in reversing policies and measures used by developing countries to achieve food security."[292]

The WTO has in fact succeeded in redefining food security from one of having increased production capacity to meet domestic food consumption to having mere access to food imports supplied by countries which can produce them cheaply.[293] The US, which instigated the launching of the Uruguay Round to capture greater share market for its agriculture exports, had exactly this

[286] Glipo "Agreement on Agriculture and Food Sovereignty Perspectives from Mesoamerica and Asia" 2003 *Global issue Papers.* http://www.boell.de/sites/default/files/assets/boell.de/images/download_de/internationalepolitik/gip3.pdf (Accessed on 16-07-14).

[287] *Ibid.* A solid example is countries like Zambia and Indonesia were fertilizer subsidies were removed.

[288] Glipo "Agreement on Agriculture and Food Sovereignty Perspectives from Mesoamerica and Asia" 2003 *Global issue Papers.* http://www.boell.de/sites/default/files/assets/boell.de/images/download_de/internationalepolitik/gip3.pdf (Accessed on 16-07-14).

[289] *Ibid.*

[290] *Ibid.*

[291] Glipo "The WTO-AoA: Impact on Farmers and Rural Women in Asia" http://www.glow-boell.de/media/de/txt_rubrik_5/sus_arze_ruralwomen.pdf (accessed on 16-07-14).

[292] *Ibid.*

[293] *Ibid.*

concept in mind.[294] But as the implementation experience of developing countries would attest, trade liberalization in agriculture has led in fact to increased hunger, starvation and poverty among the rural poor.[295]

2 7 CONCLUSIONS

A logical trace of the history of the regulation of subsidies clearly depicts the political sensitivity of the area. The agricultural negotiations were dominated by the developed countries and developing countries were to some extent side-lined.[296] The US and the EU dominated the agricultural markets, hence their contributions to the formulation of the AoA during the Uruguay Round was fiercely respected.[297] This obviously also had to do with their political prowess.[298] The AoA was fashioned in a way that would protect the interests of the developed world.[299] This included continual protection of agricultural markets by developed countries whilst the developing countries were opening their markets.[300]

Another weakness of the agreement is its silence on the enforcement measures.[301] It is apparent that developed countries continued to protect their agricultural sector by providing massive subsidies.[302] However, the AoA only prohibits trade distorting subsidies but it does not provide any clear enforcement mechanism.[303] It can therefore be submitted that the AoA is biased towards the developed countries that were at the centre stage of negotiating the agreement.[304] It was crafted to address their problems, ensure food security and to avoid potential political instability in their

---

294 Cavanagh "A Report of the IFG International Forum on Globalization (IFG). Alternatives to Economic Globalization". This was echoed by no less than John Black, the US Agriculture Secretary at that time, when he said at the start of the Uruguay Round negotiations in 1986 that the " idea that developing countries should feed themselves is an anachronism from a bygone era. They could better ensure their food security by relying on US agricultural products, which are available, in most cases, at much lower cost."

295 *Ibid.*

296 See Kwa "The WTO and Developing Countries: a Foreign policy in Focus Brief on WTO" http://focusweb.org/node/62 (accessed on 04-11-14). Also see Deardorff "What Should the Developing Countries Do in the Context of the Current Impasse of the Doha Round?" http://www.fordschool.umich.edu/rsie/workingpapers/wp.html (Accessed on 15-10-14).

297 Matthews "The Agricultural Negotiations in the Uruguay Round and the Developing Countries" 1988. http://www.trocaire.org/sites/trocaire/files/resources/policy/1988-agriculture-developing-countries-uruguay-round.pdf . (Accessed on 29/07/14).

298 Khor *Ibid.*

299 Khor *ibid.* Also see WTO "The History and the Future of the World Trade Organization" 2013 *WTO Documents.*

300 *Ibid.*

301 Lal Das "Strengthening Developing Countries in the WTO" 2012 *Trade and Development.*

302 See Glipo for more on this.

303 Einarsson "The Disagreement on Agriculture" http://www.grain.org/article/entries/309-the-disagreement-on-agriculture (accessed on 04-11-14).

304 Matthews *ibid.*

countries.[305] This was done at the expense of developed countries that strongly adhered to the agreement in an attempt to get absorbed in the emerging global trade trends.[306] The flaws in the negotiating process led to a lot of loopholes in the agreement which have distressingly affected developing countries.[307]

[305] Glipo 2003.
[306] *Ibid.*
[307] *Ibid.*

CHAPTER 3

Agreement on Agriculture: Key Elements and the Problematic Provisions

3 1 INTRODUCTION

The Agreement on Agriculture (AoA) has made significant changes in World agricultural trade. Its inception established a basis for initiating a process of reform of trade in line with the objectives of the negotiations set out in *Punta de Este* Declaration.[308] However, the agreement itself did not completely come with salvation for developing countries. Some of its provisions have been manipulated by developed countries who were at the core of the agricultural negotiations in Uruguay.[309] The AoA seem to have been crafted to safeguard the needs and address the concerns of developed countries.[310] Even though the AoA aims at providing for substantial progressive reductions in agricultural support and protection as well as correcting and preventing restrictions and distortions in world agricultural markets, developing countries are still experiencing a massive influx of subsidized exports and continue to lose their share of global agricultural markets.[311]

The AoA seeks to reduce restrictions on trade in agricultural products by introducing disciplines to increase markets access, reduce domestic support measures and reduce subsidised exports.[312] It applies only to agricultural products. Agricultural products are defined in Annex 1 of the Agreement. The definition of agricultural product covers not only basic agricultural products such as wheat, milk and live animals, but the products derived from them such as bread, butter, oil and meat, as well as all processed agricultural products such as chocolate, yoghurt and sausages.[313]

---

308 See the preamble of the AoA.

309 Blandford "Should the Green Box be Modified?" http://www.agritrade.org/Publications/DiscussionPapers/Green_Box.pdf (accessed on 21/09/14).

310 McMahon *Research Handbook on the WTO Agriculture Agreement: New and Emerging Issues in International Agricultural Trade Law* (2012) 5-15.

311 *Ibid.*

312 This chapter will mainly focus on the provisions of the AoA. However, this does not specifically mean that the AoA is the only agreement with agricultural provisions in the WTO. Other WTO agreements also discipline trade in agricultural products. Those with an impact on trade in agricultural products are: the General Agreement on Tariffs and Trade (GATT) 1994; the Agreement on Safeguards or the Safeguards Agreement; the Agreement on Import Licensing Procedures or the Import Licensing Agreement; the Agreement on the Application of Sanitary and Phyto-sanitary Measures (SPS); the Agreement on Technical Barriers to Trade or the (TBT) Agreement and, the Agreement on Trade Related Aspects of Intellectual Property Rights (TRIPs) Agreement. The reason why this study will primarily focus on the AoA is because article 21 of the AoA provides that, the provisions of GATT 1994 and of other Multilateral Trade Agreements in Annex 1A to the WTO Agreement shall apply subject to the provisions of this AoA. This of course applies to all the above agreements that deal with agricultural products.

313 See Annex 1 of the AoA. The list is however not exhaustible.

The coverage also includes wines, spirits and tobacco products, fibres such as cotton, wool and silk, and raw animal skins destined for leather production.[314]

The reform programme propelled by the AoA was made up of some degree of rulemaking and the adoption of specific commitments to increase market access and to reduce domestic support and export subsidies, which would, in the words of the preamble, lead to "substantial reductions in agricultural support and protection sustained over an agreed period of time".[315] The agreed implementation period for the commitments undertaken as part of the Uruguay Round negotiations was six years[316], save in the case of Article 13, the Peace Clause, which limited the possibility of disputes for a period of nine years.[317] Apart from this, Article 20 of the AoA establishes an agenda for further negotiations so as to achieve the long term objective of 'substantial progressive reductions in support and protection'.[318]

3 2 THE MAIN PILLARS OF THE AOA

3 2 1 Market Access

Market access can be defined as the right of exporters have to access a foreign market.[319] The WTO does not absolutely prohibit its members from protecting their markets.[320] Practically, market access refers to the ways in which that protection can be implemented. In the WTO legal context, market access broadly refers the government imposed conditions under which a product may enter a country and be released for free circulation within that country under normal conditions.[321] The legal border measures to protect markets allowed under the AoA are tariffs and tariff rate quotas.[322] A tariff can be defined as a duty or tax. Although there are several different

[314] The list also includes goods made/manufactured from agricultural products. This is a catch all provision which is meant to avoid potential abuse of the agreement through exporting manufactured agricultural products.

[315] See the Preamble of the AoA for a comprehensive explanation of the aims and objectives of the agreement. For the purposes of this study, market access, domestic support and export subsidies commitments will be used as the main pillars of the AoA.

[316] This did not apply to developing countries. The agreed implementation period for the commitments undertaken as part of the Uruguay negotiations was ten years for developing countries. However the peace clause expired in 2000 so both developed and developing countries are equally bound by the agreement.

[317] See Article 1(f) of the AoA.

[318] The reform process is currently underway in Doha and Bali. This will be fully explained in chapter 5 of the study.

[319] United Nations Conference on Trade and Development (UNCTD) "Agriculture" http://unctad.org/en/docs/edmmisc232add32_en.pdf (accessed on 15/09/14).

[320] *Ibid.* In some instances, members are allowed to protect their markets, for example, when implementing countervailing measures or anti-dumping measures.

[321] UNCTD 2003.

[322] NTBs are prohibited because they are difficult to discern and protective in nature. Tariffs are transparent and easy to monitor.

forms of tariffs, the major ones used in agriculture are *ad valorem*,[323] specific and mixed.[324] A tariff rate quota is a specific volume at which a product can enter a market at a tariff rate which is different than the over quota tariff.[325]

In terms of rulemaking, a major achievement of the AoA on market access was the elimination of nearly all types of Non-Tariff Barriers (NTBs), which were to be converted into tariff equivalents, under a process known as tariffication.[326] According to Article 4 (2) of the AoA members shall not maintain, resort to, or revert to any measures of the kind which have been required to be converted into ordinary custom duties, except as otherwise provided for Article 5 and Annex 5.[327] This can be argued as the most significant aspect of the entire AoA, since it means that virtually all agricultural protection is now in the form of tariffs, which are more transparent and easier to negotiate than non-tariff measures.[328]

The panel in *Chile – Price Band System* described article 4 (2) as central to "the establishment and protection of a fair and market-orientated agricultural trading system in the area of market access".[329] The Appellate in the same dispute noted that Article 4 (2) recorded the intention of negotiators of the Agreement that in principle custom duties would become the only form of border protection.[330] Moreover, members also undertook specific commitments in the area of agriculture markets access, which included the binding and reduction of tariffs and other commitments.[331] The reduction commitments apply to both traditional tariffs and new tariffs which have resulted from

---

323 These are tariffs calculated as a percentage of the value of the goods.

324 Specific tariffs, refers to a unit tax based on quantity and mixed a combination of *ad volorem* and specific tariffs.

325 Khorana "Tariff Rate Quotas: A Market Access Barrier for Developing Countries Products? The Case of Switzerland." http://www.researchgate.net%2Fprofile%2FSangeeta_Khorana2%2Fpublication%2F228777194_Tariff_Rate_Quotas_A_Market_Access_Barrier_for_Developing_Countries_Products_The_Case_of_Switzerland%2Flinks%2F02e7e5296354e09744000000&ei=N7cWVKT8LdOf7AbJ54HoCQ&usg=AFQjCNFdGaQUqQpId5L9BJ4G5amRiwIqXg&sig2=X6bscVmQfoYejWjbHIB9YQ&bvm=bv.75097201,d.ZGU (accessed on 14/09/14).

326 Sandrey *Agriculture and the World Trade Organization – what happened since 1995?* (2009).

327 These measures include quantitative import restrictions, variable import levies, minimum import prices, discretionary import licensing, non-tariff measures maintained through state-trading enterprises, voluntary export restraints, and similar border measures other than ordinary customs duties, whether or not the measures are maintained under country-specific derogations from the provisions of GATT 1947, but not measures maintained under balance-of-payments provisions or under other general, non-agriculture-specific provisions of GATT 1994 or of the other Multilateral Trade Agreements in Annex 1A to the WTO Agreement.

328 McMahon *Research Handbook on the WTO Agriculture Agreement. New and Emerging Issues in International Agricultural Trade Law* (2012) 12-16.

329 See *Chile – Price Band System* (DS207/R.7.15).

330 *Ibid.*

331 See Article 4.1 of the AoA.

the process of tariffication.[332] However, this study will not extensively deal with market access commitments since it is specifically dealing with agricultural subsidies.

3 2 2 Domestic support commitments

The AoA disciplines, rules and restraints on domestic support and also minimises trade protectionism by directing the domestic policies that are most trade-distorting towards lesser or minimum distortions.[333] Under WTO legal framework, domestic support policy instruments are normally classified into three categories, now often known as the traffic light system.[334] Support policies that are supposedly the least or minimally trade distorting are placed in the "Green Box," and can be exempted from reduction commitments.[335] Apart from this, also belonging to the same category are certain domestic investments and input subsidies in developing countries that qualify as Special and Differential which are equally exempted. Domestic support instruments deemed to be the most trade distorting are classified as "Amber Box" policies, and these are subject to reduction in sections. Direct payments under production-limiting programs are contained in the "Blue Box," with distorting effects between those instruments in the Green and Amber Boxes.[336]

The Uruguay Round agricultural package profoundly changed the way domestic support in favour of agricultural producers was treated under the GATT 1947.[337] Its main objective has been to discipline and reduce domestic support while at the same time leaving great scope for governments to design domestic agricultural policies in the face of, and in response to, the wide variety of the specific circumstances in individual countries and individual agricultural sectors.[338] The AoA also

---

[332] For developed country members the average reduction was to be 36 per cent over a period of six years from the inception of the AoA, whereas for developing countries the average reduction was to be 24 per cent which was to be implemented over a ten year span. Least developed countries were required to bind their tariffs but not to undertake any reduction commitments.

[333] FAO "The implications of the Uruguay Round Agreement on Agriculture for developing countries." http://www.fao.org/docrep/004/w7814e/w7814e05.htm (accessed on 18 September 2014).

[334] More on this will be explained below. The categories are the green box, amber box and blue box subsidies.

[335] Green Box category is supposed to have a minimal trade distorting effect. However its effect on developing countries as noted in chapter 2 of this study distorting trade.

[336] The Blue Box measures are exempt from commitments if such payments are made on fixed areas and yield or a fixed number of livestock.

[337] WTO "Agriculture: Explanation of the Agreement on Agriculture" 2012 *WTO Documents* generally.

[338] *Ibid.*

aims at ensuring that the specific binding commitments in the areas of market access and export competition are not undermined through domestic support measures.[339]

3 2 3 Export Subsidies

The main objective of the reform programme on export subsidies is the commitments to reduce subsidized export quantities, and the amount of finances spent subsidizing exports.[340] Apart from this, the AoA also looks at anti-circumvention questions.[341] The increase of export subsidies in the years proceeding to the Uruguay Round was one of the key issues that were addressed in the agricultural negotiations.[342] Prior to the WTO, export subsidies for industrial products were prohibited all along, and agricultural primary products such subsidies were only subject to limited disciplines which moreover did not prove to be operational.[343]

Under the WTO, the right to use export subsidies is now limited to four situations: (i) export subsidies subject to product-specific reduction commitments within the limits specified in the schedule of the WTO Member concerned; (ii) any excess of budgetary outlays for export subsidies or subsidized export volume over the limits specified in the schedule which is covered by the "downstream flexibility" provision of Article 9.2(b) of the AoA; (iii) export subsidies consistent with the special and differential treatment provision for developing country Members (Article 9.4 of the Agreement);[344] and (iv) export subsidies other than those subject to reduction commitments provided that they are in conformity with the anti-circumvention disciplines of Article 10 of the

339 FAO *Multilateral Trade Negotiations on Agriculture: Food and Agriculture Organization of the United Nations* (2000) generally.

340 Gorter "Export Subsidies: World Bank Documents". http://siteresources.worldbank.org/INTRANETTRADE/Resources/239054112681241927O/8.ExportSubsidies.pdf . (Accessed on 19/08/14).

341 WTO "Agriculture: Explanation of the Agreement on Agriculture" 2012 *WTO Documents* generally.

342 *Ibid.*

343 According to Article XVI of the GATT, a contracting party grants or maintains any subsidy, including any form of income or price support, which operates directly or indirectly to increase exports of any product from, or to reduce imports of any product into, its territory, it shall notify the contracting parties in writing of the extent and nature of the subsidization, of the estimated effect of the subsidization on the quantity of the affected product or products imported into or exported from its territory and of the circumstances making the subsidization necessary. In any case in which it is determined that serious prejudice to the interests of any other contracting party is caused or threatened by any such subsidization, the contracting party granting the subsidy shall, upon request, discuss with the other contracting party or parties concerned, or with the contracting parties, the possibility of limiting the subsidization. The contracting parties recognize that the granting by a contracting party of a subsidy on the export of any product may have harmful effects for other contracting parties, both importing and exporting, may cause undue disturbance to their normal commercial interests, and may hinder the achievement of the objectives of this Agreement.

344 According to Article 9 (4) of the AoA, during the implementation period, developing country Members shall not be required to undertake commitments in respect of the export subsidies listed in subparagraphs (d) and (e) of paragraph 1 of article 9, provided that these are not applied in a manner that would circumvent reduction commitments.

Agreement on Agriculture. In all other cases, the use of export subsidies for agricultural products is prohibited.[345]

3 3 AGRICULTURAL SUBSIDIES

One of the main objective of the AoA is to ensure that agricultural trade is not distorted through the use of agricultural subsidies.[346] The agreement classifies agricultural support measures/subsidies into two major groups' namely domestic support and export subsidies. One of the key features of the AoA is to allow WTO Members to use subsidies in derogation from the SCM Agreement.[347] A key objective of the AoA is also to discipline and reduce all subsidies, while at the same time leaving scope for governments to design effective agricultural policies.[348] Export subsidies are regulated by the provisions in Articles 8, 9, 10 and 11 of the agreement. Domestic subsidies are regulated by the provisions of Articles 6 and 7 along with Annexes 2, 3 and 4 of the AoA.

3 4 DOMESTIC SUPPORT MEASURES: GREEN BOX SUBSIDIES

Under the AoA, all Green Box support measures must have no, or at most minimal, trade-distorting effects, nor positive effects on production.[349] Green Box support should be provided through varmint-planned investments rather than through price hikes on consumer goods; it should not have the effect of providing price support to producers.[350] Green Box measures must comply with the government schemes rather than direct support to particular products.[351] The AoA imposes no limitations on the use of Green Box subsidies as long as they accord with relative criteria.[352] Green

---

[345] These include export subsidies mentioned in Articles 3.3, 8 and 10 of the Agreement on Agriculture.

[346] According the preamble of the AoA, one of the long-term objectives of the AoA is to provide for substantial progressive reductions in agricultural support and protection sustained over an agreed period of time, resulting in correcting and preventing restrictions and distortions in world agricultural markets.

[347] United Nations Conference on Trade and Development (UNCTD) "Agriculture" http://unctad.org/en/docs/edmmisc232add32_en.pdf (accessed on 15/09/14).This basically means that Agricultural Subsidies will be treated with an exemption from or relaxation from some of the provisions of the SCM.

[348] *Ibid.*

[349] There are no monetary limits imposed on green box subsidies, annex 2 of the AoA details disciplines to avoid including amber or blue box type payments in this category. The green box includes measures that "have no, or at most minimal, trade distorting effects or effects on agricultural production.

[350] OECD "Green Growth and Developing Countries: A Summary for Policy Makers" 2012. http://www.oecd.org/E7B4340B-417C-491A-9A43-DED57EC05D26/FinalDownload/DownloadId-AB05B1393B2C4AA02938345A7A286A6A/E7B4340B-417C-491A-9A43-DED57EC05D26/dac/50526354.pdf . (Accessed on 23/09/14).

[351] Blandford "Should the Green Box be Modified?" 2007. http://www.agritrade.org/Publications/DiscussionPapers/Green_Box.pdf (Accessed on 02/08/14).

[352] Blandford "Should the Green Box be Modified?" 2007. http://www.agritrade.org/Publications/DiscussionPapers/Green_Box.pdf (Accessed on 02/08/14).

Box measures are generally applicable to all members, both developed and developing countries.[353]

The AoA sets out a number of general and measure-specific criteria which, when met, allow measures to be placed in the Green Box. These measures are exempted from reduction commitments and, indeed, can even be increased without any financial limitation under the WTO.[354] The general criteria is that, the measures must have no, or at most minimal, trade-distorting effects or effects on production. They must be provided through a publicly-funded government programme[355] which excludes transfers from consumers and must not have the effect of providing price support to producers.

Apart from this, the green box also covers government service programmes including general services provided by governments, public stockholding programmes for food security purposes and domestic food aid as long as the general criteria and some other measure-specific criteria are met by each measure concerned.[356] The Green Box thus provides for the continuation as well as the enhancement of programmes such as research, including general research, research in connection with environmental programmes, and research programmes relating to particular products.[357] Many of the regular programmes of governments are thus given the "green light" to continue as long as they do not have or have minimal trade distorting effects.

---

353 *Ibid.* The application of Green Box measures to both developed and developing countries is legally a general rule. The exception is in the case of developing countries, where special treatment is provided in respect of governmental stockholding programmes for food security purposes and subsidized food prices for urban and rural poor.

354 Team "Studies Green Box Subsidies A Theoretical and Empirical Assessment" WTO Documents 2008. http://wtocentre.iift.ac.in/DOC/Studies_GreenBoxSubsidiesATheoreticalAndEmpericalAssessmen.pdf (Accessed on 02/08/14).

355 This also includes government revenue foregone.

356 FAO "After Bali. WTO rules Applying to Food Security" 2014. http://www.wti.org/fileadmin/user_upload/wti.org/news/140130_Haeberli_Stockpiles_Final_for_FAO.pdf (accessed on 30/09/14). Also see WTO "Agriculture: Explanation of the Agreement on Agriculture". http://www.wto.org/english/tratop_e/agric_e/ag_intro03_domestic_e.htm (accessed on 07/08/14).

357 These include pest and disease control programmes, including general and product-specific pest and disease control measures; agricultural training services and extension and advisory services; inspection services, including general inspection services and the inspection of particular products for health, safety, grading or standardization purposes; marketing and promotion services; infrastructural services, including electricity reticulation, roads and other means of transport, market and port facilities, water supply facilities, among others; expenditures in relation to the accumulation and holding of public stocks for food security purposes; and expenditures in relation to the provision of domestic food aid to sections of the population in need.

The Green Box regulations also provide for the use of direct payments to producers which are however not linked to production decisions.[358] The conditions exclude any *sine qua non* between the amount of such payments, on the one hand, and production, prices or factors of production in any year after a fixed base period.[359] In addition, no production shall be required in order to receive such payments. Additional criteria to be met depend on the type of measure concerned which may include: decoupled income support measures; income insurance and safety-net programmes; natural disaster relief; a range of structural adjustment assistance programmes; and certain payments under environmental programmes and under regional assistance programmes.[360]

3 4 1 Green Box Subsidies: The Concept

The concept of Green Box was introduced in the Uruguay Round to incorporate government payments that were considered trade-neutral, or at least minimally trade-distorting.[361] It therefore serves the same purpose as the class of permitted subsidies in the non-agricultural area, as defined by the SCM.[362] In the Uruguay Round of negotiations, WTO members realized that they would not be able to agree on disciplines for all agricultural payments.[363] Negotiating members agreed however that rules regulating border instruments would not be adequate to correct the trade-distorting impact of farm programs, and felt that it was essential to impose some discipline on domestic agricultural policies.[364] Hence, it was important to espouse a classification of agricultural subsidies that distinguished between those that are trade-distorting and those that are relatively trade-neutral, in order to include all domestic support instruments under WTO disciplines.[365]

---

[358] The process is known as decoupling. This means that, although the farmer receives a payment from the government, this payment does not influence the type or volume of agricultural production.

[359] See WTO "Agriculture: Explanation of the Agreement on Agriculture". http://www.wto.org/english/tratop_e/agric_e/ag_intro03_domestic_e.htm (accessed on 07/08/14).

[360] *Ibid.*

[361] Blandford "Should the Green Box be Modified?" 2007. http://www.agritrade.org/Publications/DiscussionPapers/Green_Box.pdf (accessed on 02/08/14). The concept of agricultural subsidies that have no or at most minimal production and trade-distorting effects was introduced in the Uruguay Round Agreement on Agriculture (URAA). It provided a direct link between the parallel processes of domestic agricultural policy reform, and reform of the multilateral trading system. The process of moving from price support to direct payments has been an essential part of domestic reforms, offering better targeting of support and reducing surplus production.

[362] Blandford 2007.

[363] Aggarwal "Dynamics of Agricultural Negotiations in the World Trade Organisation" 2005 *Journal of World Trade* 741-761.

[364] Aggarwal 2005 742-761.

[365] Aggarwal 2005 742-758.

The most important criterion for classifying a subsidy as "trade-distorting" is linkage between the subsidy and the incentive to produce.[366] Agricultural subsidies that directly affect output or input prices, or vary with the quantity of output, are most likely to provide an incentive to expand production.[367] However, those have no direct link to prices or output, were viewed as less likely to expand production. Hence, the Green Box is tied intricately to the notion of decoupling, and Green Box subsidies were thought to have a minimal impact on production.[368]

WTO members have taken very different positions on both the interpretation of current Green Box rules and the need for changes in the way the Green Box is defined and disciplined.[369] Those that view the Green Box positively, see the advantage of permitting the inclusion of both direct income payments and environmental subsidies, and sheltering these from challenge, even if they are not completely production neutral.[370] Proponents view shifting from highly coupled support to largely decoupled support[371] as a constructive contribution to the reform of domestic agricultural policies.[372] There is also the added advantage that decoupled payments can be "re-coupled" to reward desirable ecological practices and to provide public goods, such as rural amenities.[373]

In contrast, those who are sceptical about the Green Box are concerned that it simply provides a means for delivering income support to farmers under another guise especially in developed countries.[374] From this point of view, new justifications for support to farmers, such as the provision of public goods, are a political convenience without economic rationale.[375] Even in cases where public goods can be identified,[376] the payment provided may exceed that necessary to elicit the desired supply of a public good hence distorting trade.[377] Moreover, many other sectors of the

---

366 Blandford "Should the Green Box be Modified?" 2007. http://www.agritrade.org/Publications/DiscussionPapers/Green_Box.pdf (Accessed on 02/08/14).
367 These fall within the Amber Box category.
368 Brandford 2005.
369 ABARE "Report on EU CAP reforms – Green Box Issues" 2007. http://agfax.com/updates/misc/2007/keithgood/08/16.pdf (Accessed on 02/09/14).
370 ABARE Report 2007.
371 This is one form of box-shifting.
372 *Ibid.*
373 Brandford 2005.
374 Moon *Is agriculture compatible with free trade?* Also see Blandford, Should the Green Box be Modified? 2007.http://www.agritrade.org/Publications/DiscussionPapers/Green_Box.pdf (accessed on 21/9/14).
375 ABARE 2007.
376 For example a positive contribution to environmental quality.
377 Brandford 2005.

economy provide public goods, but are not given the same treatment as agriculture.[378] It is argued that the green box provision was incorporated in the AoA as a convenience measure to reach a consensus with all developed nations. Developed countries continue to provide trade distorting subsidies agriculture under the guise of green box.[379]

If the intention of Green Box policies is to redistribute income from taxpayers to farmers, rather than provide public goods, it therefore raises question as to whether such an objection is relevant.[380] If governments choose to redistribute national income among various groups, that is principally a domestic political issue which should not be dictated by trade rules.[381] A more substantial claim is that Green Box payments, whatever their rationale, are likely to distort trade[382] and therefore need to be disciplined. In that case, shifting from Amber to Green Box support may simply keep resources in agriculture that would otherwise be used elsewhere, negating the beneficial adjustment and trade effects of a reduction in Amber Box subsidies.[383]

However, the general perception by many is that, the current Green Box criterion allows policies that have significant trade-distorting effects.[384] Others consider that Green Box definitions do not allow for the development of a full range of legitimate domestic programs, such as those relating to environmental issues, without payments being counted against domestic support limits.[385] Apart from this, others also claim that the Green Box does not take into account the difficulties that developing countries have in providing direct payments, and underplay the desirability of

---

378 Blandford "Should the Green Box be Modified?" 2007. http://www.agritrade.org/Publications/DiscussionPapers/Green_Box.pdf (Accessed on 02/08/14).

379 Khor "The WTO Agriculture Agreement: Features, Effects, Negotiations, and what is at Stake?" www.twn.org . Khor further argues that, AoA's classification of subsidies into trade distorting and non-trade distorting, caused the developed countries to shift their existing trade distorting subsidies into acceptable boxes that are exempted from reduction such as the green and blue boxes.

380 ABARE Report 2007.

381 ABARE Report 2007. Rules that ensure that domestic agricultural programs are more consistent with open international markets will continue to allow for the development of a more satisfactory multilateral trade system. The designation in the URAA of certain types of agricultural payments that are free from reduction commitments put in the Green Box is thus pivotal for the continuation of domestic policy reform and for acceptance by other countries that the policies adopted are desirable for the development of international trade.

382 This means that they are unlikely to be fully decoupled.

383 See Brandford 2005. Clearer rules are needed to prevent countries from switching the method of payment or how payments are labelled simply to avoid subsidy constraints. That type of box shifting may do little to remove trade impacts.

384 Matthews *Decoupling and the Green Box: International Dimensions of the Reinstrumentation of Agricultural Support* (2006) 5-11.

385 Blandford, Should the Green Box be Modified? IPC Discussion Paper, Food & Agricultural Trade, March 2007. http://www.agritrade.org/Publications/DiscussionPapers/Green_Box.pdf (accessed on 21 March 2007 at 09:38:31 PM).

payments coupled to production and price in the context of rural development.[386] Another concern is that widespread use of Green Box measures by developed countries gives them a competitive edge, even if direct output effects are difficult to determine.[387]

As a result of these concerns, several countries have called for a review of Green Box payments.[388] The main users of the Green Box, the US and the EU, have argued against re-opening definitional issues.[389] As a result, the Framework Agreement of August 2004 called for negotiations to review and clarify the existing criteria, a step short of actually changing the definitions themselves.[390] Discussions on the topic took place before the Doha negotiations were suspended in July 2006, and by then it was not certain whether the Green Box would form a major part of the talks after the resumption of the negotiations.[391]

The lack of focus on Green Box criteria did not, however, mean that the issue was unimportant.[392] On the contrary, the Green Box was significant because its existence was tied to the reduction of Amber and Blue Box payments.[393] As these more trade-distorting forms of subsidies are reduced, the conditions under which payments can qualify for the Green Box become crucial.[394] A credible WTO outcome to the Doha Round that includes deep cuts in trade-distorting support requires agreement on criteria for policies considered non-trade-distorting.[395] Thus, even if Green Box issues will not form a major part of the Doha talks if they resume, WTO members may need to agree on a "built-in" agenda to tackle these issues upon conclusion of the Round.[396]

---

386 Meléndez-Ortiz, *Agricultural Subsidies in the WTO Green Box: Ensuring Coherence with Sustainable Development Goals* (2009) at 561-562.

387 Meléndez-Ortiz 2009.

388 Blandford 2007.

389 Josling "Biofuel Subsidies and the Green Box" www.ictsd.org/downloads/2008/12/josling-and-blandford.doc. (Accessed on 06 October 2014).

390 VanGrasstek, *The History and Future of the World Trade Organization,* (2013).

391 Meléndez-Ortiz 2009.

392 Blandford 2007.

393 Matthews *Decoupling and the Green Box: International Dimensions of the Reinstrumentation of Agricultural Support* (2006) at 11-14.

394 Blandford 2007.

395 WTO "Agriculture: Explanation of the Agreement on Agriculture". http://www.wto.org/english/tratop_e/agric_e/ag_intro03_domestic_e.htm (Accessed on 07/08/14).

396 Blandford "Should the Green Box be Modified?" http://www.agritrade.org/Publications/DiscussionPapers/Green_Box.pdf (Accessed on 02/08/14).

3 4 2 Green Box: Legal Issues

Most of the discussions of the compatibility of existing programs with the Green Box measures are by nature speculative.[397] There has been no WTO dispute panel ruling specifically on Green Box compatibility except the *US Cotton* case where a notification was questioned by a Panel.[398] No government has challenged the Green Box notifications of others. Besides this one case, no country has demanded that the US re-notify past domestic support (AMS) totals.

Lack of successful challenges thus far does not mean that none is possible in the future.[399] One such challenge could be on the basis that a payment for environmental services that does not simply compensate producers for compliance costs or income foregone may have a non-trivial impact on output.[400] Most programs that involve payments for environmental services include an incentive component.[401] As such, this may be actionable under the SCM. The United States has argued for a renewal of the Peace Clause in part to avoid such challenges. But this may only be effective if the policies are Green-Box compatible.[402] The likelihood of establishing a Peace Clause that covers AMS payments is more remote.[403] So, the possibility of such a challenge remains. Legislation needs to be crafted with this in mind.[404] In particular, payments should not be restricted to specific farms, though they can be regionally based, and should involve a mechanism through which a reasonable level for the payment can be determined.[405]

---

[397] De Schutter "The World Trade Organization and the Post-Global Food Crisis Agenda: Putting Food Security First in the International Trade System" https://www.wto.org/english/news_e/news11_e/deschutter_2011_e.pdf (Accessed on 14/06/14).

[398] The *US Upland Cotton* case was specifically about export subsidies (Article 13 of the AoA). However, the issue of green box subsidies was also considered in the case. The AB upheld the Panel's finding, in paragraphs 7.388, 7.413, 7.414, and 8.1(b) of the Panel Report, that production flexibility contract payments and direct payments were not green box measures that fully conform to paragraph 6(b) of Annex 2 of the Agreement on Agriculture; and, therefore, are not exempt from actions under Article XVI of GATT 1994 and Part III of the SCM Agreement by virtue of Article 13(a)(ii) of the Agreement on Agriculture; and declined to rule on Brazil's conditional request that the Appellate Body find that the updating of base acres for direct payments under the FSRI Act of 2002 means that direct payments are not green box measures that fully conform to paragraph 6(a) of Annex 2 of the Agreement on Agriculture; and, therefore, are not exempt from actions under Article XVI of GATT 1994 and Part III of the SCM Agreement by virtue of Article 13(a) (ii) of the Agreement on Agriculture.

[399] Blandford 2011.

[400] *Ibid.*

[401] This means an element that rewards producers for adopting environmentally-friendly practices.

[402] Meléndez-Ortiz *Agricultural Subsidies in the WTO Green Box: Ensuring Coherence with Sustainable Development Goals* (2009).

[403] *Ibid.*

[404] *Ibid.*

[405] Meléndez-Ortiz *Agricultural Subsidies in the WTO Green Box: Ensuring Coherence with Sustainable Development Goals* (2009).

The more serious challenge is not that of "serious prejudice" under the SCM, but of non-compliance with the Green Box definition in the AoA.[406] Payments for environmental services would clearly meet the general conditions of not being tied to production or prices.[407] The specific conditions are more problematic. One might argue that rewards for ecosystem services from the farm are payments above and beyond the costs of complying with an existing government program.[408] However, this may depend on the way in which the program is formulated. If the farmer has a choice between joining an environmental stewardship program and keeping eligibility for current farm income payments then income forgone includes the amount of those payments.[409] And if the payments are calculated with the cost to the farmer in mind, it would be difficult to argue that they are not equivalent to the "extra costs" involved in complying with the program.[410] So all, or most, of the stewardship payments might be notified as Green Box payments.[411]

The WTO ruling on the dispute between Brazil and the United States over *US upland cotton* programs called into question the legality of certain Green Box payments.[412] The essence of the case was that a wide range of US domestic subsidies, as well as some export programs, had caused serious prejudice to Brazil by depressing world cotton prices and increasing the U.S. share of world exports.[413] The domestic programs challenged included some notified as Amber Box support, some Green Box payments, and some not yet notified but potentially includable in an expanded Blue Box.[414] The United States disputed Brazil's allegations, arguing that the Peace Clause sheltered many of these programs from challenge under the subsidy rules, and furthermore, serious prejudice had not been the result of US programs.[415] The WTO Panel found that the export

---

406 Josling "Biofuel Subsidies and the Green Box" www.ictsd.org%2Fdownloads%2F2008%2F12%2Fjosling-andblandford.doc&ei=auAzVOKsJ8LPaJDJgtAL&usg=AFQjCNEBTn38NQx5vezUb8nghgFsyzvCkg&sig2=hT7WVniiZwrEOQnemFBaBA&bvm=bv.76943099,d.d2s. (Accessed on 07/10/14).

407 *Ibid.*

408 Blandford "Should the Green Box be Modified?" 2007. http://www.agritrade.org/Publications/DiscussionPapers/Green_Box.pdf (Accessed on 21 March 2007).

409 *Ibid.*

410 *Ibid.*

411 *Ibid.*

412 See WTO 2004b Report and 2005a Report.

413 WTO *United States—Subsidies on Upland Cotton* Reports of the Appellate Body WT/DS265/AB/R, WT/DS266/AB/R, & WT/DS267/AB/R (adopted March 21).

414 This included marketing loans (amber box), direct payments (green box) and counter-cyclical payments which fall under the blue box subsidies.

415 See United States—*Subsidies on Upland Cotton* 2005.

programs were in breach of US limits for such subsidies and that many of the domestic programs did in fact cause serious prejudice.[416]

As the panel was considering the extent to which US direct payments were correctly notified under the Green Box, they concluded that some do not satisfy the fundamental requirement, because they are linked to production.[417] In the panel's judgment, this linkage was created by limitations on planting flexibility for land upon which the payments are based.[418] Producers who wish to receive payments cannot plant fruits and vegetables on eligible land.[419] This was interpreted to mean that there is, in fact, a linkage between payments and production and that, consequently, they do not qualify for the Green Box.[420] This judgment is highly significant for the design of programs that countries wish to be exempt from reduction commitments – since it appears to imply that any direct linkage established between payments and production decisions would make their Green Box status potentially open to challenge.[421]

The distinction between the political decision in the AoA to classify subsidies on the basis of whether they were considered trade distorting, and therefore had to be reduced, on the one hand, and the political decision in the Agreement on SCM to distinguish among prohibited and allowed subsidies on the other, is at the heart of the problem.[422] Subsidies can be notified to the Agriculture Committee as Green Box by the country concerned and not be challenged.[423] But a policy could still be actionable even if allowable, and it could be found to cause serious prejudice.[424] Moreover,

---

[416] This decision was a huge step towards addressing the concerns of developing countries. From a developing country perspective, the decision was a major success towards addressing some of the loopholes in the AoA. It was the first time for a developing country to challenge a developed country's protectionist measures in terms of the AoA.

[417] Blandford "Should the Green Box be Modified?" 2007. http://www.agritrade.org/Publications/DiscussionPapers/Green_Box.pdf (accessed on 15/10/14).

[418] Blandford "Should the Green Box be Modified?" 2007. http://www.agritrade.org/Publications/DiscussionPapers/Green_Box.pdf (accessed on 15/10/14).

[419] WTO *United States—Subsidies on Upland Cotton*, Reports of the Appellate Body, WT/DS265/AB/R, WT/DS266/AB/R, & WT/DS267/AB/R (adopted March 21).

[420] *Ibid.*

[421] Blandford "US Environmental Programs and Green Box Provisions under the WTO Agreement on Agriculture" 2006.

[422] Blandford 2007.

[423] Blandford 2007.

[424] According to Blandford, a panel could find that the policies in question did not fit under the definition of the Green Box as happened in the U.S. cotton case, and thus were incorrectly notified. But this would only be a signification violation if it caused a country to exceed its scheduled subsidy commitments.

the treatment of agricultural subsidies in the AoA was premised on a firm distinction between domestic support and export subsidies, but both were legal if within scheduled commitments.[425]

In the WTO *Canada dairy case* doubt was cast on the validity of that distinction in that, when applying WTO rules, domestic programs can have the effect of providing an export subsidy.[426] Apart from this, the EU *Sugar case*, rested on the same premise and the result was similar.[427] The SCM includes export subsidies as one of two types of prohibited subsidies.[428] Thus, any such subsidy is actionable since the Peace Clause expired and the challenge does not have to show impacts on other countries.[429] So, a panel can declare a policy deemed to fall under the heading of domestic support in the URAA to be an export subsidy when viewed through the lens of the SCM.[430]

The SCM Agreement gives a legal definition of the term "subsidy that must have three basic elements: It must be a financial contribution; it must be made by a government or any public body within the territory of a Member; and it must confer a benefit.[431]

---

425 Puyana "The Cumulative Application of thee Agreement on Agriculture" http://www.javeriana.edu.co/juridicas/pub_rev/documents/07-JoseFernandoPlataPuyana_000.pdf (accessed on 09/09/14).

426 WTO *Canada – Measures Affecting the Importation of Milk and the Exportation of Dairy Products* (Panel report, as modified by the Appellate Body), WT/DS/103/AB/R.

427 See WTO European *Communities – Export Subsidies on Sugar*, Report of the Appellate Body, WT/DS265/AB/R, and WT/DS266/AB/R & WT/DS283/AB/R.

428 WTO "Subsidies and Countervailing Measures: Overview Agreement on Subsidies and Countervailing Measures" 2012 WTO Documents.

429 Andersen, *Brazil's WTO Challenge to U.S. Cotton Subsidies: The Road to Effective Disciplines of Agricultural Subsidies*, (2010).

430 Blandford "Should the Green Box be Modified?" http://www.agritrade.org/Publications/DiscussionPapers/Green_Box.pdf (accessed on 21/09/14).

431 Article 1 of the SCM stipulates that: "Definition of a Subsidy: For the purpose of this Agreement, a subsidy shall be deemed to exist if: (a)(1) there is a financial contribution by a government or any public body within the territory of a Member (referred to in this Agreement as "government"), i.e. where: (i) a government practice involves a direct transfer of funds (e.g. grants, loans, and equity infusion), potential direct transfers of funds or liabilities (e.g. loan guarantees); (ii) government revenue that is otherwise due is foregone or not collected (e.g. fiscal incentives such as tax credits)(1); (iii) a government provides goods or services other than general infrastructure, or purchases goods; (iv) a government makes payments to a funding mechanism, or entrusts or directs a private body to carry out one or more of the type of functions illustrated in (i) to (iii) above which would normally be vested in the government and the practice, in no real sense, differs from practices normally followed by governments; or (a) (2) there is any form of income or price support in the sense of Article XVI of GATT 1994; and (b) a benefit is thereby conferred. 1.2. A subsidy as defined in paragraph 1 shall be subject to the provisions of Part II or shall be subject to the provisions of Part III or V only if such a subsidy is specific in accordance with the provisions of Article 2.

However, even if a measure is a subsidy under the definition of the SCM Agreement, it is not subject to the disciplines of the SCM Agreement unless it is a specific subsidy.[432] Specific subsidies fall into two categories: those that are prohibited and those that are allowed.[433] Two types of subsidies are prohibited: export incentive subsidies that are contingent on export performance, and local content subsidies granted for use of domestic inputs over imported goods.[434] The SCM Agreement provides a clear process through which to identify actionable subsidies.[435] All specific subsidies are actionable under the SCM agreement.[436] But the SCM agreement deals differently with prohibited subsidies and other actionable subsidies, depending on the trade distorting nature of specific subsidies.[437] For non-prohibited actionable subsidies, a member can initiate remedial measures only if it can prove there is a serious prejudice to its interests.[438]

The AoA, on the other hand, permits domestic subsidies and existing export subsidies.[439] However, Members undertake not to provide export subsidies except as specified in that Member's schedule, and gradually to reduce overall levels of domestic support, measured by the total Aggregate Measure of Support.[440] The classification of policy instruments into export subsidies and domestic support is crucial to the current Round of negotiations.[441] Export subsidies are expected to be phased out and domestic support payments are to be further reduced.[442] But countries do not currently know what subsidies are likely to pass the test if examined by a panel. This has implications for current negotiations on disciplines on the boxes.[443] Why negotiate separate

---

[432] See Article 2 of the SCM".

[433] WTO "Subsidies and Countervailing Measures: Overview" 2011. http://www.wto.org/english/tratop_e/scm_e/subs_e.htm (accessed on 09/10/14).

[434] Meléndez-Ortiz Agricultural *Subsidies in the WTO Green Box: Ensuring Coherence with Sustainable Development Goals* (2009).

[435] *Ibid.*

[436] *Ibid.*

[437] Josling "Implications of WTO Litigation for the WTO Agricultural Negotiations" 2006 15.

[438] See Pal, Subsides and Countervailing Measures in WTO. http://www.networkideas.org/eco/may2005/print/prnt030505_WTO.htm (accessed on 10/10/14 at 12:32 am). Serious prejudice may arise in any case where one or more of the following apply: displaced domestic imports; displaced exports to the third country; significant price undercutting; and increase in world market share.

[439] Josling "Implications of WTO Litigation for the WTO Agricultural Negotiations" 2006 15-20.

[440] Blandford "Should the Green Box be Modified?" 2007. http://www.agritrade.org/Publications/DiscussionPapers/Green_Box.pdf (accessed on 21/09/14).

[441] Meléndez-Ortiz 2009.

[442] Macrory *The World Trade Organization: Legal, Economic and Political Analysis* (2005) 35-47.

[443] *Ibid.*

restraints if these are not found relevant by WTO panels? These are the challenges that the cotton and sugar cases have raised.[444]

In summary, the Green Box, as agreed to in the AoA, has both an economic and a political rationale. As an economic concept, constraints on domestic support were designed to limit support provided through subsidies and deficiency payments on output, and subsidies on inputs.[445] As a result, the focus centred on creating a class of "decoupled" subsidies that did not directly stimulate output. In political terms, the notion of the Green Box as a "safe haven" for subsidies decoupled from current price or output was a necessary step in the process of introducing disciplines on domestic farm programs.[446] It helped to move countries along a path in line with domestic policy reform: better targeting of payments and a shift in the focus of support from commodities to farmers. Though some countries are still sceptical of the extent and consequences of this shift, some observers conclude that it is a move toward better policies.[447]

3 5 DOMESTIC SUPPORT MEASURES: AMBER BOX SUBSIDIES

On Amber Box measures, the AoA stipulates that those countries that provided such support during the base period will establish a base level of support and undertake specific reduction commitments in their Schedules, which will be carried out over the agreed implementation period, those countries that did not provide such measures during the base period will not be allowed to maintain or introduce them in the future except within the terms of a few narrowly defined exceptions.[448] The centrepiece of the commitments in the area of domestic support is the concept of the Aggregate Measurement of Support, which is defined in Article 1(A).[449] Annex 3 of the agreement gives

[444] Macrory *The World Trade Organization: Legal, Economic and Political Analysis* (2005) 35-47.

[445] Baffes Disciplining Agricultural Support through Decoupling http://econpapers.repec.org/paper/wbkwbrwps/3533.htm (Accessed on 17/06/14).

[446] Josling "Implications of WTO Litigation for the WTO Agricultural Negotiations" 2006 *IPC Issue Brief* 6-14.

[447] Meléndez-Ortiz *Agricultural Subsidies in the WTO Green Box: Ensuring Coherence with Sustainable Development Goals* (2009).

[448] See Article 7.2(b) of the AoA. "Each Member shall ensure that any domestic support measures in favour of agricultural producers which are not subject to reduction commitments because they qualify under the criteria set out in Annex 2 to this Agreement are maintained in conformity therewith. (b). Where no Total AMS commitment exists in Part IV of a Member's Schedule, the Member shall not provide support to agricultural producers in excess of the relevant *de minimis* level set out in paragraph 4 of Article 6".

[449] Article 1 (A) defines it as defined as "the annual level of support, expressed in monetary terms, provided for an agricultural product in favour of the producers of the basic agricultural product or non-product specific support provided in favour of agricultural producers in general other than support provided under programmes that qualify as exempt from reduction under Annex 2 to this Agreement, which is: (i) with respect to support provided during the base period, specified in the relevant tables of supporting material incorporated by reference in Part IV of a Member's Schedule; and (ii) with respect to support provided during any year of the implementation period and thereafter,

detailed guidance on the calculations of the AMS by requiring a calculation of the value of market price support, non-exempt direct payments and other non-exempt policies.[450]

According to the provisions of this annex, the AMS is to be calculated on a product specific basis for each product receiving any type of non-exempt support.[451] Paragraph 1 of Annex 3 provides that non product specific support is to be aggregated into one number, which is to be included in the total AMS.[452] By virtue of paragraph 7 of Annex 3 the AMS is to be calculated as close as practicable to the point of first sale of the basic agricultural product concerned, although measures directed at agricultural processors are to be included only to the extent that a benefit accrues to the producers of the basic agricultural product.[453]

Market price support, a method of supporting agriculture by direct governmental or regulatory intervention in the workings of the market, usually by setting minimum or guaranteed prices, is a classic example of a trade-distorting domestic support device that belongs to the Amber Box.[454] The AMS for market price support is to be calculated according to paragraph 8 of Annex 3 by 'using the gap between a fixed external reference price and applied administrative price multiplied by the quantity of production eligible to receive the applied administrative price'.[455] Payments made to maintain the gap are to be excluded and those cover such payments as storage costs.

Annex 3 goes on to define what the fixed external reference price, which is based on the years 1986 to 1988, is to be foc a net exporting country, generally the average f.o.b. value for the product

---

calculated in accordance with the provisions of Annex 3 of this Agreement and taking into account the constituent data and methodology used in the tables of supporting material incorporated by reference in Part IV of the Member's Schedule".

[450] According to annexure 3 (1) of the AoA, "subject to the provisions of Article 6, an Aggregate Measurement of Support (AMS) shall be calculated on a product-specific basis for each basic agricultural product receiving market price support, non-exempt direct payments, or any other subsidy not exempted from the reduction commitment ("other non-exempt policies"). Support which is non-product specific shall be totaled into one non-product-specific AMS in total monetary terms. (13) stipulates that, Other non-exempt measures, including input subsidies and other measures such as marketing-cost reduction measures: the value of such measures shall be measured using government budgetary outlays or, where the use of budgetary outlays does not reflect the full extent of the subsidy concerned, the basis for calculating the subsidy shall be the gap between the price of the subsidized good or service and a representative market price for a similar good or service multiplied by the quantity of the good or service".

[451] *Ibid.*

[452] *Ibid.*

[453] Annex 3 Para 7 of the AoA says that "the AMS shall be calculated as close as practicable to the point of first sale of the basic agricultural product concerned. Measures directed at agricultural processors shall be included to the extent that such measures benefit the producers of the basic agricultural products".

[454] McMahon *Research Handbook on the WTO Agriculture Agreement: New and Emerging Issues in International Trade Law* (2012) at 5-20.

[455] McMahon *The Negotiations for a New Agreement on Agriculture* (2011) generally.

and for a net importing country generally the average c.i.f. value for the product, adjusted if necessary for quality differences.[456] In those situations where a fixed external reference price cannot be calculated, Annex 4 of the Agreement provide for the calculation of an Equivalent Measurement of Support (EMS), to be based on the applied administrative price and the quality of the product benefiting from this price or, if this is not possible, on budgetary outlays, which under Article 1(c) of the Agreement would include foregone revenues.[457] The applied administrative price is the price that the government determines producers should receive.

Non-exempt direct payments are defined in paragraph 10 of Annex 3 as payments that are dependent on a 'price gap' which is to be calculated on the difference between a fixed external reference price and the applied administrative price multiplied by the quantity of production that is eligible to receive the applied administrative price.[458] If the direct payments are not dependent on a price gap, the AMS calculation will be based on budgetary outlays. As for other non-exempt measures, such as input subsidies and marketing cost reduction measures, these are to be based on budgetary outlays.[459] Where budgetary outlays do not reflect the full extent of the subsidy, provision is made for calculating the difference between the price of the product benefiting from the measure and a representative market price for a similar product, which is then multiplied by the quality of the product benefiting from the measure. Levies or fees paid by producers are to be deducted from the AMS and the EMS.[460]

Having calculated the AMS by product, the next step is to calculate the total AMS. This is defined in Article 1 (h) as being the sum of all non-exempt domestic support provided to agricultural

---

[456] McMahon *Research Handbook on the WTO Agriculture Agreement: New and Emerging Issues in International Trade Law* (2012) at 5-20.

[457] According to annex 4 of the AoA, "subject to the provisions of Article 6, equivalent measurements of support shall be calculated in respect of all basic agricultural products where market price support as defined in Annex 3 exists but for which calculation of this component of the AMS is not practicable. For such products the base level for implementation of the domestic support reduction commitments shall consist of a market price support component expressed in terms of equivalent measurements of support under paragraph 2 below, as well as any non-exempt direct payments and other non-exempt support, which shall be evaluated as provided for under paragraph 3 below. Support at both national and sub-national level shall be included".

[458] Annex 3 para 10 of the AoA, "non-exempt direct payments: non-exempt direct payments which are dependent on a price gap shall be calculated either using the gap between the fixed reference price and the applied administered price multiplied by the quantity of production eligible to receive the administered price, or using budgetary outlays".

[459] *Ibid.*

[460] See Annex 3 para 10.

producers.[461] It includes all aggregate measurements of support for basic agricultural products, all non -product -specific aggregate measurement of support, and all equivalent measurement s of support for agricultural products.[462] By virtue of Article 6.1 of the Agreement, the domestic support reduction commitments are to be expressed in terms of Total Aggregate Measurement of Support and Annual and Final Bound Commitment Levels.[463] In Part IV of each Member's Schedules, a table can be found which consists of several columns.[464] The first column specifies a Base Total Commitments, which represent the effect of the implementation of the reduction commitment on the Base Total AMS.

Between these two figures are the Annual Bound Commitments, which represent the AMS commitments for each year of the implementation period. Under the Uruguay Round Modalities Agreement, each develops country member is committed to a 13.3 per cent reduction over ten years, while no reduction is required in the case of the least developed countries.[465] In order to comply with the reduction commitments, the Current Total AMS in any given year must not exceed the corresponding annual or final bound commitments specified in Part IV of the member's schedule.[466] In *Korea-Beef* case, the Appellate Body noted that two elements were required to calculate the current AMS, namely 'in accordance with methodology in Annex 3 and taking into account the constituent data and methodology used in the table incorporated into a member's schedule'.[467] By virtue of Article 3.1 the domestic support commitments made in Part IV of each member's schedule are an integral part of the GATT 1994.[468]

---

[461] In the wording of annex 1(h), "Total Aggregate Measurement of Support and Total AMS mean the sum of all domestic support provided in favour of agricultural producers, calculated as the sum of all aggregate measurements of support for basic agricultural".

[462] McMahon 2012.

[463] According to Article 6.1 of the AoA, "the domestic support reduction commitments of each Member contained in Part IV of its Schedule shall apply to all of its domestic support measures in favour of agricultural producers with the exception of domestic measures which are not subject to reduction in terms of the criteria set out in this Article and in Annex 2 to this Agreement. The commitments are expressed in terms of Total Aggregate Measurement of Support and "Annual and Final Bound Commitment Levels".

[464] WTO "Goods Schedules: Current Situation Of Schedules: Current Situation of Schedules of WTO Members". http://www.wto.org/english/tratop_e/schedules_e/goods_schedules_table_e.httm. (Accessed on 10-10-14).

[465] McMahon *Research Handbook on the WTO Agriculture Agreement: New and Emerging Issues in International Trade Law* (2012).

[466] Macrory *The World Trade Organization: Legal, Economic and Political Analysis* (2005) 59-70.

[467] *Korea - Measures Affecting Imports of Fresh, Chilled and Frozen Beef* DS62/AB/R, 112.

[468] According to Article 3 (1) of the AoA, the domestic support and export subsidy commitments in Part IV of each Member's Schedule constitute commitments limiting subsidization and are hereby made an integral part of GATT 1994.

Article 6 of the AoA exempts a number of domestic support measures form the reduction commitment.[469] The first of those reflects the agreement reached at the Mid-Term Review of the Uruguay Round that certain government measures to encourage agricultural and rural development programmes in developing countries would not have to be included in the calculation of a member's Current Total AMS.[470] Article 6.2 of the Agreement lists the three measures as being generally available agricultural investment subsidies, agricultural input subsidies generally available to low income and resource poor producers and domestic support to encourage diversification from growing illicit narcotic crops.[471]

The second exemption is provided for in Article 6.4 of the AoA under which members are not required to include either product specific or non-product specific domestic support that falls below a certain percentage of the total value of production of a basic agricultural product during the relevant year.[472] The level of *de minimis* support is set at 5 per cent for developed countries and 10 per cent for developing countries. By virtue of Article 7.2 (b) of the AoA, where a member's schedule does not include a Total AMS commitment, the level of support must not exceed the relevant *de minimis* level.[473] Article 6 (5) of the AoA exempts from the reduction commitment

---

[469] In accordance with Article 6 (5) of the AoA "Direct payments under production-limiting programmes shall not be subject to the commitment to reduce domestic support if: (i) such payments are based on fixed area and yields; or (ii) such payments are made on 85 per cent or less of the base level of production; or (iii) livestock payments are made on a fixed number of head".

[470] WTO "Agriculture: Explanation of the Agreement on Agriculture". http://www.wto.org/english/tratop_e/agric_e/ag_intro03_domestic_e.htm (accessed on 07/08/14).

[471] Article 6 (2) stipulates that, "in accordance with the Mid-Term Review Agreement that government measures of assistance, whether direct or indirect, to encourage agricultural and rural development are an integral part of the development programmes of developing countries, investment subsidies which are generally available to agriculture in developing country Members and agricultural input subsidies generally available to low-income or resource-poor producers in developing country Members shall be exempt from domestic support reduction commitments that would otherwise be applicable to such measures, as shall domestic support to producers in developing country Members to encourage diversification from growing illicit narcotic crops. Domestic support meeting the criteria of this paragraph shall not be required to be included in a Member's calculation of its Current Total AMS".

[472] According to Article 6 (4) of the AoA, "A Member shall not be required to include in the calculation of its Current Total AMS and shall not be required to reduce: (i) product-specific domestic support which would otherwise be required to be included in a Member's calculation of its Current AMS where such support does not exceed 5 per cent of that Member's total value of production of a basic agricultural product during the relevant year; and (ii) non-product-specific domestic support which would otherwise be required to be included in a Member's calculation of its Current AMS where such support does not exceed 5 per cent of the value of that Member's total agricultural production. (b) For developing country Members, the *de minimis* percentage under this paragraph shall be 10 per cent".

[473] Article 7 (2) provides that, "any domestic support measure in favour of agricultural producers, including any modification to such measure, and any measure that is subsequently introduced that cannot be shown to satisfy the criteria in Annex 2 to this Agreement or to be exempt from reduction by reason of any other provision of this Agreement shall be included in the Member's calculation of its Current Total AMS. (b) Where no Total AMS commitment exists in Part IV of a Member's Schedule, the Member shall not provide support to agricultural producers in excess of the relevant *de minimis* level set out in paragraph 4 of Article 6".

direct payments under production limiting programmes provided that they are based on fixed areas and yields, or on 85 per cent or less of the base level of production, or in the case of livestock payments, on a fixed number of head.[474] Payments under such programmes need not be decoupled from production.[475] This is notorious Blue Box.[476]

3 6 EXPORT SUBSIDIES

3 6 1 Definition of Agricultural Export Subsidies

The term export subsidies is defined under Article 1 (e) of the AoA to refer to subsidies contingent upon export performance and includes the export subsidies listed under Article 9 of the agreement.[477] Included in this list are such governmental acts as the provision of direct subsidies contingent upon export performance, the sale or disposal for export of non-commercial stocks of agricultural products at prices lower than on the domestic market, payments on the export of an agricultural product financed by virtue of governmental action, the provision of subsidies to reduce the costs of marketing agricultural exports, and subsidies on agricultural production contingent on their incorporation in exported products.[478]

---

[474] Article 6 (5) of the AoA says that, "direct payments under production-limiting programmes shall not be subject to the commitment to reduce domestic support if: (i) such payments are based on fixed area and yields; or (ii) such payments are made on 85 per cent or less of the base level of production; or (iii) livestock payments are made on a fixed number of head".
(b) The exemption from the reduction commitment for direct payments meeting the above criteria shall be reflected by the exclusion of the value of those direct payments in a Member's calculation of its Current Total AMS.

[475] McMahon *Research Handbook on the WTO Agriculture Agreement: New and Emerging Issues in International Trade Law* (2012) 25-30.

[476] See Article 6 para 5 of the AoA for more about the blue box. This is the "amber box with conditions" conditions designed to reduce distortion. Any support that would normally be in the amber box is placed in the blue box if the support also requires farmers to limit production. At present there are no limits on spending on blue box subsidies. In the current negotiations, some countries want to keep the blue box as it is because they see it as a crucial means of moving away from distorting amber box subsidies without causing too much hardship. Others wanted to set limits or reduction commitments, some advocating moving these supports into the amber box.

[477] In the actual wording of Article 1 (e) "export subsidies" refers to subsidies contingent upon export performance, including the export subsidies listed in Article 9 of this Agreement.

[478] The following export subsidies are subject to reduction commitments under the AoA "the provision by governments or their agencies of direct subsidies, including payments-in-kind, to a firm, to an industry, to producers of an agricultural product, to a cooperative or other association of such producers, or to a marketing board, contingent on export performance; (b) the sale or disposal for export by governments or their agencies of non-commercial stocks of agricultural products at a price lower than the comparable price charged for the like product to buyers in the domestic market; (c) payments on the export of an agricultural product that are financed by virtue of governmental action, whether or not a charge on the public account is involved, including payments that are financed from the proceeds of a levy imposed on the agricultural product concerned or on an agricultural product from which the exported product is derived; (d) the provision of subsidies to reduce the costs of marketing exports of agricultural products (other than widely available export promotion and advisory services) including handling, upgrading and other processing costs, and the costs of international transport and freight; (e) internal transport and freight charges on export shipments,

An export subsidy is, first and foremost, a subsidy. However, the Agriculture Agreement does not define the root term subsidy. To that extent, the definition of an export subsidy as a subsidy contingent upon export performance does not serve much useful purpose.[479] The question of 'what is it that should be contingent upon export performance for an export subsidy to exist' needs to be answered first. Fortunately, in the SCM agreement, annexed to the WTO Agreement, this historically elusive and controversial term has been defined for the first time. Both the AoA and the SCM being part of the multilateral agreements annexed to the WTO Agreement, the package deal principle stated under Article XIV of the WTO Agreement mandates that an acceptance of the WTO Agreement applies to all the multilateral agreements annexed thereto as well.[480] In practice, this means that a country party to the AoA is also bound by the SCM.[481] As parts of a bigger whole, terms defined by one agreement may conveniently be used to interpret the provisions of another agreement, provided, of course, that the scope of application of one such a provision is not explicitly limited to specified areas.[482]

It is thus possible to go to Article 1 of the AoA and adapt the definition given to subsidies in order to understand the meaning of the term export subsidies as defined under Article l(e) of the AoA. According to Article 1 of the SCM, it refers to a financial contribution or any other form of income or price support in the sense of Article XVI of the GATT 1994 contingent upon export performance made by a government or any public body and conferring a benefit on the recipient.[483] As a supplement to the definition, Article 9 of the AoA presents a list of practices falling under the

provided or mandated by governments, on terms more favourable than for domestic shipments; (f) subsidies on agricultural products contingent on their incorporation in exported products".

479 US Department of Commerce Report to the Congress on Review And Operation Of The WTO Subsidies Agreement 1999.

480 Gao *China's Participation in the WTO: A Lawyer's Perspective* (2007) 19.

481 *Ibid.*

482 Van Grasstek *The History and Future of the World Trade Organization* (2013) generally.

483 According to SCM, "a subsidy shall exist if there is a financial contribution by a government or any public body within the territory of a Member (referred to in this Agreement as "government"), i.e. where: a government practice involves a direct transfer of funds (e.g. grants, loans, and equity infusion), potential direct transfers of funds or liabilities (e.g. loan guarantees); government revenue that is otherwise due is foregone or not collected (e.g. fiscal incentives such as tax credits) a government provides goods or services other than general infrastructure, or purchases goods; a government makes payments to a funding mechanism, or entrusts or directs a private body to carry out one or more of the type of functions illustrate (i) to (iii) above which would normally be vested in the government and the practice, in no real sense, differs from practices normally followed by governments; or there is any form of income or price support in the sense of Article XVI of GATT 1994; and a benefit is thereby conferred".

umbrella of the term export subsidies as defined under Article l(e) of the same Agreement that are subject to reduction commitments.[484]

3 6 2 Export Subsidies Listed in Article 9 as Supplementing the Definition

According to Article 1 (e) of the Agriculture Agreement, export subsidies refers to subsidies contingent upon export performance, including the export subsidies listed in Article 9 of this Agreement. As such, the list supplements the definition provision and helps to answer a number of the contentious issues regarding both the conception as well as the calculation of subsidies.[485] Issues like the form of governmental involvement required for the existence of a subsidy, e.g. whether the government should suffer a charge to its accounts, have been resolved. Article 9: l(c) explicitly provides that what matters for the existence of an export subsidy and for the application of the discipline of the Agriculture Agreement thereupon is the mere presence of some form of governmental action whether or not a charge on the public account is involved.[486]

Similarly, the wording of Article 9 (l) (e) also clears another important problem in relation to the exact role that should be played by the government for the existence of subsidies.[487] It is stated that 'internal transport and freight charges on export shipments, provided or mandated by governments, on terms more favourable than for domestic shipments' are also included as export subsidies. This means, for example, that it is sufficient for a subsidy to exist if a government simply issues a directive mandating that all freight transport companies maintain a fare differential of, say, 10 dollars per unit between domestic and export shipments of the same volume or weight in favour of the latter.[488] The government suffers no expenses to its accounts; nor does it carry out the task of transporting freight by itself; yet, there is an export subsidy subject to the newly introduced discipline in the same way as direct transfers of public funds are subjected to it.[489]

---

[484] The practises are mentioned above.
[485] Desta *Agricultural Export Subsidies under the WTO Agriculture Package: A Legal Analysis* (1997) 7-10.
[486] According to Article 9 (1) (c) of the AoA, "The following export subsidies are subject to reduction commitments under this Agreement: "payments on the export of an agricultural product that are financed by virtue of governmental action, whether or not a charge on the public account is involved, including payments that are financed from the proceeds of a levy imposed on the agricultural product concerned or on an agricultural product from which the exported product is derived…"
[487] In the wording of Article 1 (e) of the AoA, "internal transport and freight charges on export shipments, provided or mandated by governments, on terms more favourable than for domestic shipments subsidies are subject to reduction commitments under the AoA".
[488] Desta 1997 7-10.
[489] *Ibid.*

The enumeration of Article 9 (1) does not, however, affect the generality of the definition given earlier. There are practices that fit in with the definition of the term but that are not covered by any of the items enumerated thereunder.[490] The legal status of those practices which fall within the definition but outside the list has already begun to entertain divergent views around scholars and will be discussed below.

3 6 3 Categories of Agricultural Export Subsidies: Listed vs. Non-Listed

The AoA has created two categories of export subsidies those that are listed under Article 9 (1) as export subsidies subject to reduction commitments, and those that are export subsidies as defined under Article l(e) but do not fall in any of the enumerations of Article 9 (1), and hence not subject to reduction commitments.[491] Accordingly, there is no uniform discipline applying to all forms of export subsidies that may be found to exist under the definition of the term mentioned above.[492]

Article 8 of the AoA provides that each member undertakes not to provide export subsidies otherwise than in conformity with this AoA and with the commitments as specified in that Member's Schedule on Commitments.[493] This provision is merely a commitment without sanctions. It is submitted that, this provision is problematic in the sense that perpetrators of export subsidies are not deterred from subsidising export products and will continue to do it as long as there is no repercussions for their actions. It is further argued that most developing countries are poor to such an extent that starting a legal battle with developing countries can overstretch their budgets.

Article 8 of the AoA also implies that, Members are not strictly precluded by the agreement from providing export subsidies, but the subsidies should be provided in conformity with the rules of the agreement and their respective schedules of commitments.[494] Unlike export subsidies on non-

---

[490] Desta *Agricultural Export Subsidies under the WTO Agriculture Package: A Legal Analysis* (1997) 7-10.
[491] Listed subsidies involve, "payments on the export of an agricultural product that are financed by virtue of governmental action, whether or not a charge on the public account is involved, including payments that are financed from the proceeds of a levy imposed on the agricultural product concerned or on an agricultural product from which the exported product is derived, and the non-listed export subsidies involve, internal transport and freight charges on export shipments, provided or mandated by governments, on terms more favourable than for domestic shipments subsidies are subject to reduction commitments under the AoA".
[492] Desta *Agricultural Export Subsidies under the WTO Agriculture Package: A Legal Analysis* (1997) 8-12.
[493] Article 8 of the AoA is titled "Export Competition Commitments". It stipulates that "each Member undertakes not to provide export subsidies otherwise than in conformity with this Agreement and with the commitments as specified in that Member's Schedule".
[494] See article 8 read together with article 9 of the AoA.

agricultural products, therefore, members are free to use agricultural export subsidies in any manner they like, provided that certain conditions are satisfied.[495] It is on the basis of the nature of the conditions attached to the different forms of export subsidies that the two categories are formulated.[496] The export subsidies listed under Article 9(1) are specifically required to be subject to reduction commitments under this agreement. The obligation to respect the reduction commitments each Member incorporates in its Schedules constitutes the condition for the lawful use of these practices. On the other hand, the condition for the lawful use of those export subsidy practices that are not listed under Article 9 (1) appears to be the anti-circumvention requirement of Article 10 (1) of the same Agreement.[497]

3 6 4 Non-Listed Agricultural Export Subsidies and their Legal Status

The question of whether these non-listed export subsidies are permissible at all has been approached differently by writers. It is argued that, non-listed export subsidies will be subject to the SCM Agreement, which establishes three categories of subsidies prohibited, actionable, and non-actionable.[498] This would mean that the non-listed agricultural export subsidies would be prohibited if one is lay an argument on this basis. It is further argued that export subsidies will be subject to the discipline provided for in the AoA and subsidies falling outside this discipline will be subject to the discipline provided by the SCM.[499] The latter reasoning rightly suggests that those export subsidy practices that are subject to the disciplines of the AoA are governed only by that agreement and no other.[500]

According to Article 10 (1) of the AoA, export subsidies not listed in paragraph 1 of Article 9 shall not be applied in a manner which results in, or which threatens to lead to, circumvention of export subsidy commitments. This provision implies that there is no prohibitions on the use of

[495] Desta 1997 14-17.
[496] Desta *Agricultural Export Subsidies under the WTO Agriculture Package: A Legal Analysis* (1997) 8-11.
[497] Export subsidies not listed in paragraph 1 of Article 9 "shall not be applied in a manner which results in, or which threatens to lead to, circumvention of export subsidy commitments; nor shall non-commercial transactions be used to circumvent such commitments".
[498] MoMahon *The Uruguay Round and Agriculture: Charting a New Direction?* (1995) 430.
[499] See Marsilla "Recent Stimulus Packages and WTO Law on Subsidies" 2009 *World Customs Journal.* For a detailed argument, see, Zunckel "The African Awakening in United States-Upland Cotton" (2005) *Journal of World Trade* 1071–1093.
[500] It is however important to note that, even the non-listed export subsidy practices are also subject to a disciplines created by the Agreement on Agriculture. Only the type of discipline applying to the listed and the non-listed categories varies. While the former are subject to reduction commitments, the latter are subject only to anti-circumvention requirements.

these export subsidies; it is only the manner of their use that is subject to the anti-circumvention condition, actual or potential.[501] Paragraph 2 of Article 10 goes a step further and picks three of the potentially significant export subsidy practices that fall outside the list of Article 9(1) export credits, export credit guarantees, and insurance programs and declares that members shall undertake to work toward the development of internationally agreed disciplines governing their use, and shall abide by any such agreement when, and if, it is reached.[502] As it stands to date, this is simply an agreement to maintain good faith for the current negotiations devoid of any substantive legal obligation for some time to come.[503] Until then, there exists no legal distinction in the treatment of these three practices and the other forms of export subsidies not listed under Article 9(1).[504] It is submitted that, this has resulted in the manipulation of the provisions by developed countries that provide export subsidies to their farmers at the expense of developing countries.

The relationship between the SCM and AoA concerning these issues needs to be very clear, though. First of all, we are here dealing with export subsidy cases. The regime created by the SCM for them is a simple and fiat prohibition.[505] If this regime were to apply to agriculture, this would mean that the export subsidy practices that are not listed under Article 9(1) of the AoA are flatly prohibited while those that are listed therein are simply subjected to reduction commitments.[506] The fallacy, however, is the following: if they were prohibited, why does the Agriculture Agreement talk of anti-circumvention?[507]

---

[501] Desta 1997 at 13.

[502] According to Article 10 para 2 "Members undertake to work toward the development of internationally agreed disciplines to govern the provision of export credits, export credit guarantees or insurance programmes and, after agreement on such disciplines, to provide export credits, export credit guarantees or insurance programmes only in conformity therewith".

[503] Desta *Agricultural Export Subsidies under the WTO Agriculture Package: A Legal Analysis* (1997) at 15-17.

[504] *Ibid.*

[505] Puyana "The Cumulative Application of thee Agreement on Agriculture" 2008. http://www.javeriana.edu.co/juridicas/pub_rev/documents/07-JoseFernandoPlataPuyana_000.pdf (accessed on 09/09/14).

[506] *Ibid.*

[507] See Deata 1997 15-17. This is because once prohibited, they could not be used in any manner whatsoever whether circumventor or otherwise. The case of export credits, export credit guarantees and insurance programs singled out by Article 10 (2) as subjects for a special future international agreement may help to show this fallacy more vividly. If the non-listed subsidies were subject to the Subsidies Agreement, these three practices would also be prohibited until the envisaged internationally agreed discipline is concluded in the future.

If one is to view it from an historical perspective, the scenario surrounding this situation would look the following: Before the Uruguay Round Agreements, they were 'permitted' like all other agricultural export subsidies; now they are prohibited like all non-agricultural export subsidies; and when the envisaged international discipline is reached, they will be subject to a regime short of a flat prohibition.[508] Not only is this situation inconsistent with the rule of reason; it is also out of tune with the very spirit, purpose and direction of the multilateral trading system.[509]

Article 3(1) of the SCM on prohibited subsidies also explicitly excludes agricultural export subsidies from its purview.[510] Accordingly, subsidies contingent upon export performance are prohibited except as provided in the AoA. In line with this provision of the SCM, Article 8 of the AoA limits members' obligations to the rules of the AoA.[511] As long as the provision of agricultural export subsidies conforms to the AoA and the Schedules of Commitments, therefore, there is no possibility to challenge the legitimacy of one such a practice.[512]

In a nutshell, Members are allowed to use those non-listed agricultural export subsidies on condition that they do not use them to circumvent, actually or potentially, their obligations *vis-à-vis* the listed export subsidy practices.[513] The fact that Article 10 (1) of the AoA provides that export subsidies not listed in paragraph 1 of Article 9 shall not be applied in a manner which results in circumvention implicitly endorses their use; only the manner of their use is regulated.[514] And this conclusion also applies to the three non-listed export subsidy practices for which the commitment to work toward the development of an internationally agreed discipline is undertaken

---

[508] Puyana "The Cumulative Application of thee Agreement on Agriculture" 2008. http://www.javeriana.edu.co/juridicas/pub_rev/documents/07-JoseFernandoPlataPuyana_000.pdf (accessed on 09/09/14).

[509] Considering the distortive nature of these practices, this would amount to moving away from a liberal regime into a restrictive one.

[510] According to article 3.1 of the SCM, "except as provided in the Agreement on Agriculture, the following subsidies, within the meaning of Article 1, shall be prohibited: (a) subsidies contingent, in law or in fact, whether solely or as one of several other conditions, upon export performance, including those illustrated in Annex I5; (b) subsidies contingent, whether solely or as one of several other conditions, upon the use of domestic over imported goods." However, this standard is met when the facts demonstrate that the granting of a subsidy, without having been made legally contingent upon export performance, is in fact tied to actual or anticipated exportation or export earnings. The mere fact that a subsidy is granted to enterprises which export shall not for that reason alone be considered to be an export subsidy within the meaning of this provision.

[511] Each Member undertakes not to provide export subsidies otherwise than in conformity with this Agreement and with the commitments as specified in that Member's Schedule.

[512] Desta *Agricultural Export Subsidies under the WTO Agriculture Package: A Legal Analysis* (1997) 16-18.

[513] *Ibid.*

[514] *Ibid.*

by the members.[515] When, and if, this latter agreement is reached, the direction of the move will also conform with the very purpose and direction of the multilateral trading system a progressive move from a state of distortion to one of liberalization.[516]

It is, therefore, important to always keep in mind the fact that not all agricultural export subsidies are subject to reduction commitments. Other academics, for instance, argue that contrary to the old GATT system, export subsidies are now prohibited in agriculture, except where indicated in Countries' Schedules.[517] However, academics like Desta criticises this and argues that it not entirely, true.[518] This only applies to the listed subsidies; the non-listed subsidies are not covered by the rule under Article 3 (3).[519] Subject to the anti-circumvention condition, members are always free to use any subsidies that fall outside the list of Article 9(1) of the AoA. On the other hand, in line with the argument, members are precluded from introducing any of the listed export subsidies, in principle, on any product that had not been reported as having been benefiting from any such scheme during the base period.[520]

3 7 REDUCTION COMMITMENTS

Under the AoA, export subsidies are defined as referring to subsidies contingent on export performance, including the export subsidies listed in detail in Article 9 of the Agreement.[521] As specified in more detail in Article 9 (1) of the Agreement, this list covers most of the export subsidy practices which are prevalent in the agricultural sector, notably; direct export subsidies contingent on export performance; sales of non-commercial stocks of agricultural products for export at prices lower than comparable prices for such goods on the domestic market; producer financed subsidies such as government programmes which require a levy on all production which is then used to subsidise the export of a certain portion of that production; cost reduction measures such as subsidies to reduce the cost of marketing goods for export: this can include upgrading and handling costs and the costs of international freight, for example; internal transport subsidies applying to exports only, such as those designed to bring exportable produce to one central point for shipping;

---

[515] Coppens "WTO Disciplines on Export Credit Support for Agricultural Products in the Wake of the US – Upland Cotton Case and the Doha Round Negotiations" 2010 *Journal of World Trade* 349–384.
[516] Coppens 2010 349-380.
[517] Tangermann, *The Interests of Developing Countries in the Next Round of WTO Agricultural Negotiations* (1999).
[518] Desta *Agricultural Export Subsidies under the WTO Agriculture Package: A Legal Analysis*, (1997) 18-20.
[519] *Ibid.*
[520] *Ibid.*
[521] See Article 1 of the AoA.

and subsidies on incorporated products, i.e. subsidies on agricultural products such as wheat contingent on their incorporation in export products such as biscuits.[522] All such export subsidies are subject to reduction commitments, expressed in terms of both the volume of subsidized exports and the budgetary outlays for these subsidies.[523]

3 7 1 Product categories

The reduction commitments are shown in the schedules of WTO Members on a product-specific basis.[524] For this purpose, the cosmos of agricultural products was initially divided into twenty three products/product groups, such as wheat, coarse grains, sugar, beef, butter, cheese and oilseeds.[525] Some members took commitments on a more disaggregated level.[526] The volume and budgetary outlay commitments for each product or group of products specified in a member's schedule are individually binding.[527] The reduction commitments on "incorporated products"[528] are expressed in terms of budgetary outlays only.[529] The ceilings specified in the schedules must be respected in each year of the implementation period although limited "over-shooting" in the second to fifth year of implementation was permitted.[530] It was expected that by the last year of the implementation period, members would be within their final export subsidy ceilings. However, the over shooting provision gave an unfair advantage on developing countries as they were not at par with developing countries.[531] Developing countries rather strongly followed the reduction commitments whilst developed countries manipulated the over shooting provision during the implementation period.[532]

---

[522] See Article 9 (1) for a comprehensive list of all the export subsidy practices.

[523] Hoekman "European Community—Sugar: Cross-Subsidization and the World Trade Organization" (2007).

[524] For more information visit the WTO "Members Schedules of Commitments" http://www.wto.org/english/tratop_e/schedules_e/goods_schedules_e.htm (Accessed on 08/08/14).

[525] Desta *Agricultural Export Subsidies under the WTO Agriculture Package: A Legal Analysis* 1997 18-20.

[526] *Ibid.*

[527] *Ibid.*

[528] The last item in the Article 9 list.

[529] Desta.

[530] This is known as downstream flexibility. Generally Article 9. 2(b) provides that "in any of the second through the fifth years of the implementation period, a Member may grant export subsidies in a given year in excess of the corresponding annual commitment levels, provided certain conditions are satisfied. Of the three conditions, while the first and the second concern budgetary and quantitative adjustments, respectively, the third applies to both".

[531] Matthews "Developing Countries' Position in WTO Agricultural Trade Negotiations" 2001 Vol 20 *Development Policy Review* 75-90.

[532] Matthews 2001 77-80.

3 7 2 Cut of Rates

Developed country members were required to reduce, in equal annual steps over a period of 6 years, the base-period volume of subsidized exports by 21 per cent and the corresponding budgetary outlays for export subsidies by 36 per cent.[533] In the case of developing countries, the required cuts were 14 per cent over 10 years with respect to volumes, and 24 per cent over the same period with respect to budgetary outlays.[534] Developing countries are allowed make use of a special and differential treatment provision of the in Article 9 (4) which allowed them to grant marketing cost subsidies and internal transport subsidies, provided that these are not applied in a manner that would circumvent export subsidy reduction commitments during the implementation period.[535]

3 7 3 Products with no specific reduction commitment

The AoA prohibits the use of Article 9 (1) export subsidies on any agricultural product which is not subject to a reduction commitment as specified in the relevant part of the member's schedule.[536]

3 8 ANTI-CIRCUMVENTION: ARTICLE 10

Apart from the provisions directly related to the reduction commitments, the AoA contains provisions which are designed to prevent the use of export subsidies that are not specifically listed in Article 9 of the Agreement in such a way as to circumvent reduction on other export subsidy commitments.[537] The anti-circumvention provisions include a definition of food aid in order that transactions claimed to be food aid, but not meeting the criteria in the Agreement, cannot be used to undermine commitments.[538] Food aid that meets the specified criteria is not considered to be

---

533 Amani "Critical Issues in Agricultural Trade – WTO: What does Africa want from Agriculture Negotiations?" 2004 *Tralac*.

534 See WTO "Agriculture: Explanation of the Agreement on Agriculture". http://www.wto.org/english/tratop_e/agric_e/ag_intro03_domestic_e.htm (accessed on 07/08/14).

535 See WTO "Agriculture: Agriculture: Explanation, Export competition/subsidies" (Accessed on 22/10/14) http://www.wto.org/english/tratop_e/agric_e/ag_intro04_export_e.htm .

536 This was with the exception, during the implementation, period of those benefiting from special and differential treatment.

537 Article 10 of the AoA stipulates that, Export subsidies not listed in paragraph 1 of Article 9 shall not be applied in a manner which results in, or which threatens to lead to, circumvention of export subsidy commitments; nor shall non-commercial transactions be used to circumvent such commitments. Members undertake to work toward the development of internationally agreed disciplines to govern the provision of export credits, export credit guarantees or insurance programmes and, after agreement on such disciplines, to provide export credits, export credit guarantees or insurance programmes only in conformity therewith.

538 According to Article 10 (4) "Members donors of international food aid shall ensure: (a) that the provision of international food aid is not tied directly or indirectly to commercial exports of agricultural products to recipient countries; (b) that international food aid transactions, including bilateral food aid which is monetized, shall be carried

subsidised export hence is not limited by the AoA. The Agreement also calls for the development of internationally agreed disciplines on export credits and similar measures in recognition that such measures could also be used to circumvent commitments.[539] Any member which claims that any quantity exported in excess of a reduction commitment level is not subsidized must establish that no export subsidy, whether listed in Article 9 or not, has been granted in respect of the quantity of exports in question.[540]

3 9 NOTIFICATION OBLIGATIONS: EXPORT SUBSIDIES

The AoA requires all members to notify the Committee on Agriculture annually with respect to export subsidies.[541] For the vast majority of members without reduction commitments this involves only a statement to the effect that export subsidies on agricultural products have not been used or a listing of those measures that may be used by developing country members under Article 9.4 of the Agreement if this has been the case.[542] For members with reduction commitments in their schedules, the annual notification must contain the annual use of subsidies in terms of both volume and budgetary outlays.[543]

In addition, as part of the anti-circumvention provisions, members must notify the use of food aid on an annual basis if such aid is granted.[544] Likewise, total exports of agricultural products must be notified by members with reduction commitments as well as by a number of other significant exporters as defined by the Committee.[545] As in other areas, the export subsidy notifications form part of the basis for reviewing the progress in the implementation of the commitments by the Committee on Agriculture.[546]

---

out in accordance with the FAO "Principles of Surplus Disposal and Consultative Obligations", including, where appropriate, the system of Usual Marketing Requirements (UMRs); and (c) that such aid shall be provided to the extent possible in fully grant form or on terms no less concessional than those provided for in Article IV of the Food Aid Convention 1986".

[539] *Ibid.*

[540] Article 10 (3) of the AoA provides that Any Member which claims that any quantity exported in excess of a reduction commitment level is not subsidized must establish that no export subsidy, whether listed in Article 9 or not, has been granted in respect of the quantity of exports in question.

[541] See WTO "Agriculture: Agriculture: Explanation, Export competition/subsidies" (Accessed on 22/10/14) http://www.wto.org/english/tratop_e/agric_e/ag_intro04_export_e.htm.

[542] *Ibid.*

[543] *Ibid.*

[544] *Ibid.*

[545] Desta *Agricultural Export Subsidies under the WTO Agriculture Package: A Legal Analysis* (1997) 20-21.

[546] *Ibid.*

3 10 EXPORT RESTRICTIONS

The AoA requires Members which consider to institute new export restrictions on foodstuffs to give due consideration to the effects of such restrictions on importing members' food security.[547] Members, except developing country Members which are not net exporters of the product concerned, must notify the Committee on Agriculture before introducing new export restrictions on foodstuffs and consult with affected members if so requested.[548] This requirement which has increased reliability of access to world market supply is a corollary for the opening of markets which is required by the market access provisions of the Agreement and the related specific commitments undertaken by Members.[549]

3 11 PEACE CLAUSE

The AoA contains a "due restraint" or "peace clause" provision which regulated the application of other WTO agreements to subsidies in respect of agricultural products.[550] The provisions provide that Green Box domestic support measures cannot be the subject of countervailing duty action or other subsidy action under the WTO SCM, nor can they be subject to actions based on non-violation nullification or impairment of tariff concessions under the GATT.[551] Other domestic support measures which are in conformity with the provisions of the AoA may be the subject of countervailing duty actions, but due restraint is to be exercised by members in initiating such

---

[547] Article 12 of the AoA provides that, "where any Member institutes any new export prohibition or restriction on food stuffs in accordance with paragraph 2(a) of Article XI of GATT 1994, the Member shall observe the following provisions: the Member instituting the export prohibition or restriction shall give due consideration to the effects of such prohibition or restriction on importing Members' food security; before any Member institutes an export prohibition or restriction, it shall give notice in writing, as far in advance as practicable, to the Committee on Agriculture comprising such information as the nature and the duration of such measure, and shall consult, upon request, with any other Member having a substantial interest as an importer with respect to any matter related to the measure in question. The Member instituting such export prohibition or restriction shall provide, upon request, such a Member with necessary information".

[548] The provisions of Article 12 shall not apply to any developing country Member, unless the measure is taken by a developing country Member which is a net-food exporter of the specific foodstuff concerned.

[549] Seung-Hwan *The Agreement on Agriculture, its Implementation and Case Analysis* (2007) 7-11.

[550] Article 13 of the AoA provides that, "During the implementation period, notwithstanding the provisions of GATT 1994 and the Agreement on Subsidies and Countervailing Measures domestic support measures that conform fully to the provisions of Annex 2 to this Agreement shall be: (i) non-actionable subsidies for purposes of countervailing duties4; (ii) exempt from actions based on Article XVI of GATT 1994 and Part III of the Subsidies Agreement; and (iii) exempt from actions based on non-violation nullification or impairment of the benefits of tariff concessions accruing to another Member under Article II of GATT 1994, in the sense of paragraph 1(b) of Article XXIII of GATT 1994".

[551] *Ibid.*

investigations.[552] Further, in so far as the support provided to individual products does not exceed that decided in the 1992 marketing year, these measures are exempt from other subsidy action or nullification or impairment action. Export subsidies conforming to the AoA are, to the extent relevant, covered by corresponding provisions.[553] The peace clause seem to have been a fair provision in a developing country's belvedere. It is argued that, the life of the peace clause should have been increased for developing countries who experienced the same exemptions with developed countries.

3 12 RESOLVING DISPUTES

In the case of disputes involving provisions of the AoA, the general WTO dispute settlement procedures apply.[554] Nevertheless, the Agreement also provides for certain mechanisms that can be used by members to address their concerns without recourse to these procedures. In particular, the review process of the Committee on Agriculture provides a forum for discussion and consultation.[555] This process is mainly based on the notifications and on a provision (Article 18.6) allowing any Member to raise at any time any matter relevant to the implementation of the commitments under the reform programme as set out in the Agreement.[556] There is also a counter-notification provision. Moreover, the Working Procedures of the Committee allow Members to request the Chairperson to mediate in concerns that may arise between them. The use of

[552] Domestic support measures that conform fully to the provisions of Article 6 of this Agreement including direct payments that conform to the requirements of paragraph 5 thereof, as reflected in each Member's Schedule, as well as domestic support within *de minimis* levels and in conformity with paragraph 2 of Article 6, shall be: exempt from the imposition of countervailing duties unless a determination of injury or threat thereof is made in accordance with Article VI of GATT 1994 and Part V of the Subsidies Agreement, and due restraint shall be shown in initiating any countervailing duty investigations.

[553] Export subsidies that conform fully to the provisions of Part V of this Agreement, as reflected in each Member's Schedule, shall be: (i) subject to countervailing duties only upon a determination of injury or threat thereof based on volume, effect on prices, or consequent impact in accordance with Article VI of GATT 1994 and Part V of the Subsidies Agreement, and due restraint shall be shown in initiating any countervailing duty investigations; and (ii) exempt from actions based on Article XVI of GATT 1994 or Articles 3,5 and 6 of the Subsidies Agreement.

[554] WTO dispute settlement procedures apply to all disputes related to any agreement annexed to the WTO Marrakesh agreement.

[555] Article 17 of the AoA establishes the WTO Committee on Agriculture. According to its provisions, "Committee on Agriculture is hereby established". The Committee reviews progress in the implementation of commitments negotiated under the Uruguay Round reform programme *inter alia*.

[556] Article 18 (6) of the AoA provides that, "the review process shall provide an opportunity for Members to raise any matter relevant to the implementation of commitments under the reform programme as set out in this Agreement.

instruments under the auspices of the Committee on Agriculture does not, however, prevent any member from seeking formal dispute settlement at any time.[557]

3 13 CONTINUATION CLAUSE: ARTICLE 20 OF THE AOA

The commitments taken under the AoA and within the Members' schedules are part of an on-going process.[558] At the conclusion of the Uruguay Round, Members agreed to hold further negotiations on agriculture commencing one year before the end of the six-year implementation period. The negotiations started in Doha in 2001 and aim to examine any further commitments necessary to achieve the long-term objective of substantial progressive reductions in support and protection resulting in fundamental reform.[559] The negotiations are also taking into account factors such as the experience gained during the implementation period, the effects of Uruguay Round reduction commitments on world trade in agriculture, non-trade concerns, special and differential treatment to developing country Members and the objective to establish a fair and market-oriented agricultural trading system.

---

[557] See WTO "Agriculture: Agriculture: Explanation, Export competition/subsidies" (Accessed on 22/10/14) http://www.wto.org/english/tratop_e/agric_e/ag_intro04_export_e.htm.

[558] Article 20 states that "Recognizing that the long-term objective of substantial progressive reductions in support and protection resulting in fundamental reform is an ongoing process, Members agree that negotiations for continuing the process will be initiated one year before the end of the implementation period, taking into account: (a) the experience to that date from implementing the reduction commitments; (b) the effects of the reduction commitments on world trade in agriculture; (c) non-trade concerns, special and differential treatment to developing country Members, and the objective to establish a fair and market-oriented agricultural trading system, and the other objectives and concerns mentioned in the preamble to this Agreement; and (d) what further commitments are necessary to achieve the above mentioned long-term objectives".

[559] Under the Doha ministerial Declaration, "members recognize the work already undertaken in the negotiations initiated in early 2000 under Article 20 of the Agreement on Agriculture, including the large number of negotiating proposals submitted on behalf of a total of 121 members. Members recall the long-term objective referred to in the Agreement to establish a fair and market-oriented trading system through a programme of fundamental reform encompassing strengthened rules and specific commitments on support and protection in order to correct and prevent restrictions and distortions in world agricultural markets. Negotiators reconfirm our commitment to this programme. Building on the work carried out to date and without prejudging the outcome of the negotiations the members commit themselves to comprehensive negotiations aimed at: substantial improvements in market access; reductions of, with a view to phasing out, all forms of export subsidies; and substantial reductions in trade-distorting domestic support. The members agree that special and differential treatment for developing countries shall be an integral part of all elements of the negotiations and shall be embodied in the schedules of concessions and commitments and as appropriate in the rules and disciplines to be negotiated, so as to be operationally effective and to enable developing countries to effectively take account of their development needs, including food security and rural development. The negotiators take note of the non-trade concerns reflected in the negotiating proposals submitted by Members and confirm that non-trade concerns will be taken into account in the negotiations as provided for in the Agreement on Agriculture".

3 14 SPECIAL AND DIFFERENTIAL TREATMENT

The Preamble of the Marrakesh Agreement recognise the need for positive efforts to ensure that developing and least developed countries secure a share in the growth of international trade commensurate with the need of their economic development.[560] The AoA provides some flexibility for developing countries in each of the three pillars. For example, developing countries were given an option with respect to article 4 of the AoA to go for the ceiling bindings instead of tariffication[561]. On the down side, those countries that went for this option were denied the right to introduce special safeguard measures under Article 5 of the AoA while they still required to offer minimum access commitments.[562]

In the area of domestic support developing countries were allowed a number of flexibilities, including generally available investment subsidies, input subsidies to low income farmers, and subsidies to support diversification away from the growing of illicit crops.[563] These flexibilities were further supplemented by lower reduction commitments in Amber Box measures that could be implemented over a longer period and *de minimis* levels of support that were twice those allowed for developed countries.[564] Finally, in respect of export subsidies, developing countries were allowed lower reduction commitments implemented over longer periods while LDCs were exempted altogether from reduction commitments.[565] The LDCs of course did not provide any export subsidies during the base period which left their base levels at zero and thereby made the special and differential treatment gesture in this area have no effect. [566]

Under Article 16.1 of the AoA, developed country members are required to take the action provided for in the Decision on Measures Concerning the Possible Negative Effects of the Reform

[560] In the exact words of the Agreement, the Members Recognise that there is a need for positive efforts designed to ensure that developing countries, and especially the least developed among them, secure a share in the growth of international trade commensurate with the needs of their economic development, and being desirous of contributing to these objectives by entering into reciprocal and mutually advantageous arrangements directed to the substantial reduction of tariffs and other barriers to trade and to the elimination of discriminatory treatment in international trade relations.

[561] McMahon *Research Handbook on the WTO Agriculture Agreement: New and Emerging Issues in International Trade Law* (2012) 33-40.

[562] McMahon 2012 33-35.

[563] *Ibid.*

[564] Desta "Legal Issues in International Agricultural Trade: The Evolution of the WTO Agreement on Agriculture from its Uruguay Round Origins to its Post-Hong Kong Directions" 2006.

[565] McMahon *Research Handbook on the WTO Agriculture Agreement: New and Emerging Issues in International Trade Law* (2012) 33-38.

[566] McMahon 2012 34-37.

program on Least Developed and net Food Importing Developing Countries (NFIDC), which was reached at the conclusion of the Uruguay Round.[567] By virtue of Article 16 (2), the Committee on Agriculture is to monitor the follow up to the decision.[568] The decision itself recognises that implementation of the reform package in agriculture may have negative effects on these countries in relation to the supply of food imports on reasonable terms and conditions, which would arise as a result of reductions in the level of domestic production and the restrictions on the use of export subsidies.[569]

To improve these negative effects and advance the level of food security in these countries, during the land reform programme it was agreed that the level of food aid would be reviewed periodically and that a level of food aid commitments would be set that was sufficient to meet the legitimate needs of developing countries.[570] Paragraph 3 of the decision goes on the urge the adoption of guidelines that would ensure that an increasing proportion of such aid be in grant form and/or supplied under appropriate concessional terms.[571] In addition, greater consideration would be given to providing technical and financial assistance for agricultural development and infrastructure projects in these countries.[572]

Under paragraph 4 of the decision, any future agreement on agricultural export credits would make appropriate provisions for the differential treatment of the least developed and net developing countries experiencing short-term difficulties in financing their normal level of commercial imports could draw on the resources available from international financial institutions, the IMF and World Bank, that were either existing or had been specially created to deal with this problem. As for the beneficiaries of the decision this was left to the Committee of Agriculture.[573]

---

[567] Article 16 of the AoA applies to Least-Developed and Net Food-Importing Developing Countries. It provides that developed country Members shall take such action as is provided for within the framework of the Decision on Measures Concerning the Possible Negative Effects of the Reform Programme on Least-Developed and Net Food-Importing Developing Countries.

[568] See Article 16 (2) of the AoA. It is the responsibility of the Committee on Agriculture to monitor, as appropriate, the follow-up to this Decision.

[569] McMahon 2012 37-43.

[570] Konandreas "Trade Policy Responses to Food Price Volatility in Poor Net Food-Importing Countries" 2012.

[571] McMahon 2012 37-43.

[572] McMahon 2012 42.

[573] Desta "Food Security and International Trade Law – An Appraisal of the WTO Approach" 2001 *Journal of World Trade* 449-468.

3 15 EXEMPTIONS

In addition to measures covered by the Green Box, two other categories of domestic support measures are exempt from reduction commitments under the Agreement on Agriculture (Article 6).[574] These are certain developmental measures in developing countries and certain direct payments under production-limiting programmes. Furthermore, so-called *de minimis* levels of support are exempted from reduction.

3 15 1 Developmental measures

The special and differential treatment under the Green Box aside, the type of support that fits into the developmental category are measures of assistance, whether direct or indirect, designed to encourage agricultural and rural development and that are an integral part of the development programmes of developing countries.[575] They include investment subsidies which are generally available to agriculture in developing country Members, agricultural input subsidies generally available to low-income or resource-poor producers in developing country Members, and domestic support to producers in developing country Members to encourage diversification from growing illicit narcotic crops.[576]

3 15 2 Blue Box

Direct payments under production limiting programmes (often referred to as "Blue Box" measures) are exempt from commitments if such payments are made on fixed areas and yield or a fixed number of livestock.[577] Such payments also fit into this category if they are made on 85 per cent or less of production in a defined base period.[578] While the Green Box covers decoupled payments, in the case of the Blue Box measures, production is still required in order to receive the

---

[574] Article 6 (2) further says that, "in accordance with the Mid-Term Review Agreement that government measures of assistance, whether direct or indirect, to encourage agricultural and rural development are an integral part of the development programmes of developing countries, investment subsidies which are generally available to agriculture in developing country Members and agricultural input subsidies generally available to low-income or resource-poor producers in developing country Members shall be exempt from domestic support reduction commitments that would otherwise be applicable to such measures, as shall domestic support to producers in developing country Members to encourage diversification from growing illicit narcotic crops. Domestic support meeting the criteria of this paragraph shall not be required to be included in a Member's calculation of its Current Total AMS".

[575] McMahon 2012 at 44.

[576] WTO "Agriculture: Explanation of the Agreement on Agriculture". http://www.wto.org/english/tratop_e/agric_e/ag_intro03_domestic_e.htm (accessed on 07/08/14).

[577] Kwa *Guide to the Agreement on Agriculture: Technicalities and Trade Tricks Explained* (1997) 10-15.

[578] WTO "Agriculture: Explanation of Domestic support Measures". http://www.wto.org/english/tratop_e/agric_e/ag_intro03_domestic_e.htm . (Accessed on 23/20/14).

payments, but the actual payments do not relate directly to the current quantity of that production.[579]

3 15 3 De minimis

All domestic support measures in favour of agricultural producers that do not fit into any of the above exempt categories are subject to reduction commitments. This domestic support category captures policies, such as market price support measures, direct production subsidies or input subsidies.[580] However, under the *de minimis* provisions of the Agreement there is no requirement to reduce such trade-distorting domestic support in any year in which the aggregate value of the product-specific support does not exceed 5 per cent of the total value of production of the agricultural product in question. In addition, non-product specific support which is less than 5 per cent of the value of total agricultural production is also exempt from reduction.[581] The 5 per cent threshold applies to developed countries whereas in the case of developing countries the *de minimis* ceiling is 10 per cent.[582]

3 16 NOTIFICATION OBLIGATIONS

All Members must notify the Committee on Agriculture the extent of their domestic support measures. This requires a listing of all measures that fit into the exempt categories: the Green Box, developmental measures, direct payments under production limiting programmes (Blue Box) and *de minimis* levels of support.[583] In addition, where the existence of measures requires it, AMS calculations must be undertaken by Members that have scheduled domestic support reduction commitments and the Current Total AMS must be notified.[584] Where a Member without such scheduled commitments has support measures which are not covered by one or other of the exempt categories, a notification must be made showing that such non-exempt support is within the

---

579 *Ibid.*

580 McMahon *Research Handbook on the WTO Agriculture Agreement: New and Emerging Issues in International Trade Law* (2012) 76-85.

581 McMahon *Research Handbook on the WTO Agriculture Agreement: New and Emerging Issues in International Trade Law* (2012) 77-90.

582 *Ibid.*

583 WTO "Agriculture: Explanation of Domestic support Measures". http://www.wto.org/english/tratop_e/agric_e/ag_intro03_domestic_e.htm . (Accessed on 23/20/14).

584 Amani "Critical Issues in Agricultural Trade – WTO: What does Africa want from Agriculture Negotiations?" 2004.

relevant *de minimis* levels.[585] Special formats have been developed by the Committee on Agriculture in order to facilitate compliance with the notification obligations.[586]

The requirement to notify is annual, except in the case of least-developed country Members which are only required to notify every other year.[587] Developing country Members can also request the Committee to set aside the annual notification requirement for measures other than those falling into the Green Box or the developmental or Blue Box categories.[588] In addition to the annual notification obligations, all Members must notify any modifications of existing or any introduction of new measures in the exempt categories.[589] These notifications too are examined by the Committee on Agriculture on a regular basis. As most Members do not have domestic support measures other than those falling into the exempt categories, the annual notification requirements are in many cases not particularly burdensome.[590] However, they are effective in providing a basis for policy discussions within the Committee on Agriculture and they also serve a useful purpose domestically in enabling governments to maintain an annual overview of support to their agricultural sectors.[591]

3 17 CONCLUSIONS

Most of the provisions of the AoA are lenient towards the developmental needs of developed countries at the expense of developing countries.[592] The green box provisions which are specifically designed to regulate payments that are considered trade neutral or minimally trade distorting has grossly been manipulated by developed countries at the mercy of the AoA.[593] It is argued that the current green box criterion allows members to enact policies that have a significant

[585] Notification shall be done in line with the provisions of Article 18 of the AoA. For a detailed explanation of this, see WTO "Agriculture: Explanation of Domestic support Measures". http://www.wto.org/english/tratop_e/agric_e/ag_intro03_domestic_e.htm (Accessed on 23/20/14).

[586] WTO Secretariat *Handbook on Notification Requirements under the Agreement on Agriculture* (2010) generally.

[587] *Ibid.*

[588] WTO Secretariat *Handbook on Notification Requirements under the Agreement on Agriculture* (2010) generally.

[589] Nedumpara "India's Food Security Concerns and the WTO Bali Ministerial Decision" 2014 *Global Trade and Customs Journal* 177–181.

[590] 590 Nedumpara "India's Food Security Concerns and the WTO Bali Ministerial Decision" 2014 *Global Trade and Customs Journal* 179–181.

[591] WTO "Agriculture: Explanation of Domestic support Measures". http://www.wto.org/english/tratop_e/agric_e/ag_intro03_domestic_e.htm (Accessed on 23/20/14).

[592] Khor "The WTO's Doha Negotiations and Impasse: A Development Perspective" 2006.

[593] Matthews "Decoupling and the Green Box: International Dimensions of the Reinstrumentation of Agricultural Support" http://www.researchgate.net/publication/228699618_Decoupling_and_the_green_box_international_dimensions_of_the_reinstrumentation_of_agricultural_support (Accessed on 23/07/14).

trade distorting effect.[594] It is difficult for green box definitions to allow for the development of a full range of legitimate domestic programmes without payments being counted against domestic support limits.[595] It is further argued that he green box provisions do not take into account the difficulties that developing countries have in providing direct payments, and underplay the desirability of payments coupled to production and price in the context of rural development.[596] It is not a secret that the green box measures are mostly used by developed countries, probably because of their massive financial prowess.[597] Their widespread use by developed countries provide these countries with a massive competitive edge, even if the direct output effects are difficult to determine.[598]

Developed countries continue to provide trade distorting subsidies under the guise of green box.[599] This is defeating the aims and objective of the AoA. The intended objective of the green box measures is to allow and regulate domestic support measures which have no or minimal trade distorting effects, nor positive effects on production. The output effects of these measures are difficult to determine and some argue that most of the green box measures have a positive effect on production which if true, classifies them in the amber category. It is therefore submitted that the green box provisions are another means of delivering income support to farmers under the shield of the AoA. It is further submitted that, the veil should be lifted where trade distorting support is being conferred under the guise of green box. It is suggested that the WTO should review the green box measures in order lessen the possibility of these loopholes.

Even though several developing countries had already called for review of the green box measures, these efforts have been fiercely opposed by the US and the EU, who happen to be the main users of the green box subsidies which are questionable.[600] This shows the hypocrisy of both the EU and the US. They were at the forefront of negotiating the AoA, which according to them would reduce

---

594 *Ibid.*

595 Blandford "Should the Green Box be Modified?" 2007. http://www.agritrade.org/Publications/DiscussionPapers/Green_Box.pdf (accessed on 21/10/14).

596 Meléndez-Ortiz, *Agricultural Subsidies in the WTO Green Box: Ensuring Coherence with Sustainable Development Goals* (2009) 561-562.

597 Meléndez-Ortiz, *Agricultural Subsidies in the WTO Green Box: Ensuring Coherence with Sustainable Development Goals* (2009) 561-562.

598 Meléndez-Ortiz 2009 38.

599 Blandford "Should the Green Box be Modified?" 2007. http://www.agritrade.org/Publications/DiscussionPapers/Green_Box.pdf (accessed on 21/10/14).

600 Josling "Biofuel Subsidies and the Green Box" www.ictsd.org/downloads/2008/12/josling-and-blandford.doc. (Accessed on 06/10/14).

trade distorting subsidies. Apart from the green box measures which have been used as an umbrella to shield developed countries against the disciplines of the AoA, some developed countries even continue to provide support that fall within thee amber box category.[601] However, perpetrators of these subsidies are quick to justify themselves with the green box provisions. Hence there have been a shift from amber box to green box and some amber box subsidies are being provided under the semblance of green box.[602]

The use of subsidies that are contingent on export performance has greatly affected developing countries.[603] Even though developing countries seem to have succeeded in challenging the *US Upland Cotton* programmes, developed countries have not been deterred by this and the AoA in any way since they continue to subsidize their exports. The AoA allows certain export subsidies to be provided by members.[604] Members are allowed to use those non listed export subsidies on condition that they do not use them to circumvent, actually or potentially, their obligations *vis a' vis* the listed subsidy practises. The fact that article 10 (1) of the AoA provides that export subsidies listed in paragraph 1 of Article 9 shall not be applied in a manner which results in circumvention implicitly endorses their use. What is regulated is the manner of their use.[605] The use of export subsidies by developed countries has negatively affected the agricultural sector in most developed countries.[606] It is submitted that, due to the weaknesses of the AoA, developing countries have lost their share on the global agricultural markets whilst agricultural products from developed countries continue to flood the former's markets.

---

601 Blandford "Should the Green Box be Modified?" 2007. http://www.agritrade.org/Publications/DiscussionPapers/Green_Box.pdf (accessed on 21/10/14).
602 Blandford "Should the Green Box be Modified?" 2007. http://www.agritrade.org/Publications/DiscussionPapers/Green_Box.pdf (accessed on 21/10/14).
603 Amani "Critical Issues in Agricultural Trade – WTO: What does Africa want from Agriculture Negotiations?" 2004.
604 Desta *Agricultural Export Subsidies under the WTO Agriculture Package: A Legal Analysis* (1997).
605 *Ibid.*
606 Blandford 2007.

CHAPTER 4

World Trade Organisation Jurisprudence on Agricultural Subsidies

4 1 INTRODUCTION

The agricultural sector of international trade has seen a large portion of disputes in the past fifty years.[607] This is possibly because of lack of a clear structure of rules to discipline government activity in these markets, coupled with the sensitive nature of trade in basic foodstuffs which has been the major cause of disagreement.[608] The Agreement on Agriculture (AoA) remarkably improved the framework for government policy in this area by providing *inter alia* a temporary exemption for certain subsidies from challenge in the World Trade Organisation (WTO) peace clause.[609] The expiry of the peace clause in 2003 has led to an influx of cases challenging export and domestic agricultural programmes.[610] This is partially because of slow progress in the Doha Round of trade negotiations.[611] Domestic subsidies under the AoA and the Agreement on Subsidies and Countervailing Measures (SCM) have particularly become a major subject of litigation.[612] This means that countries might have to modify their agricultural policies so as to reduce their vulnerability to challenge in the WTO.[613]

This chapter explores some WTO agricultural subsidies disputes dealing with trade distorting export and domestic subsidies. It assesses whether the interpretations adopted by the DSB and the Panel accommodate the developmental needs of developing countries. As noted above, developing countries have been largely left out in global trade. The chapter explores WTO jurisprudence on agricultural subsidies in a bid to expose possible flaws or loopholes in the WTO dispute settlement system. Not all cases dealing with agricultural subsidies will be dealt with in this study. However,

---

[607] Of the more than 367 requests for consultations made to the Dispute Settlement Body, more than 100 have primarily been about agricultural trade, a share of 27 percent.

[608] Hudec "Does the Agreement on Agriculture Work? Agricultural Disputes after the Uruguay Round." Paper presented at the Theme Day of the International Agricultural Trade Research Consortium (IATRC), San Diego, 1997. Also see Josling "Agricultural Trade Disputes in the WTO" Volume on DSU and Trade Disputes 2006.

[609] Barton *The Evolution of the Trade Regime: Politics, Law and Economics of the GATT and WTO* (2006). To support this, also see Josling, Agricultural Trade Disputes in the WTO, Volume on DSU and Trade Disputes.

[610] Steinberg "When the Peace Ends: The Vulnerability of EC and U.S. Agricultural Subsidies to WTO Legal Challenge" 2003 *Journal of International Economic Law* at 369-417.

[611] Josling, "Implications of WTO Litigation for the WTO Agricultural Negotiations" 2006.

[612] Josling 2006.

[613] Josling 2006.

the study will cover some of the most important cases resolved by the WTO panel and the Appellate Body (AB).

4 2 CANADA - MEASURES AFFECTING THE IMPORTATION OF MILK AND THE EXPORTATION OF DAIRY PRODUCTS[614]

In 1995, Canada introduced a new pricing system for dairy exports, called the "Special Milk Classes" scheme.[615] This scheme permitted Canadian exporters buy milk at significantly lower prices than otherwise available on Canada's domestic market.[616] New Zealand and the United States (US) were of the view that the scheme provided export subsidies in violation of the AoA, and requested Canada to limit its export subsidy volume commitments for dairy products.[617] New Zealand and the US argued that because Canada's exports under the "Special Milk Classes" scheme were running at around double Canada's export subsidy commitment levels, Canada was therefore in breach of the AoA.[618]

In November 1997, the US agreed with New Zealand to invoke the dispute settlement provisions of the WTO against Canada in respect of its "Special Milk Classes" regime.[619] New Zealand requested consultations under the Dispute Settlement Understanding (DSU) in December 1997.[620] As the consultations did not resolve the dispute, New Zealand requested a WTO Dispute Settlement Panel (DSP) in March 1998.[621] The US had also requested a panel in respect of the "Special Milk Classes" scheme. The Panel that was established heard both cases together.[622]

The parties to the case[623] all made written and oral submissions to the Panel in the latter part of 1998. The Panel issued its report in May 1999. It found that Canada's "Special Milk Classes" scheme did provide export subsidies, and that Canada had exceeded its export subsidy commitment

---

[614] WT/DS113.
[615] World Trade Organization, 1999. *Canada – Measures Affecting the Importation of Milk and the Exportation of Dairy Products*, WT/DS103/R and WT/DS113/R.
[616] *Ibid.*
[617] See New Zealand and United States written submissions *in re: Measures Affecting the Importation of Milk and the Exportation of Dairy Products.*
[618] *Ibid.*
[619] *Canada - Measures Affecting the Importation of Milk and the Exportation of Dairy Products* (WT/DS113).
[620] *Ibid.*
[621] New Zealand Ministry of Foreign affairs and Trade, WTO disputes with New Zealand as a principal complainant *in Canada - Measures Affecting the Importation of Milk and the Exportation of Dairy Products* (WT/DS113).
[622] *Ibid.*
[623] The parties were New Zealand, the United States and Canada.

levels in breach of the WTO AoA.[624] Canada unsuccessfully appealed the Panel's decision.[625] In its Report in October 1999, the AB upheld the Panel's key findings.[626] The Dispute Settlement Body (DSB) adopted these findings, and recommended Canada bring its measures into conformity with the WTO rules.[627]

New Zealand and the US then reached an agreement with Canada in December 1999 on the time-frame for Canada's implementation of the outcome of the case.[628] This agreement provided for a "phased" implementation over the 2000 calendar year.[629] As part of its implementation, Canada would continue to make use of the "Special Milk Classes" scheme for dairy exports, but agreed to limit export volumes under the scheme to within its commitment levels.[630] However as part of its implementation, Canada introduced a number of new dairy export mechanisms on a province-by-province basis.[631] It claimed that the new schemes did not provide export subsidies, and it would not therefore limit the volume of exports under them to within its export subsidy commitment levels.[632] New Zealand and the US officials considered that the new schemes continued to provide export illegal subsidies and that Canada had therefore failed to comply with the DSB's recommendations.[633]

In February 2001, New Zealand, the US and Canada held consultations on this issue, but Canada failed to resolve New Zealand's and US concerns.[634] Thus, later in February, New Zealand and the US formally requested that the WTO reconvene the original DSP to examine Canada's replacement

---

[624] See World Trade Organisation Panel Report - *Measures Affecting the Importation of Milk and the Exportation of Dairy Products.*

[625] World Trade Organization, 2001. *Canada—Measures Affecting the Importation of Milk and the Exportation of Dairy Products*, Report of the Appellate Body, WT/DS103&113/AB/RW.

[626] World Trade Organization, 2001. *Canada—Measures Affecting the Importation of Milk and the Exportation of Dairy Products,* Report of the Appellate Body, WT/DS103&113/AB/RW.

[627] New Zealand Ministry of Foreign affairs and Trade, WTO disputes with New Zealand as a principal complainant in *Canada - Measures Affecting the Importation of Milk and the Exportation of Dairy Products.*

[628] *Canada—Measures Affecting the Importation of Milk and the Exportation of Dairy Products*, Report of the Appellate Body

[629] New Zealand Ministry of Foreign affairs and Trade, WTO disputes with New Zealand as a principal complainant in Canada - Measures Affecting the Importation of Milk and the Exportation of Dairy Products.

[630] *Ibid.*

[631] Josling "Agricultural Trade Disputes in the WTO, Volume on DSU and Trade Disputes" *Frontiers Of Economics And Globalization* 4-11.

[632] Josling 2006 5-10.

[633] New Zealand Ministry of Foreign affairs and Trade, WTO disputes with New Zealand as a principal complainant *in Canada - Measures Affecting the Importation of Milk and the Exportation of Dairy Products.*

[634] *Ibid.*

schemes.[635] The Panel received written and oral submissions from the parties in May 2001. The European Union (EU), Mexico and Australia reserved their right to participate as third parties and made written and oral submissions to that effect.[636] The Panel issued its decision in July 2002. It found that Canada's replacement schemes continued to provide export subsidies in breach of its WTO commitments.[637]

Canada subsequently appealed this decision and in December 2001 the Appellate Body (AB) held that the Panel had applied the wrong legal test to determine whether export subsidies had been provided. The panel in *Canada – Dairy (Article 21.5 – New Zealand and US)*[638] found that Canada provided, through its "Commercial Export Milk" (CEM) mechanism, "export subsidies" within the meaning of Article 9.1(c) of the *Agreement on Agriculture.* The panel also found that Canada provided these export subsidies in excess of the quantity commitment levels specified in its Schedule and that, therefore, Canada had acted inconsistently with its obligations under Articles 3.3 and 8 of the AoA. The AB reversed the panel's findings on the grounds that the panel had erred in its interpretation of Article 9.1(c).

The AB held that the appropriate standard, in those proceedings, for determining whether "payments" are made under Article 9.1(c), is not, as held by the first Article 21.5 panel, the domestic price, but rather the producer's costs of production. However, in the light of the factual findings made by the first Article 21.5 panel, the Appellate Body was unable to determine whether the implementation measures involved such "payments" and, hence, export subsidies within the meaning of Article 9.1(c). Consequently, the AB was also unable to determine whether these measures were consistent with Articles 3.3 and 8 of the AoA.[639] In its report of 20 December 2002 the AB upheld the Panel's finding that Canada was providing export subsidies in breach of its

[635] In a meeting held on the 1st March 2001, pursuant to Article 21.5 of the DSU, the DSB referred to the original panel the matter raised by the United States and the matter raised by New Zealand (see DS113).

[636] See WTO *Measures Affecting the Importation of Milk and the Exportation of Dairy Products* on https://www.wto.org/english/tratop_e/dispu_e/cases_e/ds103_e.htm (Accessed on 09/03/15).

[637] According to the Panel Report circulated on 26 July 2002, Canada through the CEM scheme and the continued operation of Special Milk Class 5(d), had acted inconsistently with its obligations under Articles 3.3 and 8 of the AoA, by providing export subsidies within the meaning of Article 9.1(c) of the AoA in excess of its quantity commitment levels specified in its Schedule for exports of cheese and "other dairy products". It also concluded that Canada had acted inconsistently with its obligations under Article 10.1 of the AoA and that therefore Canada had acted inconsistently with its obligations under Article 8 of the AoA.

[638] Appellate Body Report, *Canada – Dairy (Article 21.5 – New Zealand and US)*, paras. 126-127.

[639] Appellate Body Report, Canada – Dairy (Article 21.5 – New Zealand and US), paras. 126-127.

WTO commitments.[640] The AB found that its replacement scheme was contrary to Canada's obligations under Article 3.3 and Article 8 of the AoA.[641] The AB's decision was adopted by the DSB on 17 January 2003.[642]

At the same time as initiating the dispute settlement process to investigate Canada's compliance with the original panel's finding, New Zealand also lodged a request seeking authorisation from the DSB to take retaliatory action against Canada by suspending tariff concessions up to the value of US$35 million a year, which was the damage calculated to be caused to New Zealand by Canada's illegal dairy export subsidy regime.[643] The retaliation related requests of New Zealand and the US were referred to arbitration. A mutually agreed solution between Canada and New Zealand was notified to the WTO on 9 May 2003.[644]

4 2 1 Conclusions and Lessons Learnt from the Canada Dairy Case

The AB upheld the Panel's findings that the supply of CEM by producers to processors involves payments within the meaning of Article 9.1 (c) of the AoA.[645] Canada had initially argued that the panel erred in finding that the payments made on the sale of CEM are financed by virtue of government action. The Panel correctly stated that there must be a demonstrable link between government action and financing of payments. A closer assessment of Canada's programmes reveals that there was a demonstrable link between Canada government actions and the financing of CEM payments. To escape this, Canada should have proved that these government actions were not demonstrably linked to the financing of payments in pursuant to article 10.3 of the AoA. Canada failed to prove that.

---

[640] World Trade Organization, Canada—*Measures Affecting the Importation of Milk and the Exportation of Dairy Products,* Report of the Appellate Body, 2001 WT/DS103&113/AB/RW.

[641] *Ibid.* Article 3.3 of the AoA provides that, "Subject to the provisions of paragraphs 2(b) and 4 of Article 9, a Member shall not provide export subsidies listed in paragraph 1 of Article 9 in respect of the agricultural products or groups of products specified in Section II of Part IV of its Schedule in excess of the budgetary outlay and quantity commitment levels specified therein and shall not provide such subsidies in respect of any agricultural product not specified in that Section of its Schedule". Article 8 of the AoA which was violated by Canada in its special milk classes provides that, "Each Member undertakes not to provide export subsidies otherwise than in conformity with this Agreement and with the commitments as specified in that Member's Schedule".

[642] See WTO *Measures Affecting the Importation of Milk and the Exportation of Dairy Products* on https://www.wto.org/english/tratop_e/dispu_e/cases_e/ds103_e.htm (Accessed on 09/03/15).

[643] The US also made a similar request to the DSB.

[644] There was a separate agreement between the United States and Canada. On 9 May 2003, Canada and the United States informed the DSB that they had reached a mutually agreed solution under Article 3.6 of the DSU.

[645] For the panel's finding see para 5.89 of the Canada Dairy Panel Report.

As regards "governmental action", the AB noted that "the text of Article 9.1(c) does not place any qualifications on the types of 'governmental action' which may be relevant under Article 9.1(c)."[646] Instead, the provision gives but one example of governmental action that is "included" in Article 9.1(c) but, this example is merely illustrative.[647] Accordingly, it was stated by the AB that Article 9.1(c) "embraces the full-range" of activities by which governments 'regulate', 'control' or 'supervise' individuals".[648] In particular, it was said that governmental action "regulating the supply and price of milk in the domestic market" might be relevant "action" under Article 9.1(c).[649] This therefore means that the governmental action may be a single act or omission, or a series of acts or omissions

The AB observed that Article 9.1(c) does not require that payments be financed by virtue of government "mandate", or other "direction". Although the word "action" certainly covers situations where government mandates or directs that payments be made, it also covers other situations where no such compulsion is involved.[650] Although the term "governmental action", when read in isolation, is somewhat open-ended, perhaps even abstract, the words "by virtue of" clarify further the meaning of this term.[651] The words "by virtue of ", therefore, express the relationship between "governmental action" and the "financing" of payments for the purpose of Article 9.1(c). The essence of that relationship is the "*nexus*" or "link" between "action" and "financing".

Thus, although Article 9.1(c) extends, in principle, to any "governmental action", not every governmental action will have the requisite nexus to the financing of payments. In the first proceedings, the AB observed that "governments are constantly engaged in regulation of different kinds in pursuit of a variety of objectives."[652] The AB, went on to say that regulation that merely

---

[646]Appellate Body Report *Canada – Dairy (Article 21.5 – New Zealand and US)* para. 112.
[647]The example given is "payments that are financed from the proceeds of a levy imposed on the agricultural product concerned or on an agricultural product from which the exported product is derived".
[648]Appellate Body Report, *Canada – Dairy (Article 21.5 – New Zealand and US)*, para. 112.
[649]*Ibid.*
[650]Article 9.1(c) of the AoA may be contrasted with Article 9.1(e) of the AoA, as well as with Article 1.1(a)(1)(iv) of the SCM and items (c), (d), (j), and (k) of the Illustrative List of Export Subsidies (the "Illustrative List") of the SCM. In these provisions, some kind of government mandate, direction, or control is an element of a subsidy provided through a third party.
[651] The AB had earlier on noted that the words "by virtue of" indicate that there must be a demonstrable link between the *governmental action* at issue and the *financing* of the payments, whereby the payments are, in some way, financed as a result of, or as a consequence of, the governmental action.
[652]*Ibid.* para 115.

enables payments to occur will not suffice for those payments to be regarded as "financed by virtue of governmental action". It stated that, where regulation merely enables payments to occur, the link between the governmental action and the financing of the payments will too tenuous for the "payments" to be regarded as "financed by virtue of governmental action" within the meaning of Article 9.1(c). Rather, there must be a tighter *nexus* between the mechanism and process by which the payments are financed. [653]

The word "financing" refers generally to the mechanism or process by which financial resources are provided to enable "payments" to be made.[654] The word could, therefore, be read to mean that government itself must provide the resources for producers to make payments.[655] However, Article 9.1(c) expressly precludes such a reading, as it states that "payments" need not involve "a charge on the public account". This is borne out by the fact that the text indicates that "financing" need only be "by virtue of governmental action", rather than "by government" itself.[656] Article 9.1(c), therefore, contemplates that "payments may be financed by virtue of governmental action even though significant aspects of the financing might not involve government." [657] This implies that payments may also be made, and funded, by private parties. [658]

4 3 PERU – ADDITIONAL DUTY ON IMPORTS OF CERTAIN AGRICULTURAL PRODUCTS

On the 12th of April 2013, Guatemala requested consultations with Peru pursuant to Article 4 of the Understanding on Rules and Procedures Governing the Settlement of Disputes (DSU), Article 19 of the AoA, Article 19 of the Agreement on Implementation of Article VII of the General Agreement on Tariffs and Trade 1994 (Customs Valuation Agreement) and Article XXIII of the General Agreement on Tariffs and Trade 1994 (GATT 1994), with respect to the imposition by Peru of an "additional duty" on imports of certain agricultural products.[659] The consultations held on 14 and 15 May 2013, failed to resolve the dispute.[660] In its request for the establishment of a

[653] *Ibid.*
[654] See para 132 of *Canada Dairy* AB report.
[655] *Ibid.*
[656] Accordingly, even if government does not fund the payments itself, it must play a sufficiently important part in the process by which a private party funds "payments", such that the requisite nexus exists between "governmental action" and "financing".
[657] Appellate Body Report, *Canada – Dairy (Article 21.5 – New Zealand and US)*, para. 114.
[658] See of *Canada Dairy* Panel Report.
[659] See request for consultations by Guatemala, document WT/DS457/1 (of 16 April 2013).
[660] See request for the establishment of a panel by Guatemala, document WT/DS457/2 (of 14 June 2013).

panel, Guatemala identified the measure at issue in this dispute as "the additional duty imposed by Peru on imports of certain agricultural products, such as milk, maize, rice and sugar" referred to as "affected products".[661]

As described by Guatemala, the measure had been in force since 22 June 2001 and it consisted of a variable levy that was imposed in addition to the ordinary customs duty.[662] The levy was determined by using a mechanism known as the "Price Range System" (PRS) which, operated on the basis of two components identified as a range made up of a floor price and a ceiling price reflecting the international price over the last 60 months for the affected product and a c.i.f. reference price published every two weeks which reflected the average international market price for the affected products.[663]

According to Guatemala, the measure resulted in the imposition of an import levy on the affected products when the international reference prices of those products were below certain floor price levels, or in tariff rebates when these reference prices are above certain ceiling price levels.[664] Both the price range and the c.i.f. reference prices varied periodically as a result of the application of certain formulas to the circumstances in the markets for the affected products and the price range varied every six months, while the c.i.f. reference prices varied every 15 days.[665] The amount of the levy was specific and was expressed in United States dollars (USD) per metric ton.[666] It was also payable upon importation of the affected products, together with the ordinary customs duties and other import taxes on the affected products.[667]

4 3 1 Issues

It was submitted by Guatemala that the duties resulting from the PRS were inconsistent with Article 4.2 of the AoA, as they constituted variable import levies or measures similar to variable

---

[661] See request for the establishment of a panel by Guatemala, document WT/DS457/2 (of 14 June 2013).

[662] Guatemala's first written submission, paras. 2.1 4-4.35 and 4.44; second written submission paras 1.18-4.21; opening statement at the first meeting of the Panel.

[663] Guatemala's first written submission, paras. 2.34-4.35 and 4.44; second written submission paras 4.18-4.21; opening statement at the first meeting of the Panel para 11

[664] Guatemala's first written submission, paras. 3.3-3.5 and 2.44; second written submission, paras. 4-4.21; opening statement at the first meeting of the Panel.

[665] *Ibid.*

[666] *Ibid.*

[667] Hereinafter, the measure will be referred to as "the duties resulting from the PRS".

import levies.[668] It was alleged that the duties resulting from the PRS were inconsistent with Article 4.2 of the AoA, as they constituted minimum import prices or measures similar to minimum import prices. The duties resulting from the PRS were duties or charges inconsistent with the second sentence of Article II: 1(b) of the GATT 1994. It was also alleged that Peru's actions were inconsistent with Article X:1 of the GATT 1994, inasmuch as it failed to publish the international prices used as a basis for calculating the floor price and the reference price, despite the fact that these international prices were an essential element of the measure at issue. It failed to publish the content of the "import costs", which was also an essential element of the measure at issue. As if it was not enough, Peru also failed to publish the methodology for determining the amounts for freight and insurance, which was a very essential element of the measure at issue.

Apart from this, Peru's actions were also allegedly inconsistent with Article X: 3(a) of the GATT 1994, because it administered the measure in question in a manner that was not reasonable given its failure to observe the requirements of its own legislation.[669] Specifically, Peru's failure to comply with its own legislation was shown by its practices of extending the validity of the Customs Tables, calculating the price ranges for dairy products by reference price intervals and not for each individual value, calculating additional duties or customs rebates for two categories of rice[670] and calculating and updating the reference price for dairy products monthly rather than fortnightly.[671]

4 3 2 The PRS and how it operated

As mentioned above, in its request for the establishment of a panel, Guatemala identified the measure at issue as "the additional duty imposed by Peru on imports of certain agricultural products" and explained that this duty was calculated by means of the PRS. This section of study describes the PRS and the duty or the tariff rebates that it can generate, together with the way in which the system operated since it was first established.

---

668 See Guatemala’s first written submissions. Also see article 4.2 of the AoA which states that, Members shall not maintain, resort to, or revert to any measures of the kind which have been required to be converted into ordinary customs duties1, except as otherwise provided for in Article 5 and Annex 5.

669 Article X: 3(a) of the GATT 1994 states that each contracting party shall administer in a uniform, impartial and reasonable manner all its laws, regulations, decisions and rulings of the kind described in paragraph 1 of this Article.

670 This only applied to pounded and paddy rice.

671 See Guatemala's first written submission for a detailed explanation on this.

The PRS was established by the Peru Supreme Decree[672] published on 22 June 2001, and was applicable to imports of various import tariff lines for rice, maize, milk and sugar.[673] According to Article 1 of the Supreme Decree, the PRS was established "for the purpose of applying variable duties additional to the tariff", when the international reference prices for the products subject to the PRS are lower than certain floor price levels, and tariff rebates as well as when those reference prices are higher than certain ceiling price levels.[674] On the website of Peru's Ministry of the Economy and Finance, it is stated that the PRS "is intended to stabilize the costs of importing the products included in the System by ensuring effective prices both for the producer, by means of a floor price, and for the consumer, through a ceiling price, and applying Variable Additional Duties or Tariff Rebates on the c.i.f. value".[675]

Guatemala also argued that the duties resulting from the PRS were inherently variable.[676] It asserts that Peru calculated the duties and tariff rebates resulting from the PRS through the PRS, which is made up of various mathematical schemes and formulas that operated in a coordinated manner to determine duties and rebates automatically and continuously.[677] Guatemala further argued that the measure at issue possessed inherent variability because the measure itself, as a mechanism, imposed the variability of the duties.[678] The duties resulting from the PRS were calculated in such a way that the authorities had no discretion to interfere in their application, since both the formulas and the manner of carrying out the calculations that produce the amounts of the resulting duties

[672] Supreme Decree No. 115-2001-EF218.

[673] See Peru's Supreme Decree No 115-2001 EF218.

[674] Supreme Decree No. 115-2001-EF (Exhibit GTM-4), Article 1.

[675] Copy of the Peruvian Ministry of the Economy and Finance's web page explaining the Price Range System. Also see the In the preamble to Supreme Decree No. 115-2001-EF which sets the objectives of the PRS and described as follows: Whereas national agricultural production is being adversely affected by distortions reflected in uncertainty and instability of domestic prices and national production and due, in particular, to the agricultural policies implemented by the main food producing and exporting countries; Whereas the Price Range System is a stabilization and protection mechanism that makes it possible to neutralize the fluctuations of international prices and limit the negative effects of the fall in those prices; Whereas the System in question constitutes an appropriate means of improving the levels of competitiveness of domestic producers, by giving the market clear signals with regard to trends in prices, thereby allowing economic agents to operate efficiently and productively.

[676] Guatemala's first written submission, paras. 4.2 4-3.3.4and 4.34; second written submission, paras. 4.18-4.21; opening statement at the first meeting of the Panel, para. 10.

[677] Guatemala's first written submission, paras. 4.34-4.35 and 4.44; second written submission, paras. 4.18-4.21; opening statement at the first meeting of the Panel, para. 11.

[678] Guatemala's first written submission, para. 4.39.

were contained in the applicable legislation.[679] Guatemala added that the mechanism guaranteed that the resulting duties would vary every 15 days.[680]

Guatemala also maintained that an empirical analysis showed the inherent variability of the duties or rebates under the PRS.[681] It contended that throughout the more than 12 years of application of the PRS, the resulting duties or rebates almost always varied with each new fortnight, the floor and ceiling prices varied with practically every publication of updated customs tables and the reference price changed every fortnight in roughly 92 to 96% of instances.[682] Any government measure in Peru could be changed by an autonomous and independent government decision, but the measure at issue enjoyed a degree of additional variability, as the text thereof included an inherent methodology requiring and necessarily implying periodic modifications.[683]

Guatemala argued that, given their very variability, the duties generated by the PRS lacked both transparency and predictability, as a natural and inherent consequence of the variable nature of those duties, since an exporter was less likely to ship to a market if that exporter did not know and couldn't reasonably predict what the amount of duties would be.[684] Guatemala asserts that the lack of transparency and predictability was clear from an empirical analysis.[685] It expounded that, as the key elements of the PRS vary, the resulting values were not predictable, and a commercial operator will have no certainty as to what will be the reference price, or as to whether an additional duty would be applied in the coming months, and what would be its amount.[686] Guatemala points out that the system in fact guarantees that the importer faces uncertainty.[687]

In its defence, Peru argued that the measure at issue was an ordinary customs duty, and that Article 4.2 of the AoA was therefore not applicable.[688] Peru also argues that the measure at issue did not

---

[679] This was in violation of Article X: 3(a) of the GATT 1994 which states that each contracting party shall administer in a uniform, impartial and reasonable manner all its laws, regulations, decisions and rulings of the kind described in paragraph 1 of this Article.
[680] Guatemala's first written submission, paras. 4.36-4.38; second written submission, paras. 4.8-4.11.
[681] See Guatemala's first written submission.
[682] Guatemala's first written submission, paras. 4.54-4.57; History of Application of the Price Range System (GTM-15), indicating the instances in which a reference price has remained the same in consecutive periods.
[683] Guatemala's second written submission, paras. 4.22-4.27.
[684] Guatemala's first written submission, paras. 4.58-4.61; opening statement at the first meeting of the Panel, para. 26 (citing Appellate Body Report, *Chile - Price Band System*, para. 234); second written submission, paras. 4.12, 4.19 and 4.50; response to Panel question No. 56, paras. 134-138.
[685] Guatemala's first written submission, paras. 4.61-4.63.
[686] Guatemala's first written submission, paras. 4.62-4.63.
[687] Guatemala's first written submission, paras. 4.61-4.63.
[688] Peru's first written submission, para. 5.41; second written submission, para. 3.13.

exhibit characteristics such as to be considered a variable import levy, a minimum import price or a measure similar to these.[689] Peru identifies a series of characteristics of ordinary customs duties, which it argued, are derived from the ordinary meaning of the text of the relevant agreements, taking into account their context, object and purpose, the supplementary means of interpretation and the previous decisions of WTO panels and the AB.[690]

Peru asserts that ordinary customs duties were subject to Most Favoured Nation (MFN) treatment, forming part of the tariff regime, applied to imports and the obligation to pay them at the time of importation. Peru also argued that the ordinary customs duties could be designed to collect revenue or to protect the domestic industry, may be *ad valorem*, specific or compound duties, could vary, but subject to an upper limit, which is the level bound in the schedule of the respective Member; and were transparent and predictable.[691] It argued that the duties resulting from the PRS met these characteristics, and were therefore ordinary customs duties.[692]

Peru claimed that lack of transparency and predictability is an additional characteristic independent of variability, and stressed that the high degree of transparency and predictability of the PRS distinguished it from variable levies and minimum import prices.[693] Peru argued that its measure was transparent and enabled commercial operators to acquaint themselves with the amounts corresponding to the applicable tariff duties.[694] Peru indicated that operators knew that the duty would never exceed the bound rate and that all the essential elements for its calculation were published.[695]

4 3 3 Main Arguments of the Third Parties

Argentina tended that Members must be particularly careful to ensure compliance with and enforcement of Article 4.2 of the AoA, and avoid taking measures that could restrict market access for agricultural products.[696] In Argentina's opinion, the duties resulting from the PRS were a

---

689 Peru's first written submission para 5.54; second written submission para 3.35.
690 Peru's first written submission paras 5.11-5.37.
691 Peru's first written submission paras 5.38-5.39.
692 Peru's first written submission, paras 5.40-5.41; opening statement at the first meeting of the Panel, para. 37.
693 Peru's first written submission paras 5.88 and 5.92; second written submission para.3.47 opening statement at the first meeting of the Panel para 44.
694 *Ibid.*
695 Peru's first written submission, paras. 5.89-5.91; second written submission, para. 3.48; opening statement at the first meeting of the Panel para 44.
696 Argentina's third-party written submission, para 10.

measure inconsistent with Article 4.2 of the AoA, since they qualified as a variable import levy, a minimum import price, or as a measure similar to these.[697] Argentina asserted that the obligation under Article 4.2 of the AoA applied from the date of the entry into force of the WTO Agreement, which would not appear to match Peru's defence to the effect that the PRS was part of Peru's tariff offer during the Uruguay Round.[698] Finally, Argentina argued that it is particularly important that transparency and predictability would prevail in trade relations, and observed that, in general terms, a PRS lessened the transparency and predictability of trade.[699]

In Brazil's view, in order to assess whether a border measure on agricultural products is consistent with market access commitments, it is not enough to establish whether the measure is consistent with the schedule of concessions of the particular Member, but it is also necessary to confirm that the measure is not one of those referred to in Article 4.2 of the AoA.[700] Brazil argued that, in assessing whether a measure is inconsistent with Article 4.2 of the AoA, it must be considered whether the challenged measure is similar to one of the measures identified in footnote 1 to the AoA, without having to check that the measure is identical. Brazil pointed out that the fact that a measure shares characteristics with the duties set out in a Member's schedule of concessions does not, *ipso facto*, turn it into an ordinary customs duty.[701] Brazil also asserted that not all the duties calculated on the basis of the value and/or volume of imports constituted ordinary customs duties.[702]

Brazil tended that some characteristics of the measure at issue appeared to be similar to those of the measures mentioned in footnote 1 to the AoA.[703] In Brazil's view, the inherent variability of the measure appeared to be undisputed. Regarding the lack of transparency and predictability, Brazil argued that a measure with these characteristics generated costs and discouraged the

---

697 Argentina's third-party written submission, para 11; third-party statement, para. 8.

698 Argentina's third-party written submission, paras.13 and 14 third-party statement, paras. 4-6.

699 Argentina's third-party written submission para 17 at 365.

700 Brazil's third-party written submission para 10.

701 Brazil's third-party written submission paras 11-12.

702 Brazil's third-party written submission para 10

703 Brazil's third-party written submission paras 14-18. The measures specified in footnote 1 of the AoA include quantitative import restrictions, variable import levies, minimum import prices, discretionary import licensing, non-tariff measures maintained through state-trading enterprises, voluntary export restraints, and similar border measures other than ordinary customs duties, whether or not the measures are maintained under country-specific derogations from the provisions of GATT 1947, but not measures maintained under balance-of-payments provisions or under other general, non-agriculture-specific provisions of GATT 1994 or of the other Multilateral Trade Agreements in Annex 1A to the WTO Agreement.

conclusion of long-term contracts.[704] It indicated that the discouraging effect was even clearer when the measure did not apply to all Members.[705] Brazil added that the fact that a measure referred to the objective of disconnecting domestic prices from international market signals beyond the normal effect of tariffs, and protecting local producers from the agricultural policies of other Members, appears to run counter to Article 4.2 of the AoA.[706]

Colombia was of the view that the AoA contains no provision suggesting that one of the fundamental characteristics of a variable levy is its inherent variability.[707] It considered that the interpretation of variable import levies by the AB is inconsistent with the customary rules of interpretation, insofar as it takes no account of the context of the entire sentence. Colombia explained that the use of the phrase "these measures include" in the footnote to the AoA is not meant to indicate that the measures must "themselves contain" variable formulas or minimum prices, but serves to list measures of the kind that should be converted into tariffs.[708]

In Colombia's view, a system like the Peruvian one may be transparent and predictable, even though it exhibits a factor of variation modulated by a methodology.[709] Colombia added that the Panel should not confine itself to the definition of predictability and transparency proposed in *Chile – Price Band System*, since that definition relates to a specific case and not a definition authorized by Members.[710] According to Colombia, the fact that a measure includes a formula with fixed terms and coefficients would make it possible to predict the final result, while the existence of clear and public rules and a stable and equally public methodology for defining the tariff made it possible to characterize the mechanism as transparent.[711]

Colombia considered that the interpretation of Article 4.2 of the AoA in *Chile – Price Band System* does not show that measures that isolate domestic markets are WTO-inconsistent.[712] Colombia maintained that, in order for a measure to be WTO-inconsistent, it is necessary that the Member

---

704 Brazil's third-party oral statement para 4.
705 Brazil's third-party oral statement para 5.
706 Brazil's response to Panel question No. 5.
707 Colombia's third-party written submission para 12 citing Appellate Body Report *Chile - Price Band System* para 233.
708 Colombia's third-party written submission para 13-14.
709 See Colombia's third-party written submission para 14.
710 Colombia's third-party written submission para 12 citing Appellate Body Report, *Chile - Price Band System* para. 233.
711 Colombia's third-party written submission para 17-23 Colombia's third-party statement, para. 11.
712 Colombia's third-party written submission para 24 citing Appellate Body Report *Chile - Price Band System*.

alleging the violation demonstrate that measures isolating domestic markets have similar or identical effects to measures that are prohibited under the provisions of the agreements. Colombia concluded that, in such cases, it is not necessary to examine whether the measure has the effect of isolating the Peruvian market from the international market.[713]

The United States tended that Peru's PRS appeared to be a variable import levy, a minimum import price, or at least a measure similar to both of these.[714] The US observed that Peru's measure had the following undisputed features; it was based on a mathematical formula such that when the reference price falls below the lower threshold, an additional duty was applied based on the difference; it employed a reference price that is updated every two weeks, based on international prices, and the lower threshold is obtained from average prices over the preceding five years; it yields duties whose amounts change every two weeks; and the further the reference price is below the lower threshold, the higher the resulting duty.[715]

The US argued that in light of those features, the PRS appeared to be inherently variable and less transparent and predictable than ordinary customs duties, apart from which its design and structure impeded the transmission of international prices to the domestic market.[716] In the United States' view, the lack of transparency and predictability are not independent characteristics that a measure must possess in order to be considered a variable import levy, since it is the presence of a formula that makes a measure inherently variable, and this feature renders the levy less transparent and predictable than ordinary customs duties.[717]

The US also pointed out that the PRS appeared to be similar to a minimum import price.[718] It considered that the existence of a target price was not required to establish that a measure is similar to minimum import prices.[719] The nature of the measure, including its tendency to distort the transmission of declines in world prices, suggested that Peru's measure was similar to minimum import prices.[720] In the US' view, Article 4.2 of the AoA did not require a finding as to whether

---

[713] Colombia's response to Panel question No 5 para 5-9.
[714] United States' third-party written submission para. 11.
[715] United States' third-party written submission para. 12.
[716] United States' third-party written submission paras. 13-16; response to Panel question No. 6, paras 21-23.
[717] United States' third-party written submission paras. 10-12.
[718] United States' third-party written submission paras. 17-19
[719] United States' third-party written submission paras. 17-18
[720] United States' third-party written submission paras. 17-19.

the measure isolates the domestic market from international prices.[721] According to the US, even if the measure never causes effects, it may be prohibited, for which reason the evidence concerning the effects will be of a secondary nature.[722]

The United States affirmed that it is not necessary to define ordinary customs duties inasmuch as, if the measure is one of those included in footnote 1 of the AoA, ordinary customs duties are defined by exclusion.[723] The US considered that the characteristics of ordinary customs duties proposed by Peru do not constitute a sound argument, since ordinary customs duties and variable import levies share certain attributes.[724] The US also pointed out that a Member's characterization of its own measure is not conclusive, apart from which the evidence presented by Peru does not demonstrate that the measure constitutes ordinary customs duties.[725] Finally, the US pointed out that Peru's schedule of concessions did not incorporate the duties resulting from the PRS and did not include the system established in 2001; even if it did, this would not remedy the violation of Article 4.2 of the AoA, since the obligations contained in that provision would prevail over the content of the schedule of concessions.[726]

The European Union (EU) was of the view that the Panel's task was to characterize the measure at issue within the framework of the categories contained in footnote 1 of the AoA, particularly with regard to variable import levies.[727] The EU referred to the two features of variable import levies identified by the AB in *Chile – Price Band System* taking into account their continuous and automatic variation and their lack of transparency and predictability.[728] The EU considered that

[721] United States' third-party written submission's reference to Article 4.2 of the AoA which stipulates that Members shall not maintain, resort to, or revert to any measures of the kind which have been required to be converted into ordinary customs duties, except as otherwise provided for in Article 5 and Annex 5. It should be noted that Article 4.2 of the AoA should be read together with footnote 1 of the AoA. According to the footnote, These measures include quantitative import restrictions, variable import levies, minimum import prices, discretionary import licensing, non-tariff measures maintained through state-trading enterprises, voluntary export restraints, and similar border measures other than ordinary customs duties, whether or not the measures are maintained under country-specific derogations from the provisions of GATT 1947, but not measures maintained under balance-of-payments provisions or under other general, non-agriculture-specific provisions of GATT 1994 or of the other Multilateral Trade Agreements in Annex 1A to the WTO Agreement.

[722] United States' response to Panel question No. 5, paras. 17-20

[723] United States' third-party written submission paras. 24-26

[724] *Ibid.*

[725] United States' third-party written submission para 27-28.

[726] United States' third-party written submission paras. 29-31 (citing Appellate Body Report, *EC - Export Subsidies of Sugar*, paras. 221-222).

[727] European Union's third-party written submission para. 42.

[728] European Union's third-party written submission paras. 43-47.

particular attention should be paid to the lack of transparency and predictability, because this is what affects traders and governments.[729] In the EU's view, if all the elements of the system were published and all the values used were publicly available, the system would be transparent and predictable, because the economic operators would be in a position to predict the nature of a change in the amount of the duties.[730]

The EU asserted that, if a Member were to change its duties every day by legislative intervention, following international prices, and not through the use of a formula, the measure would continue to lack transparency and predictability.[731] The EU noted that no decisive weight can be given to the distortion in the transmission of declines in world prices, since this is a relative analysis.[732] The EU considered that a key characteristic of variable import levies, and of all the measures included in footnote 1 of the AoA, is the fact that they prevent price competition for all imports or a part thereof, thus distinguishing them from ordinary customs duties which permit price competition on all imports.[733]

4 3 4 Assessment by the Panel: Article 4.2 of the AoA

Article 4.2 of the AoA[734] has been examined by WTO panels and by the AB in only two earlier disputes: *Chile – Price Band System* and *Turkey – Rice* and in *Chile – Price Band System.* In both the original and in the compliance proceedings, the Panels and the AB illuminated the scope of the text of Article 4.2 of the AoA and interpreted the terms "variable import levies", "minimum import prices" and "similar border measures". In *Turkey – Rice*, the Panel examined as the principal claim the consistency of the challenged measure, which was in the nature of a quantitative restriction, with Article 4.2.[735]

[729] European Union's third-party written submission paras. 43-47.
[730] European Union's third-party written submission, para. 47.
[731] European Union's third-party written submission, para. 48.
[732] European Union's third-party written submission, para. 49.
[733] European Union's third-party written submission, para. 50.
[734] Article 4.2 of the Agreement on Agriculture, together with the footnote thereto, reads as follows: Members shall not maintain, resort to, or revert to any measures of the kind which have been required to be converted into ordinary customs duties, except as otherwise provided for in Article 5 and Annex 5. The footnote states that, These measures include quantitative import restrictions, variable import levies, minimum import prices, discretionary import licensing, non-tariff measures maintained through state-trading enterprises, voluntary export restraints, and similar border measures other than ordinary customs duties, whether or not the measures are maintained under country-specific derogations from the provisions of GATT 1947, but not measures maintained under balance-of-payments provisions or under other general, non-agriculture-specific provisions of GATT 1994 or of the other Multilateral Trade Agreements in Annex 1A to the WTO Agreement.
[735] Panel Report, *EC - Seal Products* para 7.665. This panel finding was not appealed.

In two other disputes, *India – Quantitative Restrictions* and *Korea – Various Measures on Beef*, the Panels found that the challenged measure was inconsistent with Article 4.2 of the AoA, after having found an inconsistency with Article XI: 1 of the GATT 1994. In these disputes, the Panels did not interpret the content of Article 4.2, considering that a quantitative restriction on agricultural products that was inconsistent with Article XI: 1 of the GATT 1994 was necessarily also inconsistent with Article 4.2 of the AoA.[736] Along the same lines, in *EC – Seal Products*, the Panel rejected a claim in respect of Article 4.2, having already rejected a claim relating to Article XI: 1 of the GATT 1994.[737]

The interpretation of the scope of the obligation in Article 4.2 of the AoA and the meaning of the terms "variable import levies", "minimum import prices" and "similar border measures", contained in the analyses carried out by the Panels and the AB in *Chile – Price Band System* were more relevant to this dispute than those contained in the analyses of other disputes relating to Article 4.2.[738] For this reason, the Panel took those reports into account in conducting its own analysis.[739] According to the AB in the *Chile – Price Band System*, Article 4 of the AoA is the legal vehicle for requiring the conversion into ordinary customs duties of certain market access barriers affecting imports of agricultural products.[740]

With regard to the scope of Article 4.2 of the AoA, in *Chile – Price Band System*, the AB explained that the obligation not to maintain, resort to, or revert to any measures of the kind which have been required to be converted into ordinary customs duties applies from the date of the entry into force of the WTO Agreement, regardless of whether or not a Member converted any such measures before the conclusion of the Uruguay Round. The AB added that the fact that no Member singled

---

736 Panel Reports, *India - Quantitative Restrictions*, paras. 5.241-5.242; *Korea - Various Measures on Beef* para 762. These panel findings were not appealed.

737 Panel Report, *EC - Seal Products*, para. 7.665. This panel finding was not appealed.

738 In the original *Chile – Price Band System* proceedings, the Appellate Body referred to the overall objectives set out in the preamble to the Agreement on Agriculture: The preamble to the Agreement on Agriculture states that an objective of that Agreement is "to establish a fair and market-oriented agricultural trading system", and to initiate a reform process "through the negotiation of commitments on support and protection and through the establishment of strengthened and more operationally effective GATT rules and disciplines". The preamble further states that, to achieve this objective, it is necessary to provide for reductions in protection, "resulting in correcting and preventing restrictions and distortions in world agricultural markets", through achieving "specific binding commitments," *inter alia,* in the area of market access.

739 *Ibid.*

740 Appellate Body Report, *Chile - Price Band System* para 200.

out any measure of any other Member does not mean that such a measure subsequently enjoys immunity.[741]

The Panel in *Peru* also stated that footnote 1 to the AoA "lists six categories of border measures and a residual category of such measures that are included in 'measures of the kind which have been required to be converted into ordinary customs duties' within the meaning of Article 4.2."[742] The AB in *Chile - Price Band System* clarified that the list in the footnote is illustrative, and includes *inter alia* variable import levies, minimum import prices and similar border measures other than ordinary customs duties.[743] In the original proceedings, it identified the features shared by all the border measures listed in footnote 1.[744]

The Panel in *Peru* clarified that, if the measure at issue in that dispute fell within any one of the categories of measures listed in footnote 1, it would be among the "measures of the kind which have been required to be converted into ordinary customs duties", and thus could not be maintained, resorted to, or reverted to, as of the date of entry into force of the WTO Agreement.[745] The AB in *Chile - Price Band System* also explained that the fact that any variable import levies or minimum import prices result in the payment of duties does not mean that they should not have been converted into ordinary customs duties.[746] In addition, the AB referred to Article 5 of the AoA, which provides for a market access exemption in the form of a special safeguard.[747] It pointed out that Article 4.2 should not be interpreted in a way that permits Members to maintain measures that operate in a way similar to a special safeguard inasmuch as no proper meaning and effect could be given to the conditions for establishing the special safeguard.[748]

---

[741] *Ibid* para 212.
[742] *Ibid.* para. 219.
[743] *Ibid.* para. 219.
[744] According to the AB, "before looking at these categories of measures, we note that all of the border measures listed in footnote 1 have in common the object and effect of restricting the volumes, and distorting the prices, of imports of agricultural products in ways different from the ways that ordinary customs duties do. Moreover, all of these measures have in common also that they disconnect domestic prices from international price developments, and thus impede the transmission of world market prices to the domestic market."
[745] *Ibid.* para 221.
[746] *Ibid.* para 216.
[747] *Ibid.* See Article 5 of the AoA.
[748] *Ibid.* para 217.

4 3 5 The Panel's Conclusions and Recommendations

The Panel held that there was no evidence that Guatemala brought these proceedings in a manner contrary to good faith hence there was therefore no reason for the Panel to refrain from assessing the claims put forward by Guatemala.[749] It found that the duties resulting from the PRS constituted variable import levies or, at the least, shared sufficient characteristics with variable import levies to be considered a border measure similar to a variable import levy, within the meaning of footnote 1 to the AoA.[750] It further held that the duties resulting from the PRS do not constitute minimum import prices and do not share sufficient characteristics with minimum import prices to be considered a border measure similar to a minimum import price, within the meaning of footnote 1 to the AoA.[751] It was held that, by maintaining measures which constituted a variable import levy or, at the least, border measures similar to a variable import levy, and measures which were required to be converted into ordinary customs duties, Peru was acting inconsistently with its obligations under Article 4.2 of the AoA.[752]

The Panel also noted that the additional duties resulting from the PRS constituted "other duties or charges ... imposed on or in connection with the importation", within the meaning of the second sentence of Article II: 1(b) of the GATT 1994.[753] In applying measures which constitute "other duties or charges", without having recorded them in its Schedule of Concessions, Peru's actions were inconsistent with its obligations under the second sentence of Article II: 1(b) of the GATT

[749] See the Panel Report's conclusion.

[750] See the conclusion drawn by the panel on Article 4.2 of the AoA on page 92 para 4 of the Panel Report WT/DS457/R.

[751] See page 92 of the Panel Report.

[752] The Panel used in *Chile – Price Band System* in interpreting ordinary customs duties. The *Panel in Chile – Price Band System* stated that the term "ordinary customs duties" must have the same meaning in Article 4.2 of the AoA and the second sentence of Article II: 1(b) of the GATT 1994. In examining whether Chile's price band system constituted an ordinary customs duty, the Appellate Body in *Chile – Price Band System* made the following clarification with regard to the category of "other duties or charges. "We further note, in examining Article 4.2 of the AoA, that the second sentence of Article II: 1(b) of the GATT 1994, does not specify what form "other duties or charges" must take to qualify as such within the meaning of that sentence. The Panel's own approach of reviewing Members' Schedules reveals that many, if not most, "other duties or charges" are expressed in ad valorem and/or specific terms, which does not, of course, make them "ordinary customs duties" under the first sentence of Article II: 1(b)".

[753] Article 2.1(b) of the GATT deals with the Schedule of Concessions. It states that "The products described in Part I of the Schedule relating to any contracting party, which are the products of territories of other contracting parties, shall, on their importation into the territory to which the Schedule relates, and subject to the terms, conditions or qualifications set forth in that Schedule, be exempt from ordinary customs duties in excess of those set forth and provided therein. Such products shall also be exempt from all other duties or charges of any kind imposed on or in connection with the importation in excess of those imposed on the date of this Agreement or those directly and mandatorily required to be imposed thereafter by legislation in force in the importing territory on that date".

1994.[754] It was ruled that, inasmuch as the Free Trade Agreement (FTA) signed by Peru and Guatemala in December 2011 had not entered into force, it was not necessary for the Panel to rule on whether the parties could, by means of the FTA, modify as between themselves their rights and obligations under the covered agreements.[755]

In the light of the previous conclusions, the Panel did not consider it necessary to rule on Guatemala's claims that Peru's actions were inconsistent with its obligations under Article X:1 of the GATT 1994 because it failed to publish certain elements of the measure which Guatemala considered essential and that Peru's actions were inconsistent with its obligations under Article X:3(a) of the GATT 1994 because it administered the measure in question in a manner that is not reasonable, given that it failed to observe the requirements of its own legislation.[756]

Also the Panel did not consider it relevant to address Guatemala's claim that Peru acted inconsistently with its obligations under Articles 1, 2, 3, 5, 6 and 7 of the Customs Valuation Agreement (CVA) inasmuch as this claim was made by Guatemala as an alternative, and only in case the Panel were to find that the duties resulting from the PRS are ordinary customs duties.[757] Pursuant to Article 3.8 of the DSU, in cases where there is an infringement of obligations assumed under a covered agreement, the action is considered *prima facie* to constitute a case of nullification or impairment of benefits accruing under the Agreement. The Panel therefore concluded that, to the extent that Peru has acted inconsistently with the provisions of the AoA and the GATT 1994, it has nullified or impaired benefits accruing to Guatemala under those agreements.

Guatemala had requested the Panel, in the exercise of its discretionary powers afforded by the second sentence of Article 19.1 of the DSU, to suggest that Peru "completely dismantle the

[754] See the Panel's conclusion on page 92 of the Panel Report WT/DS457/R.
[755] See the Panel's conclusion on page 126 of the Panel Report WT/DS457/R.
[756] Article 10.1 of the GATT stipulates that, "laws, regulations, judicial decisions and administrative rulings of general application, made effective by any contracting party, pertaining to the classification or the valuation of products for customs purposes, or to rates of duty, taxes or other charges, or to requirements, restrictions or prohibitions on imports or exports or on the transfer of payments therefor, or affecting their sale, distribution, transportation, insurance, warehousing inspection, exhibition, processing, mixing or other use, shall be published promptly in such a manner as to enable governments and traders to become acquainted with them. Agreements affecting international trade policy which are in force between the government and a governmental agency of any contracting party and the government or governmental agency of any other contracting party shall also be published. The provisions of this paragraph shall not require any contracting party to disclose confidential information which would impede law enforcement or otherwise be contrary to the public interest or would prejudice the legitimate commercial interests of particular enterprises, public or private".
[757] See the Panel's conclusion in the Panel Report WT/DS457/R.

measure in question".[758] In Guatemala's view, this would imply the elimination of the additional variable duty and the underlying calculation mechanism, i.e. the PRS.[759] According to Guatemala, this would be the only way of enabling "Peru properly to bring its measure into conformity with WTO rules in view of the gravity, nature and manifest character of the legal violations in the measure in question".[760] The AB in *US - Oil Country Tubular Goods Sunset Review* has indicated that the power vested in panels and the AB, under Article 19.1 of the DSU, to suggest to Members ways in which they could implement recommendations and rulings is of a discretionary nature.[761] According to the provisions of Article 21.3 of the DSU, it is normally the Member to which the recommendations are addressed which has to decide on how to implement them.[762] Exceptionally, panels had accepted a request by the complaining party to suggest to the respondent Member the way in which it could comply with panel recommendations.[763]

In its request for the establishment of a panel, Guatemala had identified the measure at issue as "the additional duty imposed by Peru on imports of certain agricultural products".[764] Guatemala added that the additional duty is determined using the PRS.[765] Bearing in mind that Guatemala challenged the duties resulting from the PRS and not the system as such, the Panel did not consider

---

[758] Guatemala's first written submission, para 5.1.

[759] Guatemala's first written submission para. 5.2. See also second written submission, para. 10.2.

[760] *Ibid.*

[761] Appellate Body Reports, *US - Zeroing* (EC) (Article 21.5 - EC), para. 466; *US - Oil Country Tubular Goods Sunset Review* (Article 21.5 - Argentina), para. 182.

[762] Appellate Body Report, *US Oil Country Tubular Goods Sunset Review* (Article 21.5 - Argentina), paras. 173 and 184; Panel Report, *EC - Fasteners* (China), para. 8.8 (citing Panel Report, *US - Hot-Rolled Steel*, para. 8.13); Panel Report, *US - Steel Plate,* para. 8.8; Panel Report, EC and certain member States - *Large Civil Aircraft,* para. 8.8; Panel Report, *EU - Footwear* (China), para. 8.12.

[763] In the following cases, the panels accepted the complaining party's request to suggest a way of implementing its recommendations: *US - Underwear*, para. 8.3 (with regard to a specific transitional safeguard measure under Article 6 of the Agreement on Textiles and Clothing); *EC - Bananas III* (Article 21.5 - Ecuador), paras. 6.155-6.159 (with regard to the European Communities' banana import regime); *Guatemala - Cement* I, para. 8.6 (with regard to an anti-dumping measure); *Guatemala - Cement II*, paras. 9.6-9.7 (with regard to an anti-dumping measure); *US - Cotton Yarn*, para. 8.5 (with regard to a specific transitional safeguard measure under the Agreement on Textiles and Clothing); *US – Offset Act* (Byrd Amendment), para. 8.6 (with regard to a law on anti-dumping and countervailing duties); *Argentina - Poultry Anti-Dumping Duties*, para. 8.7 (with regard to an anti-dumping measure); and *Mexico - Steel Pipes and Tubes,* paras. 8.12-8.13 (with regard to an anti-dumping measure). In the following reports, the panels made suggestions for taking into consideration the interests of developing country Members involved in the dispute: *India - Quantitative Restrictions*, paras. 7.5-7.6; *EC - Export Subsidies on Sugar* (Australia) / *EC - Export Subsidies on Sugar* (Brazil) / *EC - Export Subsidies on Sugar* (Thailand), para. 8.7. Lastly, in the Reports *on EC - Trademarks and Geographical Indications* (US) / EC - Trademarks and Geographical Indications (Australia), para. 8.5, the Panel made a suggestion on the way in which the European Communities might implement its recommendations. In many other disputes, however, the panels refrained from making suggestions on how to implement their recommendations.

[764] See request for the establishment of a panel by Guatemala, document WT/DS457/2 (of 14 June 2013).

[765] *Ibid.*

it appropriate to suggest that the proper way of implementing its recommendation was through the elimination of the underlying mechanism for calculating the additional duties.[766] As part of the measures adopted with a view to complying with the Panel's rulings and recommendations, Peru could decide to dismantle the PRS completely.[767] According to the Panel, it was, however, in appropriate for it to make a suggestion to that effect, which would go beyond the measure as defined by Guatemala.[768] The Panel therefore rejected Guatemala's request to suggest to Peru that the way in which its recommendation should be implemented is through the elimination of the PRS.[769] Pursuant to Article 19.1 of the DSU, and having found that Peru had acted inconsistently with provisions of the AoA and the GATT 1994, the Panel recommended that Peru bring the challenged measure – namely, the duties resulting from the PRS – into conformity with its obligations under those agreements.[770]

4 4 EUROPEAN COMMUNITIES – EXPORT SUBSIDIES ON SUGAR

The impact of the Canadian dairy case on the approach taken by exporters toward agricultural policies in other countries can be seen in the challenge brought by Brazil, Australia and Thailand against the EC sugar subsidies.[771] Complaints about EC sugar policy were not new.[772] Australia had challenged the EC sugar regime in 1979 in the GATT and Brazil followed in 1980, but these were complicated by the fact that there was an International Sugar Agreement[773] that restricted exports.[774] Under such circumstances the panels were unable to determine the extent of injury that the complainants had suffered and the policies continued unchecked.[775] The US also challenged

[766] See the Panel's conclusion on 126 of the Panel Report WT/DS457/R

[767] *Ibid.*

[768] See the Panel's conclusion on 127 para 3 of the Panel Report WT/DS457/R.

[769] *Ibid.*

[770] See the Panel's conclusion on 127 para 4 of the Panel Report WT/DS457/R.

[771] The Australian and Brazilian challenges were initiated in September 2002 and Thailand joined the complaint in March 2003. The dispute numbers are DS265, DS266 and DS283, respectively. The panel report was presented on October 15, 2004 and was appealed. The Appellate Body gave their opinion on April 28, 2005 and the DSB accepted the report as modified.

[772] World Trade Organization, 2005. *European Communities – Export Subsidies on Sugar, Report of the Appellate* Body, WT/DS265/AB/R, WT/DS266/AD/R, & WT/DS283/AB/R.

[773] The EC was however not a signatory to the agreement.

[774] See Panel Report in *European Communities – Export Subsidies on Sugar*.

[775] Josling "*Production and Export Subsidies in Agriculture: Lessons from GATT and WTO Disputes Involving the US and the EC*," (2003).

the CAP sugar policy in the GATT in 1982, but no panel was established.[776] The EC indicated its willingness to join the ISA, and proceeded in turn to challenge the US sugar regime.[777]

One of the contentions of these sugar exporters in the recent WTO case was that the EC grants *de facto* export subsidies by means of the high price paid for sugar used on the domestic market.[778] The domestic market price is maintained for sugar produced under two quotas (the "A" and "B" quotas): production over those quotas (usually called "C" sugar) cannot be sold on the domestic market and receives no direct subsidy.[779] The issue was whether the "C" sugar benefited indirectly as farmers could cover their fixed costs from returns from the high-price quotas.[780] The analogy with the exported milk products from Canada is close if not exact.[781] The complainants maintained that if such subsides were included, the EC would be in breach of its export subsidy commitments under the AoA.[782]

A second contention was that the EC exports the equivalent of the 1.4 million tons of sugar that is imported under preferential agreements enshrined in the Cotonou Agreement with former colonies.[783] This sugar is sold to the EC at the internal price but re-exported at the world price.[784] This was not notified as part of the EC's schedule of exports that benefit from subsidies and it was explicitly excluded in a footnote.[785] The panel found, and the AB agreed, that the EC was in breech in both respects.[786] The exports of C sugar did benefit from the high price of A and B quotas

---

776 Josling 2003.
777 *Ibid.*
778 World Trade Organization, 2005. *European Communities – Export Subsidies on Sugar*, Report of the Appellate Body, WT/DS265/AB/R, WT/DS266/AD/R, & WT/DS283/AB/R.
779 See the World Trade Organization, *European Communities – Export Subsidies on Sugar*, Report of the Appellate Body, WT/DS265/AB/R, WT/DS266/AD/R, & WT/DS283/AB/R. Also see the submissions made by Brazil in the case.
780 World Trade Organization, 2004. *European Communities – Export Subsidies on Sugar, Reports of the Panels*, WT/DS265/R, WT/DS266/R, & WT/DS283/R
781 Josling, "Agricultural Trade Disputes in the WTO" 2007.
782 See Brazil Australia and Thailand written submissions.
783 The objectives of the agreement concluded the agreement in order to promote and expedite the economic, cultural and social development of the ACP States, with the view of contributing to peace and security and promoting a stable and democratic political environment. The partnership is centred on the objective of reducing and eventually eradicating poverty consistent with the objective of sustainable development and the gradual integration of the ACP countries into the world economy. For more information see Article 1 of The Cotonou Agreement on www.europarl.europa.eu .
784 European Communities – *Export Subsidies on Sugar, Reports of the Panels*.
785 See the EC schedule of Tariffs created in terms of the Agreement on Agriculture.
786 World Trade Organization, 2004. *European Communities – Export Subsidies on Sugar, Reports of the Panels*, WT/DS265/R.

awarded to the same farms.[787] As the C sugar was solely destined for exports, the effect was to cross-subsidize.[788] By implication, if C sugar were sold on the internal market to any extent, the argument would have required a further stage of showing that the exports were harming other exporters.[789] But as the implicit financial benefits to producers of C sugar were not notified as export subsidies they were *de facto* prohibited regardless of their market impact.[790]

Similarly, the panel found that the re-export of the ACP and Indian sugar was prohibited as it did not appear in the EC schedule.[791] Thus the *EC-sugar* case differs from that of *US cotton* in that is centres primarily on the notification of export subsidies.[792] The fact that these notifications were not challenged at the time raises questions about how the activities of the Agriculture Committee might be linked more usefully to the issue of the nature of these policies.[793] The sugar case is complicated by an additional element. If the EC cannot either re-export the ACP imports or sell C sugar on the world market, then the domestic price has to be reduced and/or the quotas have to be reduced.[794] The EC Commission realized this link with reform of the EC sugar regime, and used the argument effectively to persuade member states of the need for policy change.[795] The political decision was made by the EC's Council of Ministers on November 22, 2005, to undertake a reform that cut the sugar price support level by 36 percent and compensated farmers with "decoupled" payments.[796]

Although the support price will stay significantly above the world price level, the incentive to produce for export over and above the quota volume will be significantly reduced.[797] If the output falls as expected, the EC will come into compliance with the Panel ruling: cross subsidized

[787] See *European Communities – Export Subsidies on Sugar* Reports of the Panels Investigations of subsidies in non-agricultural markets often explore the possibility of cross-subsidization within firms. The economics of cross-subsidization is not as well accepted as the accounting conventions.
[788] Josling 2007.
[789] *Ibid.*
[790] *Ibid.*
[791] World Trade Organization, 2004. *European Communities – Export Subsidies on Sugar, Reports of the Panels* WT/DS265/R, WT/DS266/R, & WT/DS283/R.
[792] See Josling, Agricultural Trade Disputes in the WTO 2007 26 para 4.
[793] Josling 2006.
[794] See the World Trade Organization, 2005. *European Communities – Export Subsidies on Sugar Report of the Appellate Body* WT/DS265/AB/R, WT/DS266/AD/R, & WT/DS283/AB/R.
[795] *Ibid.*
[796] See the agreement on https//www.consillium.europa.eu/uedocs/cms-data/docs/87093.pdf. (Accessed on 21/04/15).
[797] This will be in line with the AoA export subsidy commitments. The term export subsidies is defined under Article 1 (e) of the AoA to refer to subsidies contingent upon export performance and includes the export subsidies listed under Article 9 of the agreement.

production will not find its way into export markets, and the ACP sugar will be absorbed largely in the domestic market.[798] Suppliers of raw sugar to the EC have also been promised compensation.[799] Under the Cotonou Agreement these suppliers benefit from guaranteed access at internal prices, and so will lose from the reduction in price levels.[800] Although this preferential access is already under threat from the opening up of tariff and quota free access to the least developed countries under the Everything but Arms Agreement of the EC, it remains of economic and political importance to a number of countries.[801] On the one hand, they will also benefit from reductions in the sales of "C" sugar on world markets.[802] Thus the link with the trade negotiations is more complex than just the connection with the reform of the EC sugar regime.[803]

4 5 UNITED STATES – SUBSIDIES ON UPLAND COTTON

The *Brazil–United States cotton* dispute was one of the biggest and popular WTO case because it involved a developing country challenging a developed country. It is a masterpiece exposition of the issue of unfair subsidies on cotton. In 2002, Brazil a major cotton export competitor expressed its growing concerns about US cotton subsidies by initiating a WTO dispute settlement case against certain features of the US cotton program.[804] On March 18, 2003, the third party panel was established to participate in the proceedings which included Argentina, Canada, China, Chinese Taipei, the European Communities, India, Pakistan, and Venezuela. Focusing on six specific claims relating to US payment programmes, Brazil argued that the US had failed to abide by its commitments in the Agreement on Agriculture (AoA) and the SCM.

[798] If it is absorbed within the EU market it will not be prejudicial to other eternal markets. However the prices of domestic sugar should not be significantly different from imported sugar. If there is a difference, this could lead to a violation of the domestic support commitment. Under the AoA, all Green Box support measures must have no, or at most minimal, trade-distorting effects, nor positive effects on production. For a detailed explanation on this point see Blandford "Should the Green Box be Modified?" 2007. http://www.agritrade.org/Publications/DiscussionPapers/Green_Box.pdf (Accessed on 21/04/15).

[799] See Josling 2006.

[800] *Ibid.*

[801] Barton *The Evolution of the Trade Regime: Politics, Law and Economics of the GATT and WTO* (2006).

[802] *Ibid.*

[803] *Ibid.*

[804] Brazil contended that these measures were inconsistent with the obligations of the United States under the following provisions: Articles 5(c), 6.3(b), (c) and (d), 3.1(a) (including item (j) of the Illustrative List of Export Subsidies in Annex I), 3.1(b), and 3.2 of the SCM Agreement; Articles 3.3, 7.1, 8, 9.1 and 10.1 of the Agreement on Agriculture; and Article III:4 of GATT 1994. Brazil was of the view that the US statutes, regulations, and administrative procedures listed above were inconsistent with these provisions as such and as applied.

The *US Cotton Case* is important in that it exposes the manipulation of the AoA by developed countries.[805] It is very essential in that, it questions the distinction between amber and green boxes.[806] The rulings of the panel can best summarized by considering the nine elements of the US programs that were the subject of the challenge by Brazil.[807] Five of these elements relate to the major instruments of agricultural policy adopted for the "program crops" in the Farm Bills that cover the period 1999-2003.[808] Two more are specific to cotton Step 2 subsidies and cottonseed payments, and the other two are of more general application crop insurance and export credit guarantees.[809] The panel ruled basically on two issues: whether these subsidies were allowed or prohibited and whether they caused "serious prejudice" even if allowed to Brazil.[810]

The two subsidies that were not price-related and which had therefore been notified by the US as being in the green box were found not to be the cause of "price suppression" in world markets.[811] They were, however, found to contain provisions that made them ineligible for the green box: specifically the restrictions on the alternative crops that farmers could grow on cotton land.[812] These, the panel decided, could keep more acres in that crop than would totally "decoupled" payments have done.[813] The three subsidies that were price-related were found to have caused price suppression through their impact on keeping cotton production high in the US at a time of low world prices.[814]

---

805 Devereaux "Case Studies in US Trade Negotiation, Resolving Disputes" 2006 Vol 2 *Institute for International Economics Washington and D.C.*

806 Josling "Agricultural Trade Disputes in the WTO" 2006. Brazil requested consultations with the United States on September 27, 2002. After three abortive discussions, a panel was established on May 19, 2003 and issued a report on June 18, 2004. This ruling was appealed by the United States, and the Appellate Body issued its report on March 3, 2005. The report as amended was adopted on March 21, 2005.

807 See World Trade Organization 2005. *United States—Subsidies on Upland Cotton* Reports of the Panel.

808 These elements are direct payments, production flexibility contract payments, market loss assistance payments, counter-cyclical payments and marketing loan payments. The two Farm Bills in question are the 1996 Fair Act and 2002 FSRI Act. Production flexibility contract payments were authorized under the Fair Act, and marketing loss assistance payments were added as emergency measures in 1998-2001. The FSRI Act replaced these with direct payments and counter-cyclical payments. Marketing loans for cotton have been in place since 1986 and Step 2 subsidies since 1990. The cottonseed payments are emergency payments authorized by the ARP Act in 2000. Crop insurance is authorized by separate legislation, the Federal Crop Insurance Act.

809 See World Trade Organization 2005 *United States—Subsidies on Upland Cotton* Reports of the Panel.

810 *Ibid.*

811 See World Trade Organization 2005 *United States—Subsidies on Upland Cotton* Reports of the Appellate Body WT/DS265/AB/R, WT/DS266/AB/R, & WT/DS267/AB/R. World.

812 See World Trade Organization 2005 *United States—Subsidies on Upland Cotton* Reports of the Panel.

813 *Ibid.*

814 The panel did not accept the US argument that the low world prices were from other causes and that the high US exports were an exception rather than the rule.

The panel ruled that the Step 2 subsidies paid to domestic users were prohibited under the Subsidies and Countervailing Measures Agreement (SCM) and the Step 2 subsidies available to export users were prohibited because they were not included in the US schedule of subsidies.[815] Moreover, the Step 2 subsidies also caused significant price suppression in world markets.[816] Cottonseed subsidies and crop insurance payments were deemed not to have caused price suppression, and were not prohibited subsidies.[817] The final aspect of the US programs on which the panel ruled was the set of export credit guarantees that are available to US firms when they sell into overseas markets where credit risks are a factor.[818] The finding in this case was that the export credit guarantees given to cotton producers constituted an export subsidy, and since no such subsidy had been included in the US schedule it was in effect prohibited.[819]

The panel ruling required the US to end the prohibited subsidies within six months of the adoption of the report or by July 1, 2005 at the latest.[820] This ruling applied to the Step 2 payments, to both domestic and export users, and to the export credit guarantees for cotton.[821] The US decided that it could make these changes in legislation without having to await the next Farm Bill at that time expected in 2007.[822] The Administration urged the US Congress to scrap the Step 2 payments, and these will cease at the end of the crop year, in August 2006.[823] The USDA has also proposed changes to the export credit arrangements by eliminating the one percent cap on the fees that are charged for borrowing through the GSM-102 program, and by terminating the GSM-103 program that provides for longer repayment periods.[824] More problematic for the US is how to adjust the programs that the panel found to cause significant price suppression.[825] Withdrawing the marketing

[815] The ruling also declared that the export credit guarantees for rice exceeded its allowed export subsidy limit, but did not find fault with other aspects of the program.

[816] See Panel ruling in World Trade Organization 2005 *United States—Subsidies on Upland Cotton* Reports of the Panel.

[817] *Ibid.*

[818] *Ibid.*

[819] Josling "Unraveling the Cotton Case" 2005.

[820] See Panel ruling in World Trade Organization 2005 *United States—Subsidies on Upland Cotton* Reports of the Panel.

[821] Josling 2005.

[822] The Farm Bill was eventually passed in early 2008.

[823] Josling "Agricultural Trade Disputes in the WTO" 2007.

[824] Josling "Agricultural Trade Disputes in the WTO" 2007.

[825] Josling "Unravelling the Cotton Case" 2005.

loan and counter-cyclical payments would require major changes in the US legislation and could not easily be done outside the context of the then proposed Farm Bill.[826]

Taking other steps to remove the adverse impacts on Brazil might seem easier to achieve, but any attempt to restrict US cotton exports could prove difficult.[827] Compensation to Brazil for lost exports would also seem politically implausible, and a deal to boost Brazilian exports of other commodities would be similarly unpopular.[828] So the prospect is for no change in these aspects of US policy at least until the 2007 Farm Bill, at which time the policies may in any case need to be modified as a result of the Doha Round.[829]

The signal importance of the cotton case for WTO jurisprudence is that it clarifies several aspects of the application of WTO rules to agricultural subsidies.[830] The Peace Clause effectively dissuaded members from challenging agricultural subsidies under the SCM before 2004.[831] Though the panel ruled that the Peace Clause did not provide shelter for the US subsidies in question, the case is best considered as the first "post-Peace Clause" challenge to farm subsidies.[832] The consistency of agricultural subsidies with the provisions of the SCM is a fertile ground for speculation.[833] But the panel indicates that, at least in this case, these restrictions are both onerous and comprehensive.[834] Though the ruling on serious prejudice was based on the impact of US subsidies on world cotton prices, the same provision of the SCM also includes the effect of

[826] *Ibid.*
[827] *Ibid.*
[828] *Ibid.*
[829] An interesting side issue raised by the panel report is the conclusion that the direct payments and production flexibility contract payments are not eligible for the green box. This would seem to indicate that countries might ask the US to resubmit notifications of domestic support for the years in question. This would almost certainly put the US in excess of its amber box limits, and raise serious problems with trading partners. If this were to be resolved by litigation (an easier task since no serious prejudice issues would be relevant) then the US would have to make major changes to its farm policy. But again, the chances are that these issues will be resolved in the context of the Doha Round.
[830] Josling 2007. Also see Barton *The Evolution of the Trade Regime: Politics, Law and Economics of the GATT and WTO* (2006).
[831] Article 13 of the AoA provided that during the implementation period, notwithstanding the provisions of GATT 1994 and the Agreement on Subsidies and Countervailing Measures (referred to in this Article as the "Subsidies Agreement"):domestic support measures that conform fully to the provisions of Article 6 of this Agreement including direct payments that conform to the requirements of paragraph 5 thereof, as reflected in each Member's Schedule, as well as domestic support within *de minimis* levels and in conformity with paragraph 2 of Article 6, shall be: exempt from actions based on paragraph 1 of Article XVI of GATT 1994 or Articles 5 and 6 of the Subsidies Agreement, provided that such measures do not grant support to a specific commodity in excess of that decided during the 1992 marketing year.
[832] Josling 2007.
[833] *Ibid.*
[834] See World Trade Organization, 2005. *United States—Subsidies on Upland Cotton,* Reports of the Panel.

subsidies in impeding exporters in domestic and developing country markets as well as the impact on market shares.[835]

Moreover, though it was not found relevant to this case, the SCM has provisions for cases where the "threat" of serious prejudice exists.[836] The case may or may not usher in a flood of similar litigation: much depends on the success of the Doha Round in reducing subsidies.[837] But the panel report certainly gives encouragement to countries that have refrained from making challenges because they felt that panels would have difficulties in finding evidence of serious prejudice.[838] In markets where there are many factors contributing to the export performance of particular countries, establishing causal relationships is problematic.[839] But the panel seemed to be un-phased by the conflicting opinions of expert witnesses on the magnitude and direction of the impact of US subsidies on world cotton prices.[840]

The Panel made its ruling on the basis of a preponderance of evidence from economic studies, that production of cotton in the US has a significant impact on the world market price.[841] Though they avoided linking their decision to any particular study, they certainly paid more attention to such evidence than many previous panels.[842] So the cotton panel continues the trend toward rulings based on economic reasoning and quantification as a way of bringing precision to terms such as "substantial" and "significant" that pepper the rules on the trade impacts of subsidies.[843]

---

[835] See Panel ruling in World Trade Organization 2005. *United States—Subsidies on Upland Cotton* Reports of the Panel.

[836] According to Article 6 of the SCM Agreement, Serious prejudice in the sense of paragraph (c) of Article 5 shall be deemed to exist in the case of: the total ad valorem subsidization of a product exceeding 5 per cent; (b) subsidies to cover operating losses sustained by an industry; (c) subsidies to cover operating losses sustained by an enterprise, other than one-time measures which are non-recurrent and cannot be repeated for that enterprise and which are given merely to provide time for the development of long-term solutions and to avoid acute social problems; (d) direct forgiveness of debt, i.e. forgiveness of government-held debt, and grants to cover debt repayment. See the entire article 6 of the SCM Agreement read together with article 5 of the same agreement.

[837] United Nations Office Of The High Representative for the Least Developed Countries, Landlocked Developing Countries and Small Island Developing Countries, List Of LDCs, LLDCs And SIDS by Regions, http://www.un.org/special-rep/ohrlls/ohrlls/allcountriesregions.pdf (last visited Feb 24 2015). In the Doha Round agricultural negotiations it has been apparent that the issue of agricultural subsidies is not strictly speaking just a trade issue. Reform of agricultural subsidies in developed countries embraces the broader issue of economic development in developing countries and a humanitarian concern for the poorest countries in the world, especially those in sub-Saharan Africa. Much on this topic will be covered in chapter 5 of this study.

[838] See Josling 2005.

[839] Josling 2007.

[840] See World Trade Organization 2005 *United States—Subsidies on Upland Cotton* Reports of the Panel.

[841] *Ibid.*

[842] Josling 2007.

[843] Josling 2005.

4 5 1 Lessons Learned from the US Cotton Case

A close review of the briefing and evidence used in Brazil's litigation of its serious prejudice-related claims in the various Cotton proceedings demonstrates how document-intensive and expert-intensive a task it is to quantify the effects of subsidies and otherwise establish the causal link to serious prejudice in agricultural commodity markets.[844] There is no doubt that future challenges will require a similar resource-intensive effort to establish causation. Nevertheless, for the reasons set forth, *infra,* it will be considerably easier for future complaining party litigants to plan and prosecute successfully their serious prejudice challenges because of the lessons learned from the Cotton decisions.[845]

First, the numerous legal interpretations by the five Cotton decisions of the SCM Agreement and the AoA have clarified issues such as the existence of a world market, the ability to use any form of subsidy to establish serious prejudice, and the meaning of significant price suppression and how it can be demonstrated causally.[846] Second, the expiration of the "peace clause" means that complaining parties can challenge the collective effects of any form of subsidy to establish serious prejudice–even subsidies falling within the so-called "green box." Nor do complaining Members need be concerned with establishing that current levels of subsidization are greater than historic levels of subsidization for particular product at issue.[847]

Third, the Cotton compliance panel and AB confirmed that the adverse effects of annually recurring agricultural subsidies can be undertaken using a long-term analysis.[848] Such an analysis would assess whether the collective effect of a number of years of annually recurring subsidies

---

[844] It is submitted that this will be too expensive for least developed countries who even struggle to bring such cases before the WTO adjudication panel. Least developed countries and other developing countries will continue to suffer prejudice in silence because the dispute settlement mechanisms appear to be resource intensive as depicted in the Cotton case.

[845] Josling 2007. However it is submitted that such an argument may be defeated by the fact that poor nations can hardly spend money on litigation before meeting immediate domestic needs.

[846] The prohibited export and local content subsidies, expired subsidies with continuing effects, green box subsidies.

[847] Brazil was forced to expend a considerable amount of resources in the original proceedings to eventually succeed in securing vitally important data to allow the establishment of a peace clause violation.

[848] In *Cotton* 21.5, 10.83 "In our view, the type of effect of a subsidy on production relevant to the analysis under Article 6.3(c) can also be demonstrated on the basis of a longer-term perspective that focuses on how the subsidy affects decisions of producers to enter or to exit a given industry.", 10.176 "Thus, it appears to us that the effect of the marketing loan and countercyclical payments on cotton farmers' production decisions could be best assessed on the basis of data covering the lifetime of the Act . . . This period of time is of sufficient length to require a medium to long-term analysis."; see also ABR Cotton 21.5, supra note 25, at 422.

contribute to farmers entering or exiting the production of the crop in question.[849] This is a very important because claims based only on short-term effects can easily collapse during the WTO proceedings if the level of subsidies contracts significantly through increases in commodity prices.[850] This rationale is particularly useful for challenges to subsidies for crops such as rice or cotton that demand specialized equipment and where certain land is only economically viable to grow a single or only several crops.[851] By contrast, the long-term causation analysis may be less useful for claims involving subsidies for commodities where it is relatively easy to shift from one crop to many other crops.[852]

Fourth, the compliance panel rejected US arguments that the absence of any temporal link between the lower world prices and the payment of marketing loan and counter-cyclical subsidies meant that the subsidies could not cause price suppression.[853] The compliance panel's finding on this point, when read in conjunction with its "long-term" approach to examining the effects of subsidies, suggests that future challenges to annual recurring agricultural subsidies need not demonstrate any temporal link between market prices and the provision of subsidies.[854] This appropriately limited an obvious defence in situations where subsidies have been provided for decades and where it would thus be difficult to identify a temporal point in which subsidies have not distorted the market.[855]

Fifth, while the original panel found that non-price contingent subsidies direct payments and crop insurance did not cause significant price suppression, dicta from the AB suggested that non-price contingent subsidies could contribute to price suppression and other forms of serious prejudice.[856]

[849] World Trade Organization 2005 *United States—Subsidies on Upland Cotton* Reports of the Appellate Body WT/DS265/AB/R, WT/DS266/AB/R & WT/DS267/AB/R.

[850] Josling 2005.

[851] *Ibid.*

[852] Josling 2007.

[853] See Panel Report Cotton, footnote 2.

[854] See World Trade Organization 2005 *United States—Subsidies on Upland Cotton* Reports of the Panel.

[855] *Ibid.*

[856] Brazil's Appellant's submission noted its disagreement with the original panel's finding that only price-contingent subsidies — but not Direct Payment, Crop Insurance, and Cottonseed payments — could be found to contribute to significant price suppression. In affirming the panel's reliance on only the "price contingent" subsidies, the Appellate Body made the following statement: "We do not exclude the possibility that challenged subsidies that are not 'price-contingent' (to use the panel's term) could have some effect on production and exports and contribute to price suppression." ABR Cotton 21.5, supra footnote 25. This statement suggests that the Appellate Body may be receptive to the collective effect of subsidies "contributing to" production — such as crop insurance and direct payments even if those subsidies are not linked to prices and implies that future serious prejudice challenges to agricultural subsidies should not shy away from including non-price contingent subsidies in the mix of subsidies to be challenged.

In addition, the rationale behind the use of a long-term effects analysis is whether the combined effect of the challenged subsidies provides revenue support to farmers that maintain them in the business of farming the commodity in question.[857] Non-price contingent subsidies that contribute to covering the costs of production or increasing the wealth of a farmer through facilitating the purchase of land or equipment can have a very similar effect on sustaining production as a price-contingent subsidy.[858]

Sixth, the Arbitrators confirmed the viability and utility of particular types of econometric models[859] to assess the effects of subsidies.[860] Similarly, the AB in each of its Cotton decisions criticized the panels for not explaining how it had taken the particular models into account, and for failing to evaluate and compare the parameters used by such models.[861] The use of such models is crucial given the counterfactual nature of the entire serious prejudice question, i.e. whether, but for the subsidies, world prices would have been higher.[862] Future complaining parties can adopt and adapt as necessary these models in preparing future challenges.[863] This will significantly facilitate the defence of such models.[864]

Seventh, the Cotton decisions highlighted the utility of a claim of price suppression in challenging such subsidies.[865] Unlike a claim of price depression, there is no requirement for a complaining party to explain what may be very wide swings in commodity prices during the reference period

[857] Panel Report Cotton footnote 18 "In our view, the type of effect of a subsidy on production relevant to the analysis under Article 6.3(c) can also be demonstrated on the basis of a longer-term perspective that focuses on how the subsidy affects decisions of producers to enter or to exit a given industry." .... "Thus, it appears to us that the effect of the marketing loan and countercyclical payments on cotton farmers' production decisions could be best assessed on the basis of data covering the lifetime of the Act . . . This period of time is of sufficient length to require a medium to long-term analysis".

[858] See World Trade Organization 2005 *United States—Subsidies on Upland Cotton* Reports of the Panel.

[859] In this case, models were generated and testimony given by Dr. Daniel Sumner of the University of California, Davis.

[860] See World Trade Organization 2005 *United States—Subsidies on Upland Cotton*, Reports of the Panel.

[861] Appellate Body Report Cotton, footnote 29, at 448 "We note that the Panel indicated expressly that it had taken the models in question into account. It would have been helpful had the Panel revealed how it used these models in examining the question of third country responses."; Appellate Body Report Cotton 21.5, supra note 25, at 348 "While the Panel appropriately examined the model, the parameters used by each party, and the arguments made by the parties, and noted the different results generated by the simulations conducted by each party, the Panel could have gone further in its evaluation and comparative analysis of the economic simulations and the particular parameters used".

[862] See World Trade Organization 2005 *United States—Subsidies on Upland Cotton* Reports of the Panel.

[863] Josling 2007.

[864] By contrast, a significant portion of Brazil's briefing before the Cotton panels and Arbitrator was focused on justifying its econometric model and the various price and elasticity parameters used by that model.

[865] See World Trade Organization 2005 *United States—Subsidies on Upland Cotton* decisions in the Panel and AB reports.

examined.[866] In the various Cotton proceedings, the US had the near impossible task of trying to demonstrate that other market factors somehow eliminated any price suppressing effects of the US subsidies.[867] However, whether the demand or supply of Chinese cotton or even subsidies to Chinese producers may have caused prices to fall was properly treated as irrelevant by all panels and AB decisions.[868] By contrast, it would be relatively easy for a defending subsidizing Member to defend against a price depression claim by demonstrating that many non-subsidy factors caused prices to fall.[869] Similarly, a claim of price undercutting would require proof that in particular transactions the actual prices of the subsidizing Member were lower than the prices of the complaining Member's producers.[870] This requires evidence that could be very difficult to obtain and would generally be highly confidential.[871]

Eighth, the compliance panel and AB's decision rejecting the distinction between subsidy payments and subsidy programs will make it much easier for those Members challenging subsidies to secure implementation by the challenged subsidizing Member.[872] Complaining Members now need only establish the existence of serious prejudice during a reference period by the effects of subsidies.[873] A positive finding of serious prejudice will mean that the losing subsidizing Member will have to make changes to the subsidy program or legislation and not simply claim that the effects of the subsidies granted during the reference period no longer cause serious prejudice.[874]

Finally, an important tactical lesson to be learned from the Cotton Arbitration decision is that the damages' focus is only upon the serious prejudicial effects suffered by a complaining party and it would be beneficial to combine as many complaining parties with the largest possible share of world production or world exports.[875] For example, if China, Brazil, and India who collectively

[866] See World Trade Organization 2005 *United States—Subsidies on Upland Cotton* decisions in the Panel and AB reports.

[867] See World Trade Organization 2005 *United States—Subsidies on Upland Cotton* Reports of the Panel and World Trade Organization 2005 *United States—Subsidies on Upland Cotton* Reports of the Appellate Body, WT/DS265/AB/R, WT/DS266/AB/R, & WT/DS267/AB/R.

[868] *Ibid.*

[869] Devereaux "Case Studies in US Trade Negotiation: Resolving Disputes" 2006 Vol 2 *Institute for International Economics*.

[870] *Ibid.*

[871] *Ibid.*

[872] Scott "Brazil's WTO Challenge to U.S. Cotton Subsidies: The Road to Effective Disciplines of Agricultural Subsidies" *Business Law Brief* 2010.

[873] *Ibid.*

[874] *Ibid.*

[875] The Cotton Club 2007 *Wall Street Journal.*

total more than fifty percent of world cotton production had joined forces to challenge US upland cotton subsidies, the total amount of retaliation allowed under the Arbitrator's formula would have been far in excess of $1 billion.[876] As a result, the United States would still have the obligation to remove all of the significant price suppression, but it would also have an arguably greater incentive to eliminate its WTO inconsistent conduct.[877] In sum, the collective effect of these Cotton decisions will considerably aid complaining parties in future disputes.[878] That is not to say that it will be easy to establish the causal link between the subsidies and particular market effects that rise to the level of serious prejudice.[879] Such cases will always be evidence and expert intensive and require considerable resources and expertise to litigate successfully.[880] However, the clarifications provided by all five of the Cotton decisions will allow the structuring and prosecution of the case in a more efficient and less resource intensive manner than Brazil was forced to endure as the first Member to challenge these subsidies.[881]

4 5 2 Implications of Cotton Decisions for Future Challenges to US and EU Agricultural Subsidy Programs

There are a number of potential challenges to US and EU agricultural subsidy programs under WTO subsidy disciplines[882] that could be based on the strategic roadmap and legal precedent of the Cotton dispute.

4 5 2 1 Challenges to US Annual Recurring Domestic Support Subsidies

The US 2008 Farm Act[883] largely maintained for a number of "program" crops representing the bulk of U.S. non-livestock agriculture, include the same "price-contingent" marketing loan and counter-cyclical subsidies that were condemned in the Cotton decisions.[884] The Farm Act also continued the Direct Payment and crop insurance subsidies, and added a new subsidy program (ACRE).[885] As noted above, the original panel found that Brazil had not sufficiently demonstrated

---

876 Scott 2010.

877 Scott "Brazil's WTO Challenge to US Cotton Subsidies: The Road to Effective Disciplines of Agricultural Subsidies" *Business Law Brief* 2010.

878 *Ibid.*

879 *Ibid.*

880 *Ibid.*

881 *Ibid.*

882 This includes claims that could be asserted under Articles 3.1, 5 and 6 of the SCM Agreement and the claims under Articles 3, 6, 7, 8, 9 and 10 of the AoA.

883 US 2008 Farm Act P.L. 110-234.

884 Josling 2005.

885 Scott 2010.

a causal link between the Direct Payment and crop insurance subsidies and significant price suppression.[886] However, by employing the "long-term" causation focus of the Cotton compliance panel and AB decisions, it will be possible under certain market circumstances to make strong arguments that the collective effect of all of these subsidies including the non-price contingent subsidies is to cause serious prejudice in the world or in third country markets in violation of Article 6.3 of the SCM Agreement.[887]

The viability of such claims will depend first on whether the prices of the particular commodity being challenged are low enough over some period of time to create payments of at least a modest amount of marketing loan and counter-cyclical subsidies.[888] Historically, commodity prices have fluctuated considerably and if, and when, they do fall from generally current high levels, then there will be much larger US marketing loan and counter-cyclical subsidies that can be challenged under the Cotton rationale.[889] Another important factor would be whether the collective amount of the subsidies is necessary to cover at least some portion of the total cost of production.[890] Congressional Research Service analysis shows that US subsidy programs have been essential for US farmers of a number of different commodities to cover their total costs of production.[891] This crucial fact, coupled with the large US world market share of exports and production of a number

---

886 See Babcock, "Breaking the Link between Food and Biofuels", 2008, available at http://www.card.iastate.edu/iowaagreview/summer_08/IAR.pdf (Accessed on 09/05/15) finding that the pattern of payments for Iowa corn proved "nearly identical to the situation for corn in other states and for wheat and soybeans in all states . . . which suggests that a large proportion of U.S. farmers will find ACRE much more attractive than current commodity programs."

887 Article 6.3 of the SCM Agreement provides that, "Serious prejudice in the sense of paragraph (c) of Article 5 may arise in any case where one or several of the following apply: (a) the effect of the subsidy is to displace or impede the imports of a like product of another Member into the market of the subsidizing Member; (b) the effect of the subsidy is to displace or impede the exports of a like product of another Member from a third country market; (c) the effect of the subsidy is a significant price undercutting by the subsidized product as compared with the price of a like product of another Member in the same market or significant price suppression, price depression or lost sales in the same market; (d) the effect of the subsidy is an increase in the world market share of the subsidizing Member in a particular subsidized primary product or commodity17 as compared to the average share it had during the previous period of three years and this increase follows a consistent trend over a period when subsidies have been granted.".

888 Scott 2010.

889 For example, billions in marketing loan subsidies were provided when prices for soybeans fell in the period 2000-2001, and corn prices collapsed in the 2005–2006 period. See Press Release, American Soybean Association, American Soybean Association Urges Agriculture Secretary to Maintain Oilseed Loan Rates (Oct. 19, 2001) (on file with the American Soybean Association), available at http://www. soygrowers.com/newsroom/releases/2001%20releases/Loan+RateOct192001.pdf; (Accessed on 09/05/15) Alexei Barrionuevo, Mountains of Corn and a Sea of Farm Subsidies, N.Y. Times, Nov. 9, 2005, at Business, available at http://www.nytimes.com/2005/11/09/ business/09harvest.html?_r=1&pagewanted=print. (Accessed on 09/05/15).

890 Scott 2010.

891 Schnepf "Potential Challenges to U.S. Farm Subsidies in the WTO: A Brief Overview" *Congressional Research Service* 2006.

of different commodities, suggests that the US will be vulnerable when prices fall for those commodities receiving significant domestic support.[892] On the other hand, it will be more difficult to challenge the US domestic support subsidies if over a 4–5 year period prices have been so high that few price-contingent subsidies were provided.[893]

Finally, subsidies provided by the E.U. would also be vulnerable to serious prejudice challenges under the Cotton rationale.[894] For example, the EU provides a wide range of subsidies tied to the production of EU processed dairy products.[895] These include export refunds and disposal subsidies, single farm payments, as well as subsidies provided contingent upon the purchase and use of EU dairy products.[896] The collective impact of these subsidies on world market prices is amplified because the EU is the largest exporter of many commoditized dairy products.[897] To the extent that these subsidies over the longer term have covered an important portion of the total production costs of milk as well as processed dairy products, it is likely that viable serious prejudice claims could be sustained.[898] Such claims under Article 6.3 of the SCM Agreement could include significant price suppression in the world market for butter, cheese, casein, skimmed milk powder, and displacement or impedance of market share of these same products in various third country export markets.[899]

4 5 2 2 Challenges to Total Aggregate Measurement of Support

Another result of the Cotton case is to increase US vulnerability to challenges under Article 3.2 of the AoA for failing to restrain the total amount of subsidies provided in favour of US domestic agricultural production to $19.1 billion of AMS.[900] The Congressional Research Service, as well

892 Schnepf "Potential Challenges to U.S. Farm Subsidies in the WTO: A Brief Overview" *Congressional Research Service* 2006.

893 *Ibid.*

894 See Scott 2010.

895 See Merrett, Refunds Return as E.C. Reconsiders Dairy Intervention, DairyReporter.com,http://www.dairyreporter.com/Industrymarkets/Refunds-return-as-EC-reconsiders-dairy-intervention (reporting the reinstatement of dairy export refunds by the E.C. (Accessed on 10/05/15).

896 See Merrett 2009.

897 *Ibid.*

898 This allowed producers to maintain and not exit production.

899 See Article 6 of the SCM Agreement.

900 Schnepf "Potential Challenges to U.S. Farm Subsidies in the WTO: A Brief Overview" *Congressional Research Service* 2006.

as a WTO challenge by Brazil[901] and Canada,[902] provided analysis suggesting that the inclusion of Direct Payments as domestic support meant the US was in violation for a number of years over the past decade of its $19.1 billion AMS limit contrary to Article 3.2 of the AoA.[903] If and when commodity prices fall, the US will again be vulnerable to future challenges regarding their total aggregate measurement of support.[904]

4 5 2 3 Challenges to Prohibited Local Content Subsidies

Both the US and the EU presently provide subsidies to processors of agricultural goods contingent *de jure* or *de facto* on the use of "local" US or EU agricultural products.[905] The Cotton decisions confirmed that such local content subsidies in the form of the Step 2 subsidies to U.S. mill users of U.S. cotton are covered by the WTO subsidies disciplines.[906] For example, the EU provides local content subsidies to EU purchasers or users of EU produced skimmed milk, skimmed milk powder, cream, butter and concentrated butter.[907] The EU also provides subsidies to purchasers or users of butter and skimmed milk powder contingent upon these products being produced in the EU.[908] Similarly, the US sugar program requires the US Government to make sugar marketing loan payments[909] to sugar processors contingent on the use of domestic U.S. sugar over imported goods.[910] Under the Cotton decision rationale, all of these forms of local content subsidies are

---

[901] Request for Consultation by *Brazil, United States–Domestic Support and Export Credit Guarantees for Agricultural Products*, WT/DS365/1 2007.
[902] Request for Consultation by *Canada, United States–Subsidies and Other Domestic Support for Corn and Other Agricultural Products,* WT/DS357/1 2007.
[903] Article 3.2 of the AoA states that, Subject to the provisions of Article 6, a Member shall not provide support in favour of domestic producers in excess of the commitment levels specified in Section I of Part IV of its Schedule.
[904] Schnepf 2006.
[905] Scott "Brazil's WTO Challenge to U.S. Cotton Subsidies: The Road to Effective Disciplines of Agricultural Subsidies" *Business Law Brief* 2010.
[906] *Ibid.*
[907] See Commission Regulation 1234/2007, Establishing a Common Organization of Agricultural Markets and on Specific Provisions for Certain Agricultural Products, 2007. A number of provisions of the Single CMO Regulation expose the EC to potential local content subsidy claims. They include EC intervention purchases of butter and skimmed milk powder, id. Article 15, 16, EC storage subsidies for storage of butter, id. Article. 28(a) (ii)-(iii), and EC disposal subsidies to the extent they are paid to processors of EC dairy products and not paid on the export of such products, id. Recitals 43, 60; art. 99-101 describing measures found in Recitals 43 and 60.
[908] See, Article 7, 10(1) (e), 10(1) (f), 100(1) providing provisions specifically indicating if milk or milk products are produced or originated "in the community".
[909] Federal Agriculture Improvement and Reform Act of 1996, 7 U.S.C. 7272 (2008).
[910] Agricultural Adjustment Act of 1938, 7 U.S.C. 1359aa (2008). Similar to a local content requirement, the current U.S. sugar program in the 2008 Farm Act contains a requirement that the size of the overall marketing allotment equal 85 percent of US human consumption of sugar. Id. This constitutes a minimum use requirement for domestic sugar, in violation of Article III of GATT 1994.

contingent on the use of domestic over imported goods, in violation of Article 3.1(b) of the SCM Agreement.[911]

4 6 CONCLUSION: LESSONS LEARNT FROM CASE LAW

The explosion of agricultural cases in the WTO reflects both the indistinct nature of the multilateral trade rules in the WTO and the sensitive nature of the trade itself.[912] In addition, the perceived vulnerability of the major agricultural programs of developed countries to challenge under the AoA and the SCM has led to some recent high profile disputes.[913] The nature of some scientific changes in food production, particularly the uneven adoption of biotech seeds, has led to other disputes.[914] Countries are still struggling with the trade policy consequences of the search for attributes in production that are desirable to consumers.[915] Apart from these and other factors, more significant is the progress in the Doha Round Agricultural negotiations which is most likely to determine whether or not there will be an increase or decrease in agricultural subsidy cases coming before the WTO dispute settlement mechanisms. Chances are more of these issues will be tested in the WTO in future years if the snail progress continues. It would be risky to predict any sharp decrease in the numbers of agricultural disputes brought before the DSB in the next decade.[916]

Of importance to developing countries is the *Cotton* decisions which has provided considerable clarity to the underhand world of WTO agricultural subsidy disciplines.[917] As the first decisions under the relatively vague and general actionable subsidy rules of the SCM Agreement, the decisions offer the analytical and evidentiary tools for government trade officials and their counsel to assess the extent of the negative impact on trade from various forms of subsidies.[918] In the case of domestic cotton subsidies, that impact is enormous $2.9 billion in worldwide price suppressing

---

[911] Article 3.1 of the SCM Agreement provides that, "except as provided in the Agreement on Agriculture, the following subsidies, within the meaning of Article 1, shall be prohibited: (a) subsidies contingent, in law or in fact4, whether solely or as one of several other conditions, upon export performance, including those illustrated in Annex I5; (b) subsidies contingent, whether solely or as one of several other conditions, upon the use of domestic over imported goods".

[912] Barton *The Evolution of the Trade Regime: Politics, Law and Economics of the GATT and WTO* (2006).

[913] One of the most stunning dispute that went to the DSP is the *US Upland Cotton* case in which a developing country successfully challenged a developed country's trade distorting agricultural policy.

[914] See Babcock "Breaking the Link between Food and Biofuels" 2008 *IOWA Agriculture Review* at 1-10.

[915] *Ibid.*

[916] In some areas of trade, complaints can trigger retaliatory filings as an element of trade strategy. This does not seem to be a problem in agriculture at present but it may emerge as more sensitive cases are litigated.

[917] Scott "Brazil's WTO Challenge to US Cotton Subsidies: The Road to Effective Disciplines of Agricultural Subsidies" *Business Law Brief* 2010.

[918] *Ibid.*

effects on cotton each year.[919] The export and local content prohibited subsidy aspects of the decision offer the hope that such highly trade distorting subsidies can be more easily identified and successfully challenged in the future or simply eliminated by WTO Members seeking to avoid a dispute settlement challenge.[920]

The enormous trade distorting effects quantified by the *Cotton* Arbitration decisions have the additional significant benefit of supporting the Doha Round negotiating efforts to further limit the amount of trade distorting domestic support and eliminate entirely highly trade distorting export subsidies for agricultural products.[921] These multilateral reform efforts are crucial to ensure long-lasting and comprehensive reform for the most trade distorting forms of agricultural subsidies.[922] The *Cotton* decisions confirmed and established as a fact the wide-ranging harm inflicted on many developing countries who struggle to compete with their heavily subsidized counterparts in world markets. Based on these established wide-ranging trade distortions, the WTO Cotton decisions compel and fully support a successful negotiated result that will alleviate the severe negative impacts of these highly trade-distorting subsidies.[923]

Cases brought against particular types of domestic support have been sporadic.[924] With inconclusive debates in the Committee for Agriculture and without the guidance of panel reports, countries were able largely to decide for themselves whether particular policies were consistent with the definitions of the green and blue boxes, and hence not subject to reductions.[925] So long as countries were way below their limits on domestic support it was not a priority to challenge the notifications themselves. But the massive funding brought in by the 2002 US Farm Act caused a reconsideration of this situation, with the possibility that the limits may have been breached if notifications had been erroneous.[926] The statement of the *US Cotton* panel that some of the

[919] Schnepf "Potential Challenges to US Farm Subsidies in the WTO: A Brief Overview" *Congressional Research Service* 2006.
[920] Josling "Unravelling the Cotton Case" 2005.
[921] Scott 2010.
[922] *Ibid.*
[923] See Josling 2005. Also see Scott 2010 for more on this point.
[924] Josling *Production and Export Subsidies in Agriculture: Lessons from GATT and WTO Disputes Involving the US and the EC* (2003). It is submitted that the position remains the same to date possibly because it is difficult to identify when a country exceeds its commitment levels until it manifest to trade distortions.
[925] Josling 2007.
[926] *Ibid.*

expenditures that the US had claimed as "green" may have been mislabelled turned this possibility into a contestable proposition.[927]

The outburst of cases of agricultural subsidies as notified under the categories used by the AoA, illustrates that the ambiguity in the agricultural rules still exists.[928] On the one hand, it depicts the enormous harm inflicted on many developing countries who are clearly struggling to compete with heavily subsidized developed countries in global markets.[929] It appears as if the possibility of a change awaits the conclusion to be reached by members in the Doha Round. However, the prospect exists that the major driver of change in the agricultural policies of developed countries could be the WTO dispute settlement process, and its decisions on the classification of subsidies.[930] So far, it is apparent that there is controversy over the role of WTO rules when they clash with powerful political interests.[931] It is submitted that trade in agricultural products might continue to provide vexing issues for the multilateral trade system and its judicial processes until a mutually acceptable agreement is reached in the Doha Round.

---

927 See World Trade Organization, *United States—Subsidies on Upland Cotton,* decisions in the Panel and AB reports 2005.

928 See Josling 2007. Also see Barton *The Evolution of the Trade Regime: Politics, Law and Economics of the GATT and WTO* (2006).

929 See Steinberg "When the Peace Ends: The Vulnerability of EC and U.S. Agricultural Subsidies to WTO Legal Challenge" *Journal of International Economic Law* 2003 at 2.

930 Josling 2007.

931 Barton 2006.

CHAPTER 5
The Doha Round Negotiations on Agricultural Subsidies: A Discussion on the Demands of Developed and Developing Countries.

"The rich world tells the poor world to get rid of subsidies, but continues to spend \$1 billion a day subsidising its own farming enterprises."[932]

5 1 INTRODUCTION

The Doha Round was initiated in 2001 and is still in progress today.[933] It is commonly known as the Doha Development Round because it undertook to put development at the core of the trade negotiations and to ensure that the outcome of the negotiations promoted the interests of developing countries.[934] More importantly, the Doha declaration pledged to enable developing countries to fully participate in world trade and to advance their economic development through improved access to developed countries' markets, by reducing import tariffs and phasing out domestic and export subsidies that often lead to dumping.[935] It was primarily the efforts of developed countries that launched this new round of negotiations after massive panic caused by

---

[932] Oxfam International "Rigged Rules: Dumping, from the Make Trade Fair Campaign" 2002. https://www.oxfam.org/en/campaigns (accessed on 15/07/15). The statement is a reflection of some of the most contentious issues at the Doha Round.

[933] "Under the Doha ministerial Declaration, members recognize the work already undertaken in the negotiations initiated in early 2000 under Article 20 of the Agreement on Agriculture, including the large number of negotiating proposals submitted on behalf of a total of 121 members. Members recall the long-term objective referred to in the Agreement to establish a fair and market-oriented trading system through a programme of fundamental reform encompassing strengthened rules and specific commitments on support and protection in order to correct and prevent restrictions and distortions in world agricultural markets. Negotiators reconfirm our commitment to this programme. Building on the work carried out to date and without prejudging the outcome of the negotiations the members commit themselves to comprehensive negotiations aimed at: substantial improvements in market access; reductions of, with a view to phasing out, all forms of export subsidies; and substantial reductions in trade-distorting domestic support. The members agree that special and differential treatment for developing countries shall be an integral part of all elements of the negotiations and shall be embodied in the schedules of concessions and commitments and as appropriate in the rules and disciplines to be negotiated, so as to be operationally effective and to enable developing countries to effectively take account of their development needs, including food security and rural development. The negotiators take note of the non-trade concerns reflected in the negotiating proposals submitted by Members and confirm that non-trade concerns will be taken into account in the negotiations as provided for in the Agreement on Agriculture.

[934] "Under the Ministerial Declaration establishing the Doha Round, members agreed that special and differential treatment for developing countries shall be an integral part of all elements of the negotiations and shall be embodied in the schedules of concessions and commitments and as appropriate in the rules and disciplines to be negotiated, so as to be operationally effective and to enable developing countries to effectively take account of their development needs, including food security and rural development".

[935] Institute of Development Studies "What is the Doha Round?" 2009 http://www.eldis.org/index.cfm?objectId=E1A93506-FCCE-F97E-205FB8451CE3EA74 (accessed on 23/05/15).

the September 11 attacks.[936] Developing countries were resistant to the idea of new trade negotiations and insisted that implementation issues from the Uruguay Round should be addressed prior to beginning a new round of negotiations.[937]

From a developing country viewpoint, the reform commitments from the Uruguay Round were pushed on them, particularly considering their limited capacity to participate in the negotiations. “From their perspective, the implementation exercise ‘had been imposed’ in an imperial way, with little concern for what it will cost, how it will be done, or if it will support their development efforts.”[938] Logically, developing countries did not wish to open up a new set of negotiations to further liberalize their economies for the benefit of developed countries, a situation that places heavy financial burdens on poorer countries to comply, without having realized the benefits of negotiated promises from the previous round.[939] In the Doha Round, developed countries continue to exert relentless pressure on developing countries to fully liberalize their economies, while they are maintaining protectionist measures at home.[940] The political sensitivity of the agricultural sector continue to hurdle the negotiations. Developed countries are still hesitant to lift their protectionist policies, using food security as an incomprehensible justification.[941]

This chapter mainly exhumes what is taking place in the proposed further negotiations. It examines the demands of both developed countries and developing countries and attempts to identify the problems affecting the negotiations. As it has been noted above, one of the main objectives of the Doha Round is to ensure that the outcome of the negotiations promote the interests of developing countries. The study assesses whether the interests of developing countries are being taken into consideration in the Doha Round and if there is a possibility of their interests being accommodated.

---

[936] Antoine “Eight Years of Doha Trade Talks: Where do we stand?” International Food Policy Research Institute, 2009. https://hal.archives-ouvertes.fr/hal-00637589v1/document (accessed on 10/06/15).
[937] Narlikar *The WTO: A Very Short Introduction* Oxford (2001) generally.
[938] Finger “Implementation of the Uruguay Round Commitments: The Development Challenge” *The World Economy* 2000. http://unctad.org/en/Docs/ux_tdxrt1d8.en.pdf. (Accessed on 07/07/15).
[939] Woods "Governing the Global Economy: Strengthening Multilateral Institutions" 2008 *International Peace Institute Policy Paper*. http://www.globaleconomicgovernance.org/sites/geg/files/Governing%20the%20Global%20Economy%20IPI.pdf (accessed on 01/05/15).
[940] Mahajan “The Common Agricultural Policy and the Doha Development Round”. EU Commission 2011. http://aei.pitt.edu/29775/1/MahajanCAPEUMAedi%5B1%5D.pdf (accessed on 29/06/15).
[941] *Ibid.*

The chapter will not look at the entire issues being dealt with in the Doha Round. It will explore only the issues dealing with agricultural subsidies since that is primarily the focus of the study.

5 2 THE DOHA DECLARATION: WHAT IS IT ABOUT?

At the World Trade Organization's (WTO) Fourth Ministerial Conference in Doha, Qatar, November 9-14, 2001, WTO member countries agreed to launch a new round of multilateral trade negotiations (MTNs), including negotiations on agricultural trade liberalization.[942] As was noted above, the round is called the Doha Development Agenda (DDA) because it underscores assimilating developing countries into the world trading system.[943] A first phase of agricultural trade negotiations had been underway since early 2000.[944] The first phase produced proposals from WTO member countries for agricultural trade liberalization, but no work program or timetable for completing negotiations as developed.[945] The new round incorporates agriculture into a comprehensive framework that includes negotiations on industrial tariffs, services, anti-dumping and countervailing duty measures, dispute settlement, and other trade issues.[946]

The Doha Ministerial Declaration mandate for agriculture calls for comprehensive negotiations aimed at substantial improvements in market access; reductions of agricultural subsidies with a view to phasing out all forms of export subsidies; and substantial reductions in trade-distorting domestic support.[947] These topics, domestic support, export subsidies, and market access have become known as the three pillars of the agricultural negotiations.[948] The Declaration also provides that Special and Differential Treatment (SDT) for developing countries would be an integral part of all elements of the negotiations.[949] The Declaration took note of non-trade concerns reflected in negotiating proposals of various member countries and confirmed that they would be taken into

---

942 See the Doha Ministerial Declaration launching the DDA negotiations at http://www.wto.org/english/tratop_e/dda_e/dda_e.htm#dohadeclaration. Para 13 and 14 of the Doha declaration set out the agricultural negotiating mandate.

943 See the Doha Ministerial Declaration preamble above.

944 Article 20 of the 1994 Uruguay Round Agreement on Agriculture called for initiating negotiations one year before the end of the URAA implementation period (the beginning of 2000). See the text of the URAA at http://www.wto.org/english/docs_e/legal_e/14-ag.pdf. (Accessed on 17/06/15).

945 WTO "The Doha Declaration Explained: Implementation-Related Issues and Concerns". https://www.wto.org/english/tratop_e/dda_e/dohaexplained_e.htm (Accessed on 11/06/15).

946 *Ibid.*

947 WTO "The Doha Declaration Explained" available on https://www.wto.org/english/tratop_e/dda_e/dohaexplained_e.htm (Accessed on 12/06/15).

948 WTO "Agriculture Negotiations: The issues, and where we are now" https://www.wto.org/english/tratop_e/agric_e/agnegs_bkgrnd_e.doc (Accessed on12/06/15).

949 *Ibid.*

account in the negotiations.[950] March 31, 2003 was set as the deadline for reaching agreement on "modalities" (targets, formulas, timetables, etc.) for achieving the mandated objectives, but that deadline was missed.[951] During the rest of 2003, negotiations on modalities continued in preparation for the fifth WTO Ministerial Conference held in Cancun, Mexico September 10-14, 2003.[952]

While the United States and the EU reached agreement on a broad framework for negotiating agricultural trade liberalization before the Cancun meeting, a group of developing countries, the G-20 which includes Brazil, China, India, and South Africa, among others, made a counter-proposal.[953] The G-20 proposal emphasized agricultural subsidy and tariff reduction for developed countries with fewer demands on developing countries. The Chairman of the Cancun ministerial circulated a draft declaration at the meeting that attempted to reconcile differences between developed (especially the United States and the EU) and developing countries (especially the G20) on the agricultural issues.[954] Neither the proposals made by the United States and the EU and the G-20 nor the Chairman's draft declaration proposed specific modalities (formulas, targets, or timetables) for reducing tariffs and trade-distorting support and for phasing out export subsidies.[955]

The Cancun Ministerial Conference thus failed to reconcile differences on agricultural issues as well as differences between developed and developing countries over expanding the negotiating agenda to include such issues as competition and investment policy.[956] The Cancun Ministerial ended without an agreement on modalities or a framework for continuing multilateral negotiations on agricultural trade liberalization.[957] The inconclusive end of the Cancun ministerial largely eliminated the prospect that the DDA would conclude by its scheduled end date, January 1, 2005.[958]

---

950 Conconi "Special and Differential Treatment of Developing Countries in the WTO" http://www.ecares.org/ecare/personal/conconi$/web/S&D.pdf (Accessed on 13/06/15).
951 WTO *WTO and the Doha Round*, (2008) 52
952 Ingco *Agriculture and the WTO: Creating a Trading System for Development* (2005) 38.
953 Hanrahan "WTO Doha Round: Agricultural Negotiating Proposals" http://fpc.state.gov/documents/organization/57217.pdf (Accessed on 13/06/15).
954 See Fergusson "World Trade Organization Negotiations: The Doha Development Agenda" https://www.fas.org/sgp/crs/misc/RL32060.pdf (Accessed on 13/06/15).
955 *Ibid.*
956 *Ibid.* Also see Baldwin, Failure of the WTO Ministerial Conference at Cancun: Reason and Remedies. Available at http://fordschool.umich.edu/rsie/Conferences/CGP/May2004Papers/Baldwin.pdf (Accessed on 14/06/15).
957 Baldwin *Ibid.*
958 See Hanrahan *Ibid.*

WTO member countries did, however, reach an agreement on July 31, 2004 on a work program which includes a framework for negotiating the agricultural trade issues in the Doha Round.[959] The July 31 work program for completing the Doha negotiations included an overall decision to complete the negotiations launched in Doha, Qatar, in November 2001 with annexes that lay out negotiating frameworks for agriculture and other DDA issues.[960] The agricultural framework, part of a work program for all the negotiating issues in the DDA, set the stage for negotiations to determine modalities, that is the specific targets, formulas, timetables, *inter alia,* for curbing trade-distorting domestic support, reducing trade barriers and eliminating export subsidies.[961] Negotiators set for themselves a deadline of July 2005 for completing a first draft of the agricultural modalities, a deadline that was subsequently missed.[962]

5 2 1 Other Areas of Negotiations

5 2 1 1 Cotton

Although not mentioned specifically in the Doha round mandate, cotton subsidies have become a key issue to resolve before DDA negotiations can be successfully concluded.[963] The framework expressly included cotton as an issue to be addressed in the agricultural negotiations. Four cotton producing African countries Benin, Burkina Faso, Chad, and Mali have proposed the complete elimination of trade-distorting domestic support and export subsidies for cotton.[964] The four countries, sometimes referred to as the C-4, call for an end to cotton export subsidies over three years, and the elimination of production related domestic support over four years, in each case from January 1 2005.[965] In addition, the proposal calls for WTO members to establish a transitional

[959] See Hanrahan "Agriculture in the WTO Doha Round: The Framework Agreement and Next Steps" http://nationalaglawcenter.org/wp-content/uploads/assets/crs/RS21905.pdf (accessed on 15/07/15).

[960] The framework agreement known as the Doha Work Programme: Decision Adopted by the General Council on August 1 2004 is at http://www.wto.org/english/tratop_e/ dda_e/ddadraft_31jul04_e.pdf. (Accessed 08/07/15).

[961] Sungjoon "Doha's Development" 2007 *Berkely Journal of International Law* 165.

[962] *Ibid.*

[963] Statement by the Chairman of the General Council. Doha Development Agenda: Informal Heads of Delegation Meeting, December 9, 2003, available at http://www.wto.org/english/news_e/news03_e/stat_gc_chair_9dec03_e.htm (accessed on 05/06/15).

[964] The original proposal WTO Negotiations on Agriculture, Poverty Reduction: Sectorial Initiative in Favour of Cotton: Joint proposal by Benin, Burkina Faso, Chad, and Mali, Committee on Agriculture, Special Session, May 16, 2003 was revised in WTO, General Council, Poverty Reduction: Sectorial Initiative on Cotton: Wording of Paragraph 27 of the Revised Draft Cancun Ministerial Text: Communication from Benin, WT/GC/W/516, October 7, 2003. These documents can be retrieved from http://www.wto.org.

[965] Hanrahan "WTO Doha Round: Agricultural Negotiating Proposals" http://fpc.state.gov/documents/organization/57217.pdf (Accessed on 13/06/15).

financial compensation mechanism for cotton-exporting developing countries affected by the subsidies.[966] The problem of how to handle the cotton issue is unresolved.[967] In contrast to a stand-alone sectoral initiative as proposed by the C-4, the United States has advocated dealing with cotton issues as part of the comprehensive agricultural negotiations.[968]

5 2 1 2 Services

A critical element of the DDA is the negotiation pertaining to foreign trade in services.[969] Trade in services has been covered under multilateral rules only since 1995 with the entry into force of the General Agreement on Trade in Services (GATS) and of the Uruguay Round Agreements creating the WTO.[970] The negotiations on services in the DDA have two fundamental objectives. One objective is to reform the current GATS rules and principles. The second objective is for each member country to liberalize or open more of its service sectors to foreign competition.[971] The WTO services negotiations also began as part of the "built-in agenda" of the WTO and have been going on for more than five years. However, as with the negotiations in agriculture and other areas, the services negotiations have proceeded slowly with missed deadlines and few results. As indicated below, the EU has linked its offer on market access for agricultural products to concessions on services by the advanced developing countries such as G-20 members.[972]

5 2 1 3 Non-Agricultural Market Access (NAMA)

In the Doha Declaration, trade ministers agreed to negotiations to reduce or eliminate tariffs on industrial or primary products, with a focus on "tariff peaks, high tariffs, and tariff escalation."[973] Tariff peaks are considered to be tariff rates greater than 15% and often protect sensitive products from foreign competition.[974] Tariff escalation is the practice of increasing tariffs as value is added

---

[966] See Hanrahan 2005.

[967] *Ibid.*

[968] For details, see The African Cotton Initiative and WTO Agriculture Negotiations, CRS Report RS21712.

[969] See Trade in Services: The Doha Development Agenda Negotiations and U.S. Goals, CRS Report RL33085

[970] WTO, "The General Agreement on Trade in Services (GATS): objectives, coverage and disciplines" https://www.wto.org/english/tratop_e/serv_e/gatsqa_e.htm (Accessed on 14/06/15)

[971] *Ibid.*

[972] *Ibid.*

[973] NAMA negotiations are discussed in World Trade Organization Negotiations: The Doha Development Agenda CRS Report RL32060 October 7 2005.

[974] Patrick "Protectionism? Tariffs and other Barriers to Trade" http://www.oecd-ilibrary.org/docserver/download/0109121ec005.pdf?expires=1438165083&id=id&accname=guest&checksum=79CB8E1796A8D6BE466B12C1A02FD732 (Accessed on 16/06/15).

to a commodity.[975] The talks are also seeking to reduce the incidence of non-tariff barriers, which include import licensing, quotas and other quantitative import restrictions, conformity assessment procedures, and technical barriers to trade.[976] The sectoral elimination of tariffs for specific product groups such as lumber has also been a focus of the negotiations. Negotiators accepted the concept of less than full reciprocity in tariff reductions for developing and least-developed countries.[977]

Doha negotiators agreed to reach modalities for the reduction or elimination of tariffs and non-tariff barriers by the end of May 2003.[978] This deadline and subsequent ones were not met. In the July 2004 Framework Agreement, negotiators adopted the use of a non-linear tariff reduction formula (one that would reduce higher tariffs more than lower ones), but in the meantime no agreement has been reached on a specific formula or coefficients.[979] The framework agreement stipulated that tariff reductions would be calculated from bound, rather than the applied, tariff rates.[980] Reductions in unbound tariff lines would be calculated from twice the currently applied rate.[981]

5 2 1 4 Rules

The Doha Declaration included an objective of "clarifying and improving disciplines" under the WTO Agreements on Antidumping (AD) and on Subsidies and Countervailing Measures (SCM).[982] The United States sought to keep negotiations on trade remedies outside of the Doha Round, but found many WTO partners insistent on including them for discussion. US negotiators did manage to insert language asserting that "...basic concepts, principles and effectiveness of these Agreements and their instruments and objectives" would be preserved. However, Congressional leaders were highly critical of this concession by US trade negotiators.[983]

---

975 Patrick "Protectionism? Tariffs and other Barriers to Trade" http://www.oecd-ilibrary.org/docserver/download/0109121ec005.pdf?expires=1438165083&id=id&accname=guest&checksum=79CB8E1796A8D6BE466B12C1A02FD732 (Accessed on 16/06/15).

976 Fergusson The World Trade Organization: The Non-Agricultural Market Access (NAMA) Negotiations. http://international-trade-reports.blogspot.com/2011/02/world-trade-organization-non.html (Accessed on 17/06/15).

977 Mathur "Multilateral Trading System and Developing Countries: Prospects and Perspectives with Special Reference to India". http://www.cid.harvard.edu/cidtrade/Papers/mathur.pdf (Accessed on 17/06/15).

978 WTO "The Doha Declaration Explained" https://www.wto.org/english/tratop_e/dda_e/dohaexplained_e.htm (Accessed on 17/06/06/15).

979 *Ibid.*

980 *Ibid.*

981 Bound rates are the rates permitted, while applied rates are those actually used. Applied rates are generally lower than bound rates.

982 See WTO *et al* "Antidumping Issues in the Doha Development Agenda.

983 Zoellick "Stance on Trade Remedy in WTO Provokes Criticism." 2001 *Inside US* 2.

The United States primarily has been on the defensive in the rules talks. Many countries have attacked the use of antidumping actions by the United States and other developed nations as disguised protectionism.[984] However, many developing countries are now using antidumping actions themselves, which may goad some countries to re-examine the necessity for discipline. Most of the proposals on trade remedies focus on providing more specificity or restrictions to the AD/SCM Agreements in terms of definitions and procedures. However, no agreements have been reached, even on what is to be negotiated.[985]

5 2 1 5 Other Negotiating Issues

A number of other issues are on the agenda of the Doha Round.[986] These include a review of dispute settlement procedures, a number of specific issues of interest to developing countries for example, access to patented medicines, implementation of existing WTO agreements, changes in special and differential treatment provisions, and trade facilitation which refers generally to harmonizing and streamlining customs procedures among WTO members.[987]

5 3 ROLE OF DEVELOPING COUNTRIES IN AGRICULTURAL NEGOTIATIONS

The active participation of developing countries in the Doha Round distinguishes it from previous multilateral trade rounds held under the auspices of the General Agreement on Tariffs and Trade (GATT), the predecessor of the WTO.[988] During the Uruguay Round, an agreement between the United States and the EU on agricultural issues in 1992 paved the way for a successful conclusion of this last GATT round.[989] However, a US-EU joint proposal on agriculture during the 2003 Cancun Ministerial meeting was greeted with strong opposition from a group of developing countries.[990] This group, led by Brazil, India, and China, known as the G-20, has remained together since Cancun and is playing a key role in the Doha agricultural negotiations.[991] The G-20 was first among the major players in the Doha Round to offer a proposal on agricultural modalities in

[984] See Zoellick 2001. Also see Palmeter *The WTO as a Legal System: Essays on International Trade Law and Policy* (2003)

[985] *Ibid.*

[986] See the Doha declaration.

[987] *Ibid.*

[988] Hanrahan, "WTO Doha Round: Agricultural Negotiating Proposals" http://fpc.state.gov/documents/organization/57217.pdf (Accessed on 13/06/15).

[989] Hassan "Agreement on Agriculture in the Uruguay Round of GATT: From Punta Este to Marrakesh" 1996 *Agricultural Economics* 30.

[990] See CRS Report RL32053 Agriculture in the WTO September 30 2003.

[991] Zeng *China and Global Trade Governance: China's First Decade in the World Trade* (2013) generally.

advance of the Hong Kong meeting, and its proposal has become a benchmark for evaluating other, developed country proposals.[992]

Not only are the more advanced developing countries like the G-20 members, but also the least developed countries (LDCs) are participating actively in the Doha negotiations. The African cotton initiative, first introduced during the Cancun Ministerial, is an example of the LDCs attempting to use multilateral trade negotiations to accomplish their policy objectives. The LDCs also were instrumental in blocking an overall agreement at Cancun when they rejected an EU proposal to enlarge the negotiating agenda to include discussion of the so-called "Singapore issues" of trade facilitation, competition policy, investment, and transparency in government procurement. Subsequent agreement to limit negotiations of Singapore issues to just one, trade facilitation, was a victory for the LDCs.

5 3 1 US Economic and Agricultural Interests

According to several economic analyses, further liberalization of world trade in the Doha Round would provide economic gains for developing and developed countries alike.[993] A World Bank study estimates that "a deal to lower global trade barriers could add more than $500 billion a year to global incomes by 2015."[994] A University of Michigan study estimates that world incomes would increase by $613 billion with reductions in world agricultural, industrial, and services trade barriers.[995] Such analyses illustrate the potential impacts of trade liberalization; real outcomes, though, may not match the studies' results if their assumptions are not matched by the actual reductions in barriers in the negotiated agreements.[996]

Much of US agriculture would be expected to benefit from further multilateral trade liberalization, but some US products might face stiffer foreign competition at home or in third-country

[992] Ismail "From the Hong Kong WTO Ministerial Conference to the Suspension of the Negotiations. Developing Countries Re-claim the Development Content of the WTO Doha Round" https://www.wto.org/...e/.../ismail_from_hong_kong_to_suspension.doc (Accessed on 19/06/15).

[993] World Bank *Global Economic Prospects: Realizing the Development Promise of the Doha Agenda* 2004 at http://www.worldbank.org/prospects/gep2004/full.pdf (Accessed on 16/06/15) School of Public Policy, CGE Modeling and Analysis of Multilateral and Regional Negotiating Options, 2001 at http://www.spp.umich.edu/rsie/workingpapers/wp.html. (Accessed on 16/06/15).

[994] *Ibid.*

[995] Hanrahan "Agriculture in the WTO Doha Round: The Framework Agreement and Next Steps" http://congressionalresearch.com/RS21905/document.php?study=Agriculture+in+the+WTO+Doha+Round+The+Framework+Agreement+and+Next+Steps (Accessed on 19/06/15).

[996] *Ibid.*

markets.[997] Benefits to US agriculture could include increased market access through tariff reduction or expanded market access quotas, not only in developed but also in the fast-growing developing country markets.[998] Competitive conditions for US agricultural exports could improve with the elimination of export subsidies, especially vis-a-vis the EU which accounts for about 90% of the world's agricultural export subsidies.[999] US agriculture could also benefit from the elimination of trade-distorting practices of State Trading Enterprises (STEs), such as the Canadian Wheat Board.[1000]

Agricultural trade liberalization also could impose adjustment burdens on some agricultural sectors, including some commodity sectors in developed countries.[1001] Particularly vulnerable to increased import competition could be such products as sugar, dairy, and livestock products. The designation of such commodities as sensitive and therefore exempt from large tariff reductions, as provided in the framework agreement, could mitigate adjustment effects that might ensue from liberalization.[1002]

If DDA negotiations do result in a trade agreement, then the US Congress would presumably take up legislation to implement it under US Trade Promotion Authority (TPA), or fast-track procedures.[1003] Under fast-track, if the President meets the trade negotiating objectives established in the legislation and satisfies consultation and notification requirements, then the US Congress would consider legislation to implement a trade agreement with limited debate, no amendments, and with an up-or-down vote. TPA, however, covers trade agreements signed by July 1, 2007, the effective deadline for US participation in the DDA round and for congressional consideration of implementing legislation. That time frame also coincides with the expiration of the 2002 Farm bill

---

[997] Hanrahan "WTO Doha Round: Agricultural Negotiating Proposal" http://fpc.state.gov/documents/organization/57217.pdf (Accessed on 19/06/15).

[998] Thompson "The WTO Trade Negotiations: Why the Emphasis on Development?" 2005. http://ageconsearch.umn.edu/bitstream/37505/2/apb%2005-01.pdf (Accessed on 15/06/15).

[999] *Ibid.*

[1000] Koo "Effects of the Canadian wheat board on the US Wheat Industry" http://www.researchgate.net/publication/23514095_effects_of_the_canadian_wheat_board_on_the_u.s._wheat_industry (Accessed on 15/06/15).

[1001] Ray "World Bank Study: Trade liberalization would shut down two-thirds of EU's grain and oilseed production" 2004 viewed at http://www.extension.iastate.edu/agdm/articles/others/RayJano4.htm. (Accessed on 17/06/15)

[1002] Hanrahan *ibid.*

[1003] Fergusson "Trade Promotion Authority (TPA) and the Role of Congress in Trade Policy" https://fas.org/sgp/crs/misc/RL33743.pdf (Accessed on 19/06/15).

in 2007. Farm bill changes may be needed to meet US commitments in a final DDA agreement on agriculture.

5 3 2 The Demise of the 2008 Geneva Ministerial Conference

Pascal Lamy (Director-General, World Trade Organization) declared the resumption of the stalled negotiations in February 2007 after trade ministers from major WTO members informally gathered at the Davos World Economic Forum in January 2007 and recommitted themselves to further negotiations.[1004] As the year 2008 dawned, the agricultural negotiations emerged with some significant developments as the Chair improved the agricultural modalities' text with each new draft, although the NAMA negotiation proved to be a tougher process.[1005] Chairs in both the agricultural sector, Crawford Falconer, and NAMA, Don Stephenson, issued a series of drafts in February, May, and July of 2008 which identified areas of convergences and divergences.[1006] These drafts were to provide negotiators with simplified options for modalities.[1007]

When the WTO's head, Pascal Lamy, summoned trade ministers to Geneva in the summer of 2008, many cautiously predicted a successful deal on modalities.[1008] Most negotiators felt compelled to complete the Doha Round in the foreseeable future, especially considering the global financial turmoil.[1009] Nonetheless, once the actual negotiation began, the general pace turned out to be rather slow-going.[1010] After days of negotiation, no clear signs of progress emerged. At long last, on the sixth day, a ray of hope shone over the stalemated negotiations.[1011] On the verge of collapse in the talks, Lamy managed to persuade negotiators to continue by presenting a critical "package

1004 Lamy Director-General World Trade Organization, Informal TNC Meeting at the Level of Head of Delegation, Chairman's Remarks, http://www.wto.org/english/ news_e/news07_e/job07_12_e.doc. (Accessed on 17/06/15).

1005 See Bridges Weekly Trade News, Slow Progress on Industrial Goods Talks in Final Push to Ministerial, 2008, available at http://ictsd.org/downloads/bridgesweekly/bridgesweekly12-25.pdf. (Accessed on 16/07/15).

1006 For a synopsis of these drafts, see Bhala, "Doha Round Schisms: Numerous, Technical and Deep" 2008. http://lawecommons.luc.edu/cgi/viewcontent.cgi?article=1057&context=lucilr. (Accessed on 20/06/15).

1007 Bridges Weekly Trade News, "Chair of WTO AG Talks Says New Draft Text Will Simplify Options for Ministers" 2008, at 2, available at http://ictsd.org/downloads/bridgesweekly/bridgesweekly12-25.pdf. Regarding the most recent Doha draft text, see World Trade Organization, "The July 2008 Package" available at http://www.wto.org/english/tratop_e/dda_e/meet08_e.htm. (Accessed on 22/06/15).

1008 Bridges Daily "Geneva Mini-Ministerial: 'Now or Never' For Real This Time?" at 1, available at http://ictsd.org/downloads/ 2008/07/bridges-daily-update-21-july1.pdf.

1009 World Trade Organization Day 1: Ministers begin final effort to agree blueprints of deal, 2008, http://www.wto.org/english/news_e/news08_e/meet08_summary_21july_e.htm. (Accessed on 23/06/15).

1010 *Ibid.*

1011 *Ibid.*

of elements,"[1012] which might have been coined the Lamy Draft. This deal-salvaging package was nothing more than a deliberate compromise proposal based on the most recent draft modalities on agriculture and NAMA.[1013]

What Lamy did was to present some concrete headline numbers on several major sticking issues, such as farm subsidies and industrial tariffs, in an articulated fashion out of the intense consultations among the seven key negotiating parties (United States, the EU, Australia, Japan, China, Brazil, and India). According to the Lamy Draft, the United States would cut the current bound level of agricultural subsidies ($48 billion) to $14 billion[1014] (which was still much higher than the actual spending in the previous year of $7 billion), and the EU would cut its agricultural subsidies by 80 percent, to approximately €22 billion.[1015] As to market access, the Draft called for a 70 percent reduction for the highest farm tariffs (above 75 percent) of developed countries.[1016] At the same time, the Draft allowed developed countries to designate 4 percent of their agricultural tariff lines as "sensitive products" which are exempt from the aforementioned tariff cut.[1017]

Under the Draft, developing countries were also allowed to shelter 12 percent of all covered products (special products) from the normal tariff reduction.[1018] As to the special safeguard mechanism (SSM), developing countries could use it only when an import surges by more than 40 percent in volume.[1019] As to NAMA coefficients, the maximum level of tariffs would be 8 percent for developed countries and 20, 22 or 25 percent for developing countries, depending on three different "flexibility mechanisms."[1020] Developing countries could choose from these flexibility mechanisms to protect some of their strategic products more than others within these limits.[1021] Finally, the Draft proposed to hold the Services Signalling Conference to gather voluntary

[1012] World Trade Organization Lamy Presents "Package of Elements" from Consultations with Ministers, July 2008, http://www.wto.org/english/news_e/news08_e/meet08_chair_26july08_e.htm. (Accessed on 24/06/15).
[1013] *Ibid.*
[1014] International Centre for Trade and Sustainable Development WTO Mini-Ministerial Evades Collapse, As Lamy Finds 'Way Forward,' 2008, at 1, available at http://ictsd.org/downloads/2008/07/daily-update-issue-6-template.pdf. (Accessed on 17/06/15).
[1015] International Centre for Trade and Sustainable Development WTO Mini-Ministerial Evades Collapse, As Lamy Finds 'Way Forward,' 2008,at 1 available at http://ictsd.org/downloads/2008/07/daily-update-issue-6-template.pdf. (Accessed on 15/06/15).
[1016] *Ibid.*
[1017] *Ibid.*
[1018] *Ibid.*
[1019] *Ibid.*
[1020] *Ibid.*
[1021] *Ibid.*

commitments in service-sector liberalization from developing countries in an effort to give some comfort to developed countries.[1022]

Frustratingly, this rather "unexpected momentum" soon evaporated as the United States wrangled with India and China over the SSM and cotton.[1023] India maintained a recalcitrant stance against tightening the eligibility of the SSM, while China severely criticized the United States for pressuring it to open its cotton market as a condition to cut the US cotton subsidies. On the ninth and final day of the talks, the core negotiating group (Australia, US, EU, Japan, China, India, and Brazil) and the G-33 bloc of food-importing developing countries (India, China, Indonesia, etc.) failed to close their gaps on some details of the SSM.[1024] Other than this holdup, the deal was close to completion because negotiators had managed to reach a consensus on nearly all other sticking points.[1025]

Jagdish Bhagwati blamed the United States as the "central spoiler" of the 2008 Geneva Ministerial Conference.[1026] According to Bhagwati, the United States refused to significantly reduce its trade-distorting farm subsidies which are "universally recognized as intolerable," while it attacked India for requesting enhanced safeguards for its mostly subsistent, rural farmers.[1027] Ironically, U.S. Trade Representative (USTR) Susan Schwab, at the time, probably did a service to the WTO since

---

[1022] International Centre for Trade and Sustainable Development WTO Mini-Ministerial Evades Collapse, As Lamy Finds 'Way Forward,' 2008,at 1 available at http://ictsd.org/downloads/2008/07/daily-update-issue-6-template.pdf. (Accessed on 15/06/15).

[1023] Financial Times, "Disputes Threaten Doha Round", July 29, 2008, available at http://www.ftchinese.com/story/001020872/en.

[1024] Bridges "WTO Mini-Ministerial Ends in Collapse" http://ictsd.org/downloads/2008/07/daily-update-issue-6-template.pdf (Accessed on 15/06/15). The United States insisted that an importing country might impose these emergency tariffs above the current WTO limits determined at the previous Uruguay Round only when imports increase more than by 40% over the preceding three years, while India wanted the trigger to be 15%. Daniel Pruzin, Trade Officials Voice Doubts on Push by Lamy to Revive Doha Round Talks, 25 Int'l Trade Rep. (BNA) 1256 (Sept. 4, 2008). Yet India argued that with a 40% threshold the SSM would be inoperable "because India's ability to monitor its imports of individual products is so haphazard that by the time the government detected a 40% import surge farmers would already be committing suicide en masse." Paul Blustein, The Nine-Day Misadventure of the Most Favored Nations: How the WTO's Doha Round Negotiations Went Awry in July 2008, Brookings Institute., Dec. 5, 2008, at 10, available at http://www.brookings.edu/articles/2008/1205_trade_blustein.aspx. (Accessed on 14/06/15). Nonetheless, the United States was adamant with this 40% threshold, permitting no compromise; it also refused Pascal Lamy's alternative proposal which would have replaced this numerical trigger with an expert review on "demonstrable harm," which India accepted.

[1025] World Trade Organization Day 9: Talks collapse despite progress on a list of issues, 2008, http://www.wto.org/english/news_e/news08_e/meet08_summary_29july_e.htm (Accessed on 11/06/15).

[1026] Jagdish Bhagwati "The Selfish Hegemon Must Offer a New Deal on Trade" 2008 *Financial Times* at 11.

[1027] *Ibid.*

any deal sealed in Geneva but killed later in Washington might have dealt a more severe blow to the WTO.[1028]

The Doha Round talks entered into yet another dormant stage after the Geneva debacle of the summer of 2008. Although during September 2009 in Pittsburgh, the G-20 leaders pledged, yet again, to conclude the Doha Round by the end of 2010,[1029] no genuine breakthrough, such as an agreement on the modalities, had been made by October 2009.[1030] The Geneva Ministerial Meeting in December 2009 ended without any substantial progress, merely reaffirming the 2010 deadline.[1031] All in all, the Doha Round still remains a failure.[1032]

5 4 REFLECTIONS ON DOHA'S FAILURE: WHAT WENT WRONG?

The question of what caused Doha's failure is debated among scholars due to the complexity of the negotiations. There may have been a unique context for the Doha Round which has militated against smooth negotiation in a consistent manner. For example, different expectations for the Doha Round between the developing world and the developed world may have complicated the entire process of negotiation.[1033] Adverse election cycles in major economies, as well as the recent global economic recession, may have also rendered any concessions (liberalization commitments) politically unpalatable.[1034] Or, as a more immediate cause, an unfortunate discordant chemistry among major negotiators may have triggered the demise.[1035] At any rate, a sobering exploration of causes and contributing factors for Doha's failure seems to be in order to alter the direction of future trade talks toward a successful round.[1036]

1028 See Blustein 2008.

1029 Palmar *etal* G-20 Leaders Pledge Quick Action on Doha Deal, 2009, http://www.reuters.com/article/idUSTRE58O5MO20090925. (Accessed on 13/06/15).

1030 Daniel Pruzin, WTO Chief Warns 2010 Deadline for Doha Hard to Meet without 'Serious Acceleration,'

1031 See WTO Ministerial Lifts Hopes for Doha, But Skepticism Lingers, *Bridges Weekly Trade News Digest* 2009, page 1–2. http://deepblue.lib.umich.edu/bitstream/handle/2027.42/94073/hopewell_1.pdf?sequence=1&isAllowed=y (Accessed on 10/06/15).

1032 The most recent attempt by negotiators to "take stock" until March 2010 to meet the end of 2010 deadline seems to have faltered, darkening the prospects of completing the Round by the end of 2010. See Jonathan Lynn, Ministers Lynn , "Won't Meet on Doha Prospects Soon", 2010, http://in.reuters.com/article/businessNews/idINIndia-46329820100220. (Accessed 24/06/15).

1033 Cho A Long and Winding Road: The Doha Round Negotiation in the World Trade Organization Available at http://scholarship.kentlaw.iit.edu/cgi/viewcontent.cgi?article=1161&context=fac_schol (Accessed on 25/06/15).

1034 *Ibid.*

1035 See Blustein 2008 depicting vehement negotiation styles of negotiators from major WTO members.

1036 See Cho 2009.

5 4 1 The Primary Cause: Irreconcilable Agendas of Development and Mercantilism

As discussed above, the Doha Round was meant to be a development round. The Doha Ministerial Declaration (2001) states that:

> "International trade can play a major role in the promotion of economic development and the alleviation of poverty. We recognize the need for all our peoples to benefit from the increased opportunities and welfare gains that the multilateral trading system generates. The majority of WTO members are developing countries. We seek to place their needs and interests at the heart of the Work Programme adopted in this Declaration."[1037]

However, the initial development focus of the Doha Round quickly blurred and faded. Some observers from developed countries even believe that the development label tended to distance powerful stakeholders (businesses and industries) who might think the Doha trade talks would be mere charity and thus find little incentive to participate.[1038] They argue that developed countries basically perceive the Doha Round as yet another commercial negotiation in which they could press for market opening by big developing countries, such as China, India, and Brazil.[1039] For example, the United States conditioned the reduction of its farm subsidies firmly on other members' concessions, not only on the EU's reduction of farm tariffs but also on developing countries' (such as China and India) disarmament of special protection for their crops, even though this special protection was for no mercantilist purposes (such as food security and livelihood concerns).[1040] While leaders of developed countries continued to advocate the vital cause of development, this rhetoric had little consequence at the negotiation table.[1041] In the meantime, developing countries refused to make concessions before developed countries tabled substantial

[1037] See the Doha Declaration para 2.

[1038] See Christy 'Round and 'Round We Go' Summer 2008, at page 19-24 contending that "affixing the label 'development' to the Round may have warmed a few hearts, but it has not filled any bellies." http://www.jstor.org/stable/40210176?seq=1#page_scan_tab_contents. (Accessed on 19/06/15). Evenett, "What Can Researchers Learn from the Suspension of the Doha Round Negotiations in 2006?" Observing that the ambiguous and confusing "development" mandate of the Doha Round discouraged corporate executives from attending WTO Ministerial Conference. http://core.ac.uk/download/pdf/6710675.pdf (Accessed on 25/06/15).

[1039] International Center for Trade and Sustainable Development "Political Positioning Dominates Opening Day of WTO Talks", www.researchgate.net/...WTO.../0deec528bc2f325b0a000000.pdf (Accessed on 27/06/15).

[1040] International Center for Trade and Sustainable Development, "G-6 Ministers Agree to Work to Conclude Doha Round by End of 2007" https://www.fas.org/sgp/crs/misc/RL32060.pdf (Accessed on 17/07/15).

[1041] See Beattie claiming that there was a "bizarre disconnect between the enthusiastic rhetoric from G8 leaders in Gleneagles on pushing ahead with trade talks and intransigence from negotiators that has brought the Doha round almost to a halt".

commitments in the area of agricultural protection.[1042] It was this brinkmanship that frequently deadlocked the negotiation process.[1043]

At the heart of the developing-developed country clash in the Doha Round laid the domestic politics of rich countries which simply could not accommodate the cause of development on political terms. In the US, the heavily battered Bush administration was simply incapable of managing protectionist pressures from Congress in its lame-duck period. In a highly symbolic gesture, in April 2007 fifty-eight US Senators jointly sent a warning letter to US President Bush stating that "our trading partners have refused to offer significant tariff reductions, and they insist on exceptions for sensitive and special products that will render meaningless the modest tariff reduction formulas they have proposed."[1044]

Likewise, Charles Grassley, a powerful US Senator from a farming state, urged that the US negotiators "pack their bags and come home" if other trading partners refused to grant US businesses substantial market access in agricultural and industrial goods.[1045] Mindful of these anti-trade sentiments in Congress, the USTR desired substantial concessions from trading partners and thus rejected any modest package, such as the "Doha-lite" proposal.[1046] Delegates from major US special interest groups, such as the American Farm Bureau and National Association of Manufacturers, were actually stationed in Geneva as they monitored and even instructed US negotiators.[1047] Such circumstances squeezed the negotiation space of the USTR which was preoccupied with the idea of sinking a deal in Geneva rather than failing to pass it in D.C.[1048] Naturally, these mercantilist stances by developed countries irked developing countries. Indian

---

[1042] See Bridges Weekly Trade News Digest July 20, 2005 at 2, Members Try to Convert Dalian Effort into Negotiations Breakthrough, (noting insistence by developing nations that some of their demands be met in agriculture before moving forward on NAMA, and citing "demands that the EU reduce subsidies and open its markets to foreign farm products").

[1043] See The Doha Round Cruising Along 2005 at 12 claiming that brinkmanship would once have led to a last-minute deal, "but the sheer breadth of the current round of trade talks, coupled with the involvement of no less than 148 countries, forecloses that option".

[1044] Letter to George W. Bush, President, United States of America (Apr. 12, 2007), https://conrad.senate.gov/issues/statements/agriculture/070412_WTO_Ag_Letter.pdf (Accessed on 20/07/15); Also see also Bhala, Doha Round Schisms, at 12 discussing the provisions on special products.

[1045] Palmer "US Farm Programmes Spared as WTO Talks Collapse", 2008, http://www.reuters.com/article/idUKL950898920080729. (Accessed on 19/07/15).

[1046] Cho "The WTO Doha Round Negotiation: Suspended Indefinitely" 2006, http://www.asil.org/insights060905.cfm (Accessed 17/01/15).

[1047] See Blustein 2008 pg 11.

[1048] *Ibid.*

Commerce Minister Kamal Nath commented that rich countries pursued only "commercial prosperity."[1049]

In particular, lavish farm protection in major developed countries, such as the United States and the EU nations, continued to undermine the DDA as the negotiation progressed. Under the EU's Common Agricultural Policy, big agribusinesses in France alone receive more than $10 billion a year.[1050] The EU's biofuels policy created a tariff equivalent of 1,000 percent for controversial environmental benefits.[1051] In the US, the renewal of the highly protectionist-oriented Farm Bill in the middle of the Doha Round negotiations disheartened many delegates.[1052] This ignominious bill, which "rewards rich farmers who do not need the help while doing virtually nothing to help the world's hungry, who need all the help they can get," was lambasted by some US media outlets.[1053] As Victor Davis Hanson trenchantly observed, lavish farm subsidies in the US are "transparent election-cycle harvests for farm-state politicians, who have small constituencies but exercise outsized national political clout."[1054] In a six-year cycle, US politicians have masqueraded this special interest legislation by phony rationalizations, as seen in the Freedom to Farm Act,[1055] the Farm Security and Rural Investment Act,[1056] and the Farm, Nutrition and Bioenergy Act.[1057]

Farm protectionism in the US and EU generates enormous distortion in the global crop market beyond the level which might be remedied through occasional WTO litigation.[1058] The fixation

---

[1049] Reuters "Instant Analysis Implications of the Failure of WTO Talks" 2008 http://www.reuters.com/article/idUKL928387320080729. (Accessed on 16/07/15). Admittedly, South-South relations were not without tensions in the Doha trade talks. For example, Brazil, one of the main agricultural exporting countries, criticized India for their recalcitrant position on the SSM. Other agricultural exporting countries, such as Argentina and Thailand, also opposed a separate exception of "special products" under which importing countries can protect certain agricultural sectors for food and livelihood security and rural development. See also Lynn, "Developing Countries Split over WTO Farm Protection" 2008, http://www.reuters.com/article/idUKL748592720080728 (Accessed on 23/07/15) discussing the division between poorer countries over proposals for a new trade deal. However, such tensions were negligible compared to deep-rooted North-South conflicts.

[1050] Messerlin "A Doha Deal Would Aid Many European Farmers" 2008 at 9. http://www.ft.com/cms/s/0/9424c1de-5667-11dd-8686-000077b07658.html (Accessed on 18/07/15).

[1051] *Ibid.*

[1052] Ryan "New Farm Bill Seen Adding Fodder for Trade Feud" 2008 http://www.reuters.com/article/idUSN0953063020080511 (Accessed on 24/07/15).

[1053] See New York Times, "A Disgraceful Farm Bill" 2008. http://www.nytimes.com/2008/05/16/opinion/16fri3.html?_r=0 . (Accessed on 10/07/15).

[1054] Victor Davis Hanson "Harvesting Money in a Hungry World" 1 Aug 2008 *New York Times* generally.

[1055] Freedom to Farm Act 1996.

[1056] Farm Security and Rural Investment Act 2002.

[1057] Farm, Nutrition and Bioenergy Act 2008.

[1058] Cho "The Demise of Development in the Doha Round Negotiations" 2010 *Texas International Law Journal* 573.

by the G-33 bloc (food-importing developing countries) on the Special Safeguard Mechanism (SSM) originated mainly from rich countries' highly subsidized, and thus cheapened, crop.[1059] Under these circumstances, "any opening up of agriculture would be doubly difficult politically because exposing one's farmers to the impact of highly subsidized foreign producers is regarded as yielding to unfair trade."[1060] The Uruguay Round outcome enabled developed countries to continue their old practice of lavish farm subsidies, but deterred developing countries from invoking the special safeguard mechanism under the Agreement on Agriculture for technical reasons.[1061] This frustrated developing countries, who now want to fix this imbalance in the Doha Round.

In sum, different expectations over the Doha Round bred enormous tensions between the developing and the developed countries in the course of trade talks.[1062] While developed countries basically demanded from the developing world unreciprocated disarmament in agricultural protection under the DDA, the developed world still wanted to use the reduction of agricultural protection, if any, as a bargaining chip for reciprocal concessions from the developed world in areas of both agricultural and industrial market access.[1063]

5 4 2 The Secondary Cause: The Sterile Environment for Trade Talks

Apart from the aforementioned deep-rooted developing-developed country tensions, a blend of adverse factors has undermined the odds for a successful round. First, as most commentators noted, the recent domestic political situations of major negotiating parties, such as the US, EU, and India, have not been amenable to trade concessions, leading to a general lack of political support for a deal.[1064] Key elections were pending in the United States and India as delegates papered over the modalities. To make things worse, the Wall Street-born financial crisis quickly spread throughout the world and froze global trade, brewing protectionist sentiments.[1065] Amid

---

[1059] Bridges Daily Update "G-7 Talks on Special Safeguard Mechanism Inconclusive as Blame Game Heats Up" 2008 available at http://ictsd.org/i/wto/englishupdates/15018/.

[1060] Bhagwati, "How the Food Crisis Could Solve the Doha Round", 2008, at 9 http://www.ft.com/intl/cms/s/0/7021839c-40bb-11dd-bd48-0000779fd2ac.html#axzz3giSrDqtP (Accessed on 21/07/15).

[1061] Cho "The Demise of Development in the Doha Round Negotiations" 2010 *Texas International Law Journal*.

[1062] *Ibid.*

[1063] *Ibid.*

[1064] Cho "A Long and Winding Road: The Doha Round Negotiation in the World Trade Organization" 2009 Available at http://scholarship.kentlaw.iit.edu/cgi/viewcontent.cgi?article=1161&context=fac_schol (Accessed on 25/06/15).

[1065] *Ibid.*

this economic hardship, some politicians intensified their acerbic rhetoric against the Doha deal.[1066] For example, French President Nicolas Sarkozy stated that the EU Trade Commission's offer would destroy the European farm sector by reducing agricultural production by 20 percent and cutting 100,000 jobs.[1067]

Another negative factor was the absence of the US government's trade promotion authority (TPA), formerly known as "fast track authority."[1068] Without the TPA, passing the Doha deal in Congress would have been a very difficult, if not impossible, task for the lame-duck administration. The US negotiators, stripped of the TPA, had to grab a deal which could impress Congress, but major developing countries, such as Brazil and India, could not simply concede such a deal without a major reduction of US agricultural subsidies.[1069]

Moreover, the US proposal of cutting the trade-distorting subsidies to US$15 billion, if implemented, would have forced the United States to dilute agricultural protection bestowed by the new Farm Bill[1070] which had recently been passed over a presidential veto.[1071] This forecast seemed to have pushed the US negotiators to resist loosening the trigger threshold of the subsidies, which would have hampered US farmers' exports to emerging markets.[1072] Tom Harkin, chair of the US Senate agriculture committee, made it clear that this proposal was conditioned on enhanced access for US farmers to foreign markets.[1073]

5 5 THE DOHA FAILURE AS THE WTO'S LEGITIMACY CRISIS

The failure of the Doha Development Round is particularly ill-timed amid the global financial crisis.[1074] One recent study revealed that the global financial crisis will cut developing countries' income by US$750 billion before the end of 2009 and leave another 50 million people in abject

[1066] Cho "The Demise of Development in the Doha Round Negotiations" 2010 *Texas International Law Journal*.
[1067] *Ibid.*
[1068] Business Roundtable Trade Resource Center, Trade Promotion Authority (TPA) Is an Important Tool, http://trade.businessroundtable.org/trade_2006/tpa/important_tool.html (Accessed on 17/07/15).
[1069] Klapper "Blame High, Confidence Low as WTO Heads into Another" 2007. www.wtocenter.org.tw/SmartKMS/fileviewer?id=92208 (Accessed on 16/07/15).
[1070] Harkin "WTO Offer Could Affect 2008 Farm Bill Programs If Trade Talks Succeed" 2008, www.agriculture.com/ag/story.jhtml?storyid=/templatedata/ag/ story/data/1216993795055.xml.
[1071] Food Conservation, and Energy Act of 2008.
[1072] Beattie "Lamy Plan Spurs Optimism at Doha Talks" 2008, at 5. http://www.ft.com/intl/cms/s/0/9e83da1e-5a97-11dd-bf96-000077b07658.html (Accessed 17/07/15).
[1073] Beattie "US Offers to Reduce Farm Subsidy Limit to $15bn", 2008, at 8 http://www.ft.com/intl/cms/s/0/efada66c-584f-11dd-b02f-000077b07658.html#axzz3giSrDqtP (Accessed 23/07/15).
[1074] See Blustein 2008 observing that the "financial crisis has greatly magnified the import of Doha's failure".

poverty.[1075] Collateral damage to the world's poor, such as the decrease of foreign direct investment and remittances, may last long after rich countries start recovering economically.[1076] A Doha success would certainly mitigate such developmental impacts to a great extent, considering that its agricultural package is two or three times larger than that of the Uruguay Round.[1077] However, a Doha failure would reduce developing countries' agricultural exports by 11.5 percent.[1078]

It is also of serious concern that a systemic failure of the WTO representing the operationally sound multilateral trading system could inflict suffering on developing countries.[1079] The Doha failure is a WTO failure in that "commitment to free trade is weakening."[1080] The Doha failure would embolden protectionism by generating a "public impression that whoever opens their markets loses."[1081] Such sentiments have already emerged. For example, the EU has recently decided to pour lavish export refunds (subsidies) on its dairy farmers, despite the fact that such subsidies are clearly against the current Doha agricultural draft.[1082] The EU, which had originally planned to repeal such export refunds, took advantage of the legal vacuum created by the Doha deadlock.[1083]

Therefore, beyond any calculable welfare loss, the Doha failure might leave an irreversible systemic impact on the credibility of the WTO legal system.[1084] As the Doha undermines the

---

1075 Bridges Monthly How to Rescue the Global Economy?, 13 2009, available at http://ictsd.org/i/news/bridges/44278/ (Accessed on 10/07/15).

1076 WTO "Worried about Developing Economies" 2009. https://www.wto.org/english/tratop_e/devel_e/d1who_e.htm (Accessed on 14/07/15).

1077 Mandelson *Doha a Posteriori, in Agreeing And Implementing The Doha Round Of The WTO* Cambridge University Press 2008. Under the current Doha package on the table, trade distorting farms subsidies will be cut by 70–80%. Also see Lamy *supra.*

1078 Bouët "The Potential Cost of a Failed Doha Round" 2008, available at http://www.ifpri.org/sites/default/files/publications/ib56.pdf. (Accessed at 09/07/15).

1079 Keck "Special and Differential Treatment in the WTO: Why, When failure and How?" https://www.wto.org/english/res_e/reser_e/ersd200403_e.doc (Accessed on 21/10/15).

1080 Ferguson "How a Local Squall Might Become a Global Tempest" 2008, pg 9. http://www.ft.com/intl/cms/s/0/2056a192-649e-11dd-af61-0000779fd18c.html#axzz3giSrDqtP . (Accessed on 23/07/15).

1081 Dowling "WTO Failure Reflects Changing Global Power Relations, SPIEGEL ONLINE, July 30, 2008, http://www.spiegel.de/international/world/0,1518,569027,00.html. (Accessed on 19/07/15).

1082 Gamberoni "Trade Protection: Incipient but Worrisome Trends" 2009, at 2, available at http://siteresources.worldbank.org/INTRANETTRADE/Resources/239054-1126812419270/Trade_Note_37.pdf .

1083 Hunt "EU Subsidies to Wreak Havoc on Global Dairy Industry" 2009 www.tilj.org/content/journal/45/num3/Cho573.pdf ; quoting the Australian trade minister Simon Crean who stated that "if the Doha round is concluded, export subsidies will be eliminated".

1084 Hunt 2009.

WTO's legal shield, powerful countries tend to downplay the WTO's authority.[1085] This would be highly detrimental to the less powerful developing countries.[1086] Under these circumstances, a small developing country's victory against a big developed country in the WTO tribunal might seem to be less secure.[1087]

It is imperative to fully realize the symbolic and dynamic impact which delivering the development round could bring to the WTO. Most quantitative studies on the welfare gains which a successful completion of the Doha Round might generate to developing countries are based on a rather static model.[1088] This is why some studies forecast fairly limited benefits to developing countries from a Doha success.[1089] However, such a model, by design, does not take into account long-term, institutional ramifications for development resulting from Doha success.[1090] Such institutional ramifications include enhanced credibility of trade for economic growth in the LDCs, further political impetus for trade liberalization, both unilateral and in developed country trade liberalization and increased domestic and foreign investment in developing countries' lifeline industries, such as agriculture.[1091]

In addition to the Doha Round's importance in staving off protectionism during the current financial crisis, it is inextricably linked to the WTO's moral agenda.[1092] Moral foundations for delivering the development round can be located in multiple sources.[1093] The idea of a "duty to assist" less fortunate nations is established in well-known literature[1094] and has been applied in the

---

1085 Hunt 2009.

1086 Elliott "Does the Doha Round Matter?" Current History, 2009. 39-42.

1087 Blustein 2008.

1088 Taylor "Projected Benefits of the Doha Round Hinge on Misleading Trade Models", 2007, at 2, available at http://www.newschool.edu/cepa/publications/policynotes/Doha%20Policy%20Note% 20Final%2003_12_07.pdf (Accessed on 15/06/15).

1089 Zepeda "The Impact of The Doha Round on Kenya" 2009 predicting that a Doha success would bring a negligible or small boost to Kenya's GDP. http://carnegieendowment.org/files/impact_doha_kenya.pdf (Accessed on 23/07/15).

1090 Tokarick "Trade Issues in the Doha Round: Dispelling Some Misconceptions" 2006, http://www.imf.org/external/pubs/ft/ pdp/2006/pdp04.pdf, (Accessed on 17/06/15) arguing that the World Bank's forecast of small scale benefits to developing countries from the Doha success US$20 billion in 2015 failed to fully appreciate dynamic effects of trade liberalization, which are hard to quantify.

1091 Kandiero "Supporting the World Trade Organization Negotiations: Looking beyond Market Access", 2009, observing that one of the benefits from the Doha Round to African countries is to "lock-in" domestic reforms. http://vox.cepr.org/index.php?q=node/4295 (Accessed on 11/07/15).

1092 *Ibid.*

1093 *Ibid.*

1094 Rawls *The Law of Peoples* 106 1999. Well-ordered peoples have a duty to assist burdened societies.

trade context.[1095] Given what developing countries potentially stand to gain from a successful development round,[1096] it is important for developed countries to fully realize that developing countries' effective access to the former's markets is a critical ingredient for the latter's development.[1097]

The moral failure of a Doha breakdown is further highlighted by the developmentally unsound outcome of the previous Uruguay Round.[1098] Under the Uruguay Round, the concessions of developing countries (such as the inclusion of trade in services and trade-related intellectual property rights) materialized immediately, while those borne by developed countries (such as further liberalization in the areas of agriculture and textiles) "remained to be negotiated."[1099] The DDA was the widely accepted acknowledgement that the WTO system "owed something to developing countries."[1100] The Doha Round, if it fails to address this unfair legacy, will leave an indelible mark of moral failure on the WTO.[1101]

5 6 A DISCUSSION ON THE BALI PACKAGE

After continuous negotiations with less than optimum outcomes, the Bali Ministerial marked the first substantive breakthrough for the WTO since the launch of the Doha Round in 2001.[1102] In December 2013, the multilateral trading system was resuscitated when the members of the WTO agreed on a package that included three important issues under the Doha Development Agenda

---

[1095] See Garcia *Trade, Inequality, and Justice: Toward a Liberal Theory of Just Trade* 2003 at 107 arguing for the special treatment of developing countries along Rawlsian lines, and advocating for Special and Differential Treatment (SDT) as a solution. However, Pauwelyn, Book Review 2005 (reviewing Garcia *Trade, Inequality, and Justice: Toward A Liberal Theory of Just Trade* 2003), critics Garcia's application of Rawls' difference principle to trade in terms of his focus on the allocation of natural endowments as ex ante disadvantages to developing countries, but agrees with the premise that developing countries deserve special treatment and suggesting equal free trade, as opposed to SDT, as a better solution. The concept of a moral obligation between states in trade related matters is worthy of a much more detailed discussion but is beyond the scope of this article.

[1096] Taylor "Projecting Benefits of the Doha Round Hinge on Misleading Trade Models" 2007, at 2, available at http://www.newschool.edu/cepa/publications/policynotes/Doha%20Policy%20Note%20Final%2003_12_07.pdf. (Accessed on 24/07/15).

[1097] Stiglitz "Two Principles for the Next Round or, How to Bring Developing Countries in From the Cold," 2000 *World Economics* at 437-452.

[1098] Cho "The Demise of Development in the Doha Round Negotiations" 2010 *Texas International Law Journal.*

[1099] Ostry *Asymmetry in the Uruguay Round and in the Doha Round in Developing Countries in the WTO*, (2009) 105-109. Ostry labeled the Uruguay Round deal as a "Bum Deal" for developing countries.

[1100] Finger *Trade and Development: Systematic Lessons from WTO Experience with Implementation, Trade Facilitation, and Aid for Trade, in Developing Countries in the WTO Legal System* (2009) 75–90.

[1101] Cho 2010.

[1102] Mukumba "Unpacking the Bali Package A Snapshot of the Bali Ministerial Decisions of the WTO Members" 2014 *Centre for International Trade, Economics & Environment* 8-13.

(DDA).[1103] The Bali Agreement was adopted by the WTO on December 7, 2013. The agreement was struck after the United States gave in to India's demand on food security and agreed to a temporary peace clause to shield the food subsidy programs of developing countries including India's food subsidy program from challenge under WTO rules for four years.[1104]

A key condition of the Bali "interim solution" was that developing countries must take steps to make sure that the stocks procured under these stockholding schemes do not distort trade, nor affect the food security of others.[1105] The deal also set a 2017 deadline to negotiate a permanent solution to the food security issue, with an interim report due in 2015.[1106] The three issues dealt with in the Bali Agreement are trade facilitation, some agriculture issues including public stockholding for food security measures, and development and least developed country issues.[1107] The Bali Package covers only a small fraction of the Doha Round mandate and leaves the more difficult trade topics for future negotiations.[1108] However, the Bali Package represents the first multilateral trade deal in nearly two decades.[1109]

In the run up to the Bali Ministerial, India and the G33 group of developing countries tabled a demand to amend the Agreement on Agriculture (AoA) to allow for developing countries to use price support to implement public stockholding for food security and domestic food aid.[1110] Simply put, the G33 countries were asking for permission from the WTO, to provide subsidies to poor farmers.[1111] The proposal was to amend the AoA, specifically its domestic support rules. Under the current rules, countries cannot go beyond the set AoA domestic support limits – 5 percent for developed countries and 10 percent for developing countries.[1112]

1103 *Ibid.*

1104 Shedd "Dispute Settlement in the World Trade Organization (WTO): An Overview" 2012 https://www.fas.org/sgp/crs/misc/RS20088.pdf (Accessed on 27/03/16).

1105 Schnepf "Agriculture in the WTO Bali Ministerial Agreement" Congressional Research Service 2014 https://www.fas.org/sgp/crs/misc/R43592.pdf (Accessed on 26/03/16).

1106 *Ibid.*

1107 WTO "Bali Package and November 2014 decisions" 2014 https://www.wto.org/english/thewto_e/minist_e/mc9_e/balipackage_e.htm (Accessed on 26/03/16)

1108 Bridges Africa "Reflections on the Bali Deal" 2014 *International Center for Trade and Sustainable Development*.

1109 Bellmann "The Bali Agreement: Implications for Development and the WTO" 2014 https://poldev.revues.org/1744 (Accessed on 25/03/16).

1110 Haberli "After Bali: WTO Rules Applying to Public Food Reserves" 2014 http://www.fao.org/3/a-i3820e.pdf .

1111 Malig "Big Corporations, the Bali Package and Beyond Deepening TNCs gains from the WTO" 2014 https://www.tni.org/files/download/wto-big_business_bali_0.pdf (Accessed on 26/03/16).

1112 India, for example, which approved the National Food Security Bill in September 2013, to provide subsidized food grains to poor members of its population, an estimated two-thirds of its 1.2 billion population, would definitely

Developed countries however declared the proposal to amend the AoA as "too big an issue for Bali."[1113] Instead, the compromise reached in Bali was a very weak peace clause that has so many loopholes that developing countries are likely to find it very difficult to use.[1114] For example, it has several restrictive conditions on what crops can be included or not included. The decision is seen to apply only to "primary agricultural products that are predominant staples in the traditional diet of a developing Member".[1115] This is problematic as agricultural products related to food security are not all necessarily considered as staple crops.[1116] Then there are the extensive, onerous and intrusive information requirements per crop. Trade observers have pointed to the dangers of India and other developing countries sharing too much information as required by this peace clause that is to say, they are opening balance of stocks, annual purchases value, quantity, purchase prices, release prices, *inter alia* because these are food security sensitive information and can be used against that country in future trade disputes around agriculture.[1117] Furthermore, it does not address the SCM and therefore still provides technical avenues for countries to be sued under the WTO DSM.[1118]

Apart from this, the peace clause states that it only applies "…in pursuance of public stockholding programmes for food security purposes existing as of the date of this Decision" which many have pointed out as highly problematic.[1119] "An important question is whether the decision introduces a "standstill" clause for any expansion of these public programs because the decision applies to programs "existing as of the date of this Decision."[1120] If so, this would have an impact on developing countries who currently do not have such programs.[1121] This future illegality of food

go over the 10 percent limit. Without the amendment, India could be taken to the WTO DSM, for violation of the AoA rules.

1113 Malig "The Return of The WTO: Why the 9th Ministerial and the Bali package threaten the people and the planet" 2013 http://smaa.asia/the-return-of-the-wto/ (Accessed on 26/03/16).

1114 *Ibid.*

1115 *Ibid.*

1116 FAO "Food Security and Trade: An Overview" 2013 http://www.fao.org/docrep/005/y4671e/y4671e05.htm .

1117 Malig "Big Corporations, the Bali Package and Beyond Deepening TNCs gains from the WTO" 2014 https://www.tni.org/files/download/wto-big_business_bali_0.pdf (Accessed on 25/03/16).

1118 *Ibid.*

1119 FAO "Sustainable Agricultural Development for Food Security and Nutrition, Including the Role of Livestock" 2015 http://www.fao.org/fsnforum/cfs-hlpe/Sust-Agr-Dev-Livestock-V0 (Accessed on 25/03/16).

1120 Sharma "Draft deal lays groundwork for future negotiations on exempting food security programs from WTO Disputes" 2013 available at: http://www.iatp.org/blog/201312/draft-deal-lays-groundwork-for-future-negotiations-on-exempting-food-security-programs-f#sthash.PFa44dt2.dpuf (Accessed on 26/03/16).

1121 Sharma "The 9th WTO Ministerial" 2013 http://www.iatp.org/blog/201312/draft-deal-laysgroundwork-for-future-negotiations-on-exempting-foodsecurity-programs-f#sthash.czggyNjL.dpuf (Accessed on 26/03/16).

security programs jeopardizes the right to food and the responsibility of governments to guarantee, through all available means, their peoples' food security.[1122]

Most importantly, in order to use the peace clause, countries need to – notify the WTO that they are breaching the limits of the domestic support rules of the AoA, tantamount to admitting 'guilt'.[1123] It is argued that, all these admissions of guilt will not be good for that Member country after the peace clause time period lapses, as other Member countries will be able to use that against them at a future date.[1124] Furthermore, the peace clause is not a permanent solution and doesn't measure up to the original demands of amending the AoA.[1125] Worse, the promise of a long-term solution is unclear and subject to further negotiations.[1126]

The peace clause also highlights the deep hypocrisy embedded within the WTO.[1127] While India and other developing countries have to beg for permission to provide food subsidies to their poor constituents, "the US and EU, through various loopholes are able to circumvent their 5 percent limit under the AoA and provide billions of dollars in domestic support to their agricultural producers – the US with 130 billion USD in 2010 and the EU with 79 billion Euros in 2009."[1128] Some developing countries argue that they do not need the WTO to decide whether they can guarantee the right to food to their people.[1129] They further argue that the right to food is a universal human right that should not be subject to trade rules.[1130]

1122 FAO "Food Security for Africa: An Urgent Global Challenge" 2012 http://agricultureandfoodsecurity.biomedcentral.com/articles/10.1186/2048-7010-1-2 (Accessed on 28/03/16).

1123 Malig "Big Corporations, the Bali Package and Beyond Deepening TNCs gains from the WTO" 2014 https://www.tni.org/files/download/wto-big_business_bali_0.pdf (Accessed on 28/03/16).

1124 *Ibid.*

1125 *Ibid.*

1126 Malig "The Return of The WTO: Why the 9th Ministerial and the Bali package threaten the people and the planet" 2013 http://smaa.asia/the-return-of-the-wto/ (Accessed on 29/03/16).

1127 Germanos "US/India WTO Agreement: How Corporate Greed Trumps Needs of World's Poor and Hungry" 2014 http://www.commondreams.org/news/2014/11/14/usindia-wto-agreement-how-corporate-greed-trumps-needs-worlds-poor-and-hungry (Accessed on 29/03/16).

1128 Louise. "In Bali, the right to Food Traded Away" 2013 http://m.thejakartapost.com/news/2013/12/16/ in-bali-right-food-traded-away.html.

1129 WTO "A Guide for Officials, Legislators, Civil Society and all Those Interested in International Trade and Global Governance" 2002 https://www.wto.org/english/thewto_e/minist_e/min01_e/wto_matters_e.pdf (Accessed on 27/03/16).

1130 *Ibid.*

5 6 1 Public Stock-holding for Food Security Purposes under the Bali Agreement

Of all the draft ministerial documents tabled at the Bali Ministerial, the proposal on public stock holding proved to be the most difficult to finalize.[1131] The proposal was based on a G-33 proposal raised at the informal meeting of the Special Session of the Committee on Agriculture in 2012.[1132] It called for the provisions on public stockholding for food security purposes already included in the Doha Round draft modalities of 6 December 2008 to be taken up for a formal decision at the ninth ministerial conference in December 2013.[1133]

In the past seven years, agricultural prices have been both high and volatile and while the rise in food prices has affected almost all agricultural products, the price volatility has been confined to mainly grains and some oil seeds that constitute the major food products of concern when discussing food security.[1134] The under-developed nature of agriculture in most developing countries has made the sector vulnerable to price fluctuations with particularly dire consequences on the poor and other vulnerable consumers who devote a high portion of their incomes to the purchase of food.[1135] For many developing countries, therefore, stock adjustments serve as a buffer for both their producers and consumers against the vagaries of price volatility especially in basic food products such as grains.[1136]

In summary although the success of the Bali Ministerial is indeed a step in the right direction, the road ahead may prove to be more tedious than the one behind.[1137] The public stockholding for food security proposal proved to be the most contentious issue at the Bali Ministerial due to the need to ensure that the final decision included language aimed at ensuring that developing countries would

---

[1131] Mukumba "Unpacking the Bali Package A Snapshot of the Bali Ministerial Decisions of the WTO Members"2014 *Centre for International Trade, Economics & Environment* 8-13.

[1132] WTO "Agriculture Negotiators Edge into Substantive Discussion for post-Bali Work Programme" 2014 https://www.wto.org/english/news_e/news14_e/agng_23jul14_e.htm (Accessed on 28/03/16).

[1133] Jafri "India (G-33) Proposal on Food Security: A wrong move can jeopardize India's food security forever" 2013 available at http://focusweb.org/content/india-g-33-proposal-food-security-wrong-move-can-jeopardize-india%E2%80%99s-food-security-forever#sthash.B2ZK0XVw.dpuf (Accessed on 27/03/16)

[1134] Emongor "Food Price Crisis and Food Insecurity In Kenya" 2013 http://elibrary.acbfpact.org/acbf/collect/acbf/index/assoc/HASH01b5.dir/Food%20crisis%20and%20food%20insecurity%20in%20Kenya.pdf (Accessed 27/03/16).

[1135] Mukumba "Unpacking the Bali Package A Snapshot of the Bali Ministerial Decisions of the WTO Members" 2014 *Centre for International Trade, Economics & Environment* 8-13.

[1136] *Ibid.*

[1137] Mukumba 2014 8-10.

be protected by an interim measure up until a permanent solution' was achieved.[1138] Therefore, it can be expected that the content as well as the process of negotiations to arrive at a consensus for the permanent solution 'will most probably be one of the primary issue areas within the post-Bali agenda.[1139]

To arrive at permanent solution, the members are going to have start work on a dynamic methodology for calculating stockholding for security purposes that takes into the consideration the concerns of developing countries regarding both the reference price.[1140] In other words, to reach a consensus on permanent solution by the 11th Ministerial Conference of the WTO Members in 2017, the post-Bali agenda would need to take into consideration not only the revision in baseline prices but also need to look into changing the formula of calculating this subsidy.[1141]

In short, this permanent solution 'cannot be achieved unless there is an agreement to necessary and sufficient changes in the formula of calculation of this subsidy from its present static nature to a dynamic one.[1142] Apart from developing a work programme on the implementation of the Bali agreement on trade facilitation, the non-binding nature of the Bali Ministerial Decisions on export competition in agriculture, cotton and the development and least developed country issues will most probably constitute another major component of the post-Bali agenda.[1143] It is argued that, developing countries have much to benefit from preferential treatment therefore there will most likely be a drive to push for more legally-binding and enforceable commitments.[1144]

5 7 THE FUTURE OF THE DOHA ROUND AND BEYOND: COULD DEVELOPMENT SURVIVE DOHA?

5 7 1 The Need for a Doha Success

Does the Doha Round have a future? Can it be salvaged? If one considers the terrible consequences that its permanent failure would likely bring, in particular to the WTO system itself,

---

[1138] Bellmann "The Bali Agreement: Implications for Development and the WTO" 2014 available at https://poldev.revues.org/1744 (Accessed on 26/03/16).

[1139] *Ibid.*

[1140] Dhar "Prospects of the Bali Ministerial Conference" 2013 http://www.unescap.org/sites/default/files/AWP%20No.%20136.pdf (Accessed on 25/03/16).

[1141] *Ibid.*

[1142] Bellmann "The Bali Agreement: Implications for Development and the WTO" 2014 available at https://poldev.revues.org/1744 (Accessed on 26/03/16).

[1143] See Mukumba 2014 at 8-9.

[1144] *Ibid.*

the better question to ask might be how, not whether, it can be saved. The global trading community simply cannot afford an eventual Doha failure against the recent background of global economic hardship.[1145] As global trade contracted in 2009 for the first time since World War II,[1146] it is submitted that, Doha a failure would further discredit the WTO system and supply sufficient ammunition to politicians leaning toward protectionism.[1147]

It appears that the timing, not the substance, of a deal will be the most decisive factor for any successful conclusion of the framework agreement on modalities, which will guide each member's efforts to articulate its own improved schedule of commitments. Former WTO Director General Pascal Lamy observed that out of twenty topics on the "to-do-list," members' positions on eighteen topics had converged before the 19th topic (the special safeguard mechanism) busted the deal.[1148] The very fact that the negotiation suddenly fell apart after members spent so much time and acquired substantial mileage signifies a lack of political will.[1149] Without recharged political capital, negotiators cannot seal the deal on modalities.[1150]

Yet the current economic landscape tends to render any political initiative for free trade unpalatable. First, the global economic crisis appears to have hardened key players' intractable positions with regards to their wish lists.[1151] For example, the US has continued to push the "sectoral" approach in industrial tariffs reduction, which it spearheaded in the July Ministerial in Geneva.[1152] Pressured by domestic interest groups, such as the National Association of Manufacturers (NAM), the US desired to draw a substantial level of tariff reduction commitments in key sectors, such as chemicals, electronics, and industrial machinery, from major importing

1145 Finger 2009.
1146 See International Monetary Fund "Open Markets Would Support Rebound in Trade" 2010 indicating that trade volume fell by 18 percent, http://www.imf.org/external/pubs/ft/survey/so/2010/SurveyartB.htm . (Accessed on 14/07/15)
1147 Dickinson "The Doha Development Dysfunction: Problems of the WTO Multilateral Trading System" 2013 *The Global Business Law Review Journal.*
1148 World Trade Organization "Day 9: Talks Collapse despite Progress on a List of Issues", July 29, 2008, http://www.wto.org/english/news_e/news08_e/meet08_summary_29july_e.htm (Accessed on 15/07/15).
1149 Castle "After 7 Years, Talks on Trade Collapse" 2008 http://www.nytimes.com/2008/07/30/business/worldbusiness/30trade.html?_r=0 (Accessed on 24/04/15).
1150 *Ibid.*
1151 Yerkey 2008.
1152 *Ibid.*

countries, including China.[1153] China also repeated its previous position, strongly opposing the US approach, that participation in the sectoral liberalization program should be "voluntary."[1154]

Second, every trade deal tends to inevitably accompany certain churning effects and therefore leaves domestic constituencies that will be negatively affected by increased competition from abroad.[1155] Adding this trade-generated dislocation to recession-generated unemployment might be difficult for any government to implement.[1156] Against this backdrop, having acknowledged that "there was no readiness to spend the political capital needed," Lamy cancelled the pre-scheduled ministerial meeting in December 2008 where negotiators were supposed to deliver a breakthrough on modalities.[1157]

Nonetheless, forsaking the Doha Round at this stage is not an option since it would likely broaden the room for protectionism. As discussed above, major governments have competitively responded to some of the consequences of the current economic crisis by simply relying on protectionist measures, such as subsidies.[1158] If left unchecked, this competition may turn into a dreadful trade war, invoking the old spectre of economic balkanization on a global scale.[1159] The conclusion of the Doha Round can effectively deter such proclivity of major members. In fact, the news of a Doha deal will instil a strong sense of hope in the global business community.[1160]

Preconditions for a Successful Round:

To resume the Doha negotiations, it is vital to mobilize necessary political capital both domestically and internationally. Doing so will require monumental leadership from global

---

1153 *Ibid.*
1154 Cho 2009.
1155 Cho 2009.
1156 *Ibid.*
1157 Yerkey Unfortunately, major players, in particular the United States, found it hard to gather the political capital necessary to sell the Doha deal to recession-battered domestic constituencies. See Bridges "US Not Prepared for High-Level Doha Engagement Before Fall" 2009 at 11 http://www.ictsd.org/bridges-news/bridges/news/us-not-prepared-for-high-level-doha-engagement-before-fall-us-official (Accessed on 29/06/15).
1158 See Blustein claiming that the economic downturn discouraged countries from removing trade barriers and subsidies. Also see Evenett "The Global Overview: Has Stabilisation Affected the Landscape of Crisis-Era Protectionism?" observing that the recent sign of stabilization has not ended protectionism in major countries). Available at http://www.globaltradealert.org/sites/default/files/evenett_gta4.pdf (Accessed on 29/06/15).
1159 *Ibid.*
1160 World Trade Organization "Ministers Continue to Attach Highest Priority to the Round's Conclusion" 2009, http://www.wto.org/english/news_e/news09_e/tnc_chair_report_03feb09_e.htm . The point raised is trade with its multiplier effect must be an integral part of the stimulus packages that are being adopted. A successful outcome of the Doha Development Round can therefore be part of the solution to the economic downturn.

leaders. In particular, the United States is uniquely situated to offer such an important public good with a progressive president in office.[1161] As the world's most powerful and affluent country and as the country responsible for engendering the previous global financial crisis, the US should recognize and shoulder its historic responsibility.[1162] As President Obama stated in his inaugural speech, the United States has duties to the world which it "does not grudgingly accept but rather seizes gladly."[1163] Other major trading nations, such as Canada, Japan, and those of the EU should join the United States in a move toward bold trade liberalization. In fact, to these countries trade liberalization means the saving of public money and the repealing of wasteful rent-seeking programs.[1164] They are nothing but a form of domestic economic reform.

It is true that the current economic landscape could complicate any trade deal. For example, the US special interests' reciprocal demands from the Doha Round intensified as the recession worsened.[1165] Yet the Obama administration should be more proactive in exercising political capital and leadership that the exigency of the current financial crisis has called for.[1166] The United States must embrace multilateralism as a critical global public good over myopic parochial interests.[1167] If the US provides constructive leadership and revitalizes the largely dormant Doha Round negotiation, WTO members can soon deliver a genuine breakthrough deal on the

---

[1161] Kindleberger *The World in Depression 1929–1939* 40th ed (1973) at 297–98.

[1162] Cho 2009.

[1163] White House "President Barack Obama, Inaugural Address" transcript available at http://www.whitehouse.gov/blog/inaugural-address/. (Accessed on 27/06/15).

[1164] Cho 2010.

[1165] See Barfield "The Politics and Likely Trade Policies of the Obama Administration: Speech before the Japanese Ministry of Economy, Trade and Industry" 2009 noting how current economic conditions have made parties less willing to negotiate, available at http://www.rieti.go.jp/en/events/bbl/09022601.html (Accessed on 24/07/15) . Palmer, "Business Groups Tell Lamy Need More from Doha" 2009, http://uk.reuters.com/article/idUKTRE52N7KY20090324 (Accessed on 24/07/15) reporting the US Congress' resistance to the idea of resuming the Doha talks from the last year's draft. Also see Stokes, "Rousing Doha from Its Doze" 2009 http://www.europeanvoice.com/ article/imported/rousing-doha-from-its-doze/63918.aspx, observing that US businesses view the summer 2008 package as no longer acceptable.

[1166] See Barfield "What President Obama Can Learn from President Clinton" 2009, available at http://www.american.com/archive/2009/july/what-president-obama-can-learnfrom-president-clinton (Accessed on 13/06/15) arguing that President Obama should abandon his ambivalent trade policy positions by disconnecting himself from anti-trade Democrats in the Congress as President Clinton did.

[1167] Bouët "The Doha Round: A Safety Net in Stormy Weather" 2009, http://www.voxeu.org/index.php?q=node/3564 (Accessed on 14/06/15) arguing that "the WTO is an international public good that acts as an insurance scheme against potential trade wars. Also see Palmer, "U.S. Trade Freeze Could Be Slowly Thawing" 2009 citing Jeffrey Schott who observed that with the U.S. economy improved and its social safety net reinforced, Obama will be in a better position to promote free trade policies.

modalities, given the progress the negotiations have made thus far.[1168] Once WTO members conclude the modalities deal, the rest of the process, including the actual composition of national schedules based on the modalities and the subsequent verification, would be finalized rather expeditiously, potentially within several months.[1169] This means that WTO members can finalize the Doha Round by the end of 2015 or 2016 if all goes well.[1170]

Nonetheless, any attempt to ignore the penultimate deal as well as the whole modalities structure would gravely jeopardize the Doha Round.[1171] Reflecting the increasing impatience from the major US export industries, US Trade Representative Ron Kirk has recently floated the idea of skipping the modalities deal and instead directly conducting bilateral negotiations to generate market-opening concessions.[1172] This idea has gathered little support from other members, especially from developing countries, which fear being forced into a disadvantageous position in a bilateral setting with developed countries.[1173]

Likewise, it seems to be vital that WTO members preserve the original scope of negotiation and defy any unreasonable ambition regarding what the Doha Round talks might achieve. In fact, the main reason why the last deal was so close in July 2008 was that WTO DG Pascal Lamy was able

---

[1168] See Rampton "'Like Waiting for Godot,' WTO Awaits Next US Move", 2009, http://af.reuters.com/article/topNews/idAFJOE54703V20090508?sp=true (Accessed on 13/06/15) discussing halt in progress on talks until United States determines how to proceed. The WTO head Pascal Lamy observes that eighty percent of a Doha Round deal has been secured thus far 2009. Welfare Payments Better than Trade Barriers—WTO Chief, 2009, http://in.reuters.com/article/ economicNews/idINIndia-40092320090604 (Accessed on 13/06/15).

[1169] See Shacinda "WTO's Lamy Says Doha Deal in Sight" 2009 quoting Pascal Lamy who observed that it would take six or eight months to complete the round once WTO members agree on the modalities. Available at http://af.reuters.com/article/topNews/idAFJOE5360JJ20090407?sp=true (Accessed on 27/07/15).

[1170] Bridges "Doha Talks Get New Energy at Cairns Group Meeting" 2009 observing that WTO members seem to have set a new deadline of the end of 2010 for the completion of the Doha Round. Available at http://www.ictsd.org/bridges-news/bridges/issue-archive/doha-talks-get-new-energy-at-cairns-group-meeting (Accessed on 26/07/15). See also Reuters "G8 plus G5 Agree to Conclude Doha in 2010" 2009, WTO chief Pascal Lamy said that a deal could be clinched in 2010 because the mood of the negotiations had improved since the appointment this year of US Trade Representative Ron Kirk and India trade minister Anand Sharma whose countries are seen as key to unlocking a deal. Available at http://blogs.reuters.com/financial-regulatory-forum/2009/07/07/g8-plus-g5-agree-to-conclude-doha-in-2010-draft/ (Accessed on 26/017/15).

[1171] Office of the United States Trade Representative, "The President's Trade Policy Agenda For 2009", 2009 available at http://www.ictsd.org/bridges-news/bridges/issue-archive/doha-talks-get-new-energy-at-cairns-group-meeting (Accessed on 27/07/15).

[1172] Bridges "Kirk's Geneva Visit Signals US Engagement on Doha" 2009 available at http://www.ictsd.org/bridges-news/bridges/news/kirk%E2%80%99s-geneva-visit-signals-us-engagement-on-doha (Accessed on 16/07/15).

[1173] Klapper "New US Trade Chief Finds Few Takers on Doha Plan" 2000 reporting on the vehement opposition to Kirk's proposal to skip the modalities due largely to its potential effect on developing countries. Available at http://www.thestreet.com/story/10500359/1/new-us-trade-chief-finds-few-takers-on-doha-plan.html (Accessed on 27/07/15).

to narrow down the zone of negotiation by excluding potential deal-breakers such as services, rules (antidumping), and geographical indications.[1174] Although these issues have been technically part of the Doha trade talks, they do not belong to essential agendas, such as agricultural trade and industrial tariffs.[1175] Those issues, albeit important to many members, have not fully ripened for a possible deal mainly because members' positions diverge to a great degree and they often cannot agree on basic concepts.[1176] Under these circumstances, to force engagement on these issues may risk yet another collapse or provide recalcitrant negotiators with subterfuges for deal-blocking.[1177] One commentator aptly encapsulated the desirable path of the Doha Round as follows: "It is time to step back and build political support for a limited, scaled-down conclusion to the Doha Round and then plot a course for the long-term survival of the multilateral system and the WTO."[1178]

5 7 2 With or Without Doha: Developing Countries' Own Initiatives

As discussed above, developed countries' leadership, in particular that of the US, is vital in reviving the stalled Doha Round. Given the state of negotiations, the US could not avoid criticisms for the Doha failure both from the developing and other developed countries.[1179] Developed

---

[1174] Cho 2010.

[1175] *Ibid.*

[1176] Indeed, this position does not necessarily restrict the WTO's future agenda. Regarding positions in favor of the expansion of the WTO's agenda, see Subramanian, "A Crisis Calls for a 'Crisis Round" 2009 *Wall Street Journal,* 14 urging the launch of a "Crisis Round" of trade talks at the April 2009 G-20 summit.

[1177] See Cho, "Constitutional Adjudication in the World Trade Organization", observing widely diverging views on zeroing among negotiators. Available at http://www.ssrn.com/link/SIEL-InauguralConference.html. See also Deere, *Use Transparency to Keep Trade Flowing, in Rebuilding Global Trade: Proposals for a Fairer, More Sustainable Future* (2009) 75 proposing not to "call for new items on the WTO's over-loaded agenda. Also see Subramanian, supra proposing to replace the current Doha Round by a new "Crisis Round" which mainly targets new protectionism such as antidumping measures, government procurement, and climate change policies.

[1178] Barfield, "The Doha Endgame and the Future of the WTO", 2009, http://www.voxeu.org/index.php?q=node/2806 (Accessed on 25/07/15). See also Blustein, "G20 Should Be Pragmatic about Protectionism", 2009. Arguing that WTO members "should recast the Doha talks as an emergency anti-protectionism round" and postpone controversial issues http://www.brookings.edu/research/opinions/2009/03/30-protectionism-blustein (Accessed on 26/07/15). Also see Palmer "Remove Environmental Goods Talks from Doha: US Groups" 2009 reporting that US businesses urged the Obama administration to remove the negotiation on environmental goods and services from the current Doha Round negotiation. Available at http://www.reuters.com/article/2009/08/03/us-usa-trade-environment-idUSTRE5725Z520090803 (Accessed on 25/07/15). Miller, "Few Expect Progress on Doha at WTO Talk" 2009 *Wall Street Journal* at 14 quoting Fredrik Erikson from the European Center for International Politics and Economy who observed that for a Doha success "trade ministers could jettison the idea of liberalizing trade in services, such as law firms and banking".

[1179] See Elliot "President Obama Has Failed to Kick-Start World Trade Talks" 2009, citing Gareth Thomas, the British top trade negotiator who criticized President Barack Obama for his failure to galvanize the Doha Round negotiations. Available at http://www.timesonline.co.uk/tol/news/politics/article6939446.ece (Accessed on 27/07/15). Also see Times of India "India Blames US for Delay in Doha Deal" 2009 criticizing the "non-serious" U.S. attitudes to the Doha Round talks in which it failed to appoint trade negotiators for the Round. http://articles.economictimes.indiatimes.com/2009-12-09/news/28476495_1_doha-round-trade-talks-wto (Accessed on 13/07/15).

countries should realize that certain SDT, which the special products exemption and the special safeguard mechanism embody, are necessary for developing countries to cushion the overall liberalization impact on poor countries' subsistence farmers and to address food security concerns.[1180] In fact, these SDT do not significantly affect other countries' gains from the Doha Round.[1181]

At the same time, however, developing countries, including low-income developing countries such as LDCs, should, on their own initiatives, mainstream open trade as their top development strategy and endeavour to integrate themselves into the global market, rather than relying solely on SDT.[1182] "Retreat from openness would unacceptably delay the development transformation that developing countries sorely need."[1183] This awakening may start from a sobering reality check on the genuine effectiveness of pre-existing SDT for developing countries. While a garden variety of development assistance initiatives with different labels, such as SDT and aid for trade, may symbolize the development mandate within the WTO system, in particular under the DDA, their practical value is still questionable.

First of all, the very concept of SDT is incomprehensible.[1184] While it may offer useful rhetoric, it fails to generate any concrete legal rights and obligations among WTO members.[1185] The fact

---

1180 Nash 'How Freer Trade Can Help Feed the Poor", 2005, 34-36, available at http://www.imf.org/external/pubs/ft/fandd/2005/03/pdf/nash.pdf. (Accessed on 25/07/15).

1181 Polaski *Winners and Losers: Impact of the Doha Round on Developing Countries* (2006) submitting only a modest gain for developing countries from a Doha success). Even among developing countries positions on special products tend to diverge between food-exporting countries such as Thailand, Malaysia, and Costa Rica and food-importing countries such as Brazil, China, and India.

1182 See Bhagwati *Two-Edged Sword: Demands of Developing Countries and the Trading System, in Power, Passions, and Purpose: Prospects for North-South Negotiations* 1984, 201–203 describing developing country demands for special and differential treatment as a "two-edged sword," implying that it eventually damages developing countries themselves via the destruction of free trade regime. Anderson "The Cost of Rich and Poor Country Protection to Developing Countries", 2001 http://jae.oxfordjournals.org/content/10/3/227.abstract (Accessed on 27/07/15) finding that around sixty percent of all trade barriers in the global trading system originate from developing countries, not developed countries. United Nations "United Nations Conference on Trade and Development, Bangkok, Thailand" 2000, highlighting the importance of openness and nondiscrimination in light of reducing the opportunities for corruption and arbitrariness. Available at http://unctad.org/en/pages/MeetingsArchive.aspx?meetingid=4288 (Accessed on 25/07/15).

1183 Stiglitz "Two Principles for the Next Round or, How to Bring Developing Countries in From the Cold" 2000 *The World Economy Journal* 437-452.

1184 World Trade Organization, "Aid for Trade at a Glance 2009: Maintaining Momentum" 2009, acknowledging that the scope and definition of aid for trade is not clear. Available at http://www.wto.org/english/res_e/booksp_e/aid4trade09_e.pdf (Accessed on 29/06/15).

1185 *Ibid.*

that even the Doha agenda calls for "more precise, effective and operational" SDT[1186] is testimonial to its innate nebulous nature.[1187] Yet such opacity, which certainly tends to jeopardize its effectiveness, cannot be easily fixed.[1188] Some developing countries desire to convert the current hortatory structure of SDT into a legally binding mechanism.[1189] However, it is unlikely that such a drastic proposal would find supporters among other WTO members, especially developed countries. In fact, this proposal goes beyond the level of SDT: it touches on the very constitutional nature of the WTO system as a whole. The current WTO structure would not permit such a far-reaching redistributive mechanism.

The practical effects of SDT are also controversial. Non-reciprocal (free-riding) concessions from the North to the South may not necessarily be translated into poor countries' effective access to rich countries markets.[1190] Those products subject to reduced MFN tariffs may not match exports of low-income developing countries.[1191] For example, suppose that the US import duties for passenger cars are reduced to zero due to the US negotiations with South Korea in the WTO. Even though Zimbabwe may theoretically benefit from such concession via the MFN principle, it will not practically help Zimbabwe since it does not produce and export any cars to the US.

Furthermore, developing-exporting countries should demystify unilateral preferential tariffs such as the Generalized System of Preferences (GSP) and other regional preferential trade programs.[1192] Empirical studies demonstrate that real preferential value of those programs may be relatively small.[1193] For sub-Saharan African countries, for example, such value is only four percent of their

---

[1186] World Trade Organization "Ministerial Declaration of 14 November 2001" 2002 para.44. https://www.wto.org/english/thewto_e/minist_e/min01_e/mindecl_e.htm (Accessed on 29/06/15).
[1187] *Ibid.*
[1188] World Trade Organization "Ministerial Declaration of 14 November 2001" 2002 para 44. https://www.wto.org/english/thewto_e/minist_e/min01_e/mindecl_e.htm (Accessed on 29/06/15).
[1189] See World Trade Organization, "Proposal for a Framework Agreement on Special and Differential Treatment: Communication from Cuba, Dominican Republic, Honduras, India, Indonesia, Kenya, Malaysia, Pakistan, Sri Lanka, Tanzania, Uganda, and Zimbabwe", 2001 para. 15, proposing that S&D treatment "shall be mandatory and legally binding through the dispute settlement system of the WTO. https://www.wto.org/english/thewto_e/minist_e/min01_e/proposals_e/wt_gc_w442.pdf (Accessed on 30/06/15).
[1190] Page "Special and Differential Treatment of Developing Countries in the World Trade Organization" www.worldfuturecouncil.org/fileadmin/.../40725_Gl_Dev_Stud_2.pdf (Accessed on 22/08/15).
[1191] Thomas *Editor's Introduction to Developing Countries in the WTO Legal System* (2009).
[1192] Regarding an earlier argument in favor of MFN-based trade liberalization over trade preferences see Hudec, *Developing Countries in the GATT Legal System* (1987). From the standpoint of public choice theory, Hudec warned that trade preferences programs were vulnerable to capture and abuse in their arrangement.
[1193] Thomas 2009.

exports to the EU market and 1.5 percent to the US market.[1194] Such shocking statistics may be explained by the facts that (1) many developing country products have low or non-existent tariffs before the application of any preferences, (2) products with high duties are typically excluded from preferences, and (3) uncertainty surrounding preferences often dampen incentives to invest.[1195] Likewise, the US Caribbean Basin Initiative (CBI) strictly limits the import of sugar from Caribbean countries which earn more than a half of their foreign currency income from exporting sugar.[1196] The cost of compliance with those preferential programs, such as the rules of origin, is also quite high.[1197] According to Francois *et al*, these costs may amount to four percent of beneficiary countries' total exports from preference regimes.[1198] Finally, importers, not poor countries' farmers or producers, may reap most of the benefits from those preferential tariffs programs.[1199] In sum, it seems fair to say that the economic benefits of preferential programs have been disappointing in general.[1200]

A mercantilist assumption behind SDT that no reciprocal tariff reduction somehow leads to development, as seen in the argument for the infant industry protection, remains debatable.[1201] Maintaining high tariffs may in fact harm developing countries since it deprives them of potential gains from domestic trade liberalization.[1202] As a matter of fact, this non-reciprocity tends to induce tariff peaks maintained by rich importing countries against the main exports of low-income

---

[1194] See Das *The Doha Round of Multilateral Trade Negotiations: Arduous Issues and Strategic Responses* (2005) 95 observing that the preference programs are rife with "restrictions, product exclusions and administrative rules.

[1195] See Brenton *The Value of Trade Preferences for Africa, in Trade, Doha, and Development: A Window into the Issues* (2006) 223-227.

[1196] Dunoff "Dysfunction, Diversion, and the Debate over Preferences: Do Preferential Trade Policies Work in Developing Countries in the WTO" 2007 Social Science Research Network 51–52. Also see, Oxfam, "Rigged Rules and Double Standards—Trade, Globalization, and the Fight against Poverty" 2002 pointing out the exclusion of sensitive products from liberalization under the US African Growth and Opportunity Act. Available at http://www.iatp.org/files/Rigged_Rules_and_Double_Standards_Trade_Global.htm (Accessed on 27/07/15).

[1197] *Ibid.*

[1198] Francois "Preference Erosion and Multilateral Trade Liberalization" 2005 http://elibrary.worldbank.org/doi/abs/10.1596/1813-9450-3730 (Accessed on 13/07/15).

[1199] See, Olarrega "AGOA and Apparel: Who Captures the Tariff Rent in the Presence of Preferential Market Access?" 2005, World economic Journal 63, explaining that while trade regimes like the AGOA purport to encourage trade and direct investment in LDCs they have the effect of benefiting importing industrialized countries rather than LDCs.

[1200] UN Conference on Trade and Development (UNCTAD), "Trade Preferences for LDCs: An Early Assessment of Benefits and Possible Improvements", 2004. Available on http://unctad.org/en/docs/itcdtsb20038_en.pdf (Accessed on 16/07/15).

[1201] Group of Thirty "Sharing the Gains from Trade: Reviving the Doha Round" 55 (2004). http://www.group30.org/images/PDF/G30_SharingGainsofTrade.pdf (Accessed on 15/06/15).

[1202] See Das 2005 There is also a collective benefit from trade liberalization: developing countries should open their markets among one another to fully achieve "export-market diversification."

developing countries.[1203] Such "reverse SDT," which refers to a number of exemptions from free trade principles that developed countries retain in practice, may outweigh any benefits from SDT.[1204] This is nothing but a "Faustian Bargain"[1205] to developing countries: it is developmentally pernicious because it undermines economic efficiency domestically due to the maintenance of high tariffs and impedes developing countries' market access abroad due to developed countries' lingering tariff barriers to developing countries' main exports.[1206]

Most importantly, lowering tariffs for developing countries' exports is not a panacea to their development. A plethora of the so-called non-tariff barriers (NTBs) or behind-the-border measures can effectively block the access of developing countries' exports even after tariffs are eliminated. For example, both the United States and the EU launched a large number of antidumping investigations against low- and lower-middle-income developing countries from 1995 to 2008: out of the 418 US antidumping investigations, 179 were against low- or lower-middle-income developing countries; out of the 391 EU investigations, 208 were also aimed at such countries.[1207] In a developmentally devastating pattern, these antidumping initiations have concentrated on those products in which low-income developing countries retain comparative advantages vis-à-vis developed countries, such as primary commodities and labour-intensive manufacturing goods.[1208]

Taxing regulatory standards in the areas of environment and food safety that are imposed by rich importing countries also hinder poor countries' effective access to the former's markets. Most low-income developing countries, such as LDCs, simply cannot afford those sophisticated

---

1203 Thomas 2009.

1204 Ouedraogo "Deputy Director-General, World Trade Organization, Closing Remarks at Seminar on Special and Differential Treatment for Developing Countries", 2000 transcript available at http://www.wto.org/english/news_e/pres99_e/pr150_e.htm (Accessed on 15/06/15)

1205 Balassa *New Directions in the World Economy* (1989) 360, quoting Sidney Weintraub, who observed that the developed countries' exclusion of most competitive exports from trade preferences was a price for non-reciprocal maintenance of tariffs retained by developing countries. These figures were derived from antidumping investigations data on individual countries from the WTO website after applying the World Bank's list of low- and lower-middle-income economies. World Trade Organization, Statistics on Antidumping, http://www.wto.org/english/tratop_e/adp_e/adp_e.htm (Accessed on 15/06/15).

1206 *Ibid.*

1207 These figures were derived from antidumping investigations data on individual countries from the WTO website after applying the World Bank's list of low- and lower-middle-income economies. World Trade Organization, Statistics on Antidumping, http://www.wto.org/english/tratop_e/adp_e/adp_e.htm (Accessed on 15/06/15).

1208 *Ibid.*

standards, nor do they have the necessary technology to meet them.[1209] More often than not, some rich countries' prohibitively demanding standards, based on a zero-tolerance policy, unduly harm poor countries' exports. For example, the EU's aflatoxin regulation, which is more austere than a relevant international standard, could reduce African food exports by over sixty percent, while it might save only 1.4 deaths per billion a year.[1210] These structural issues, such as capacity gap, cannot be fully addressed by SDT provisions alone without any serious redistributive measures such as financial aid and technology transfer.

The aforementioned reality check offers a new perspective on the prospects of the Doha Round as a development round. While the Doha Round's developmental potential as it stands under the current proposed package may not be insignificant, at the same time one should not overestimate it. Developing countries, in particular low-income developing countries, such as LDCs, should look beyond Doha's promises.[1211] Departing from the hitherto largely passive, recipient's standpoint, developing countries themselves should take more active and innovative stances toward their development, with or without the DDA.[1212]

First, developing countries may reconsider representing themselves in big groups, such as the G-77 or G-90.[1213] Each developing country's developmental agenda is unique. A more targeted approach country or product-specific in the trade negotiation may prove more effective than a big group approach.[1214] Here, a litigation threat under the WTO dispute settlement mechanism may boost individual developing countries' leverage in the trade negotiations.

[1209] See Wilson *Standards and Global Trade: A Voice for Africa* (2003) providing case-by-base analyses of the struggles Kenya, Mozambique, Nigeria, South Africa, and Uganda have experienced complying with regulatory standards. Available at http://www.unido.org/fileadmin/import/12960_WorldBank_StandardsGlobalTrade_voiceForAfrica.pdf (Accessed on 16/06/15).

[1210] Wilson *Standards, Regulation, and Trade: WTO Rules and Developing Country Concerns, in Development, Trade, and the WTO: A Handbook.* (2002) 428-431. Also see Otsuki "Saving Two in a Billion: A Case Study to Quantify the Trade Effect of European Food Safety Standards on African Exports" http://siteresources.worldbank.org/INTRANETTRADE/Resources/Topics/aflatoxins.pdf (Accessed on 16/06/15).

[1211] See Cho "Beyond Doha's Promises: Administrative Barriers as an Obstruction to Development" 2007 Berkeley Journal of International Law 395, arguing that developing countries' exports are still subject to various non-tariff barriers, such as antidumping measures, rule of origin and regulatory standards, imposed by developed countries even though the Doha Development Agenda fully materializes.

[1212] *Ibid.*

[1213] Rolland "Developing Country Coalitions at the WTO: In Search of Legal Support" *Harvard International Law Journal* at 484-500.

[1214] *Ibid.*

Second, developing countries themselves should boldly embrace market opening[1215] and thus situate themselves in a better position to pressure developed countries to drop chronic protectionism, such as tariff peaks.[1216] In particular, freer South-South trade, which many commentators on international trade have long advocated,[1217] is an essential component for development. The developmental potential of some anecdotal South-South trade attempts, regional or plurilateral, appear to be largely limited in that they remain closed and exclusive.[1218] Possible export decreases due to preference erosion could be compensated by export increases of non-preferential products.[1219] Concomitantly, in what may be called "strategic liberalization,"[1220] a developing country should set its own trade liberalization course, including a case-specific liberalization sequence, modality, and speed,[1221] taking into account its own socio-economic context.[1222] Often, developing countries are compelled to restrict trade due to the lack of adequate adjustment assistance programs as well as certain policy concerns such as food security.[1223] These inevitable restrictions should be regarded not as a mercantilist exemption but rather as a justifiable

---

1215 United Nations "The 2002 U.N. International Conference on Financing for Development" http://www.un.org/esa/ffd/ffdconf/ (Accessed on 17/06/15). The conference featured many speeches highlighting the essential role which open trade can play in achieving development. These speeches were delivered by then World Bank President James Wolfensohn stressing that all trading nations would eventually benefit from more open trade, IMF Managing Director Horst Koehler describing trade as the most import avenue for self-help, and then WTO Director-General Mike Moore pointing out that "poor countries need to grow their way out of poverty and trade can serve as a key engine of that growth. Also see Bridges Weekly Trade News Digest, "Mixed Reaction on Trade in Financing for Development Outcome" http://www.ictsd.org/bridges-news/bridges/news/mixed-reaction-on-trade-in-financing-for-development-outcome (Accessed on 17/06/15).

1216 *Ibid.*

1217 See Bhala "Resurrecting the Doha Round: Devilish Details, Grand Themes, and China Too" 2009 *Texas International Law Journal* 45 agreeing with United States that South-South trade must increase poor countries must lift themselves out of poverty in part by trading more with each other.

1218 See Cho "Breaking the Barrier between Regionalism and Multilateralism: A New Perspective on Trade Regionalism" http://scholarship.kentlaw.iit.edu/cgi/viewcontent.cgi?article=1167&context=fac_schol (Accessed on 17/06/15) observing that South-South regional trading blocks tend to generate only limited development impacts due to the lack of diversity in trade patterns.

1219 Amiti "Will the Doha Round Lead to Preference Erosion?" https://www.imf.org/external/pubs/ft/wp/2006/wp0610.pdf (Accessed on 18/06/15).

1220 Redden *Introduction, in Trade and Poverty Reduction in The Asia-Pacific Region: Case Studies and Lessons from Low-Income Communities* (2009) at 1-19.

1221 *Ibid.*

1222 See McMillan *The Economic Effects of Trade on Poverty Reduction: Perspectives from the Economic Literature in Trade and Poverty Reduction* (2009) 58–59 observing that the effects of trade on developing countries are context-specific and depend on many non-economic variables such as history and geography. This is also true in the area of development aid, such as the Aid for Trade program. See Maintaining Momentum, supra emphasizing the notion of "country owned development.

1223 *Ibid.*

moderation in market opening; this is particularly true as long as rich countries' lavish subsidies continue to distort the global market.[1224]

Finally, developing countries themselves, more than the WTO, should aggressively tap into development agencies, such as the World Bank and the United Nations Conference on Trade and Development (UNCTAD), to receive trade related technical assistance for capacity building.[1225] At the same time, donor governments may work directly with the developing countries' private sector without the intermediation of recipient governments.[1226] Developed countries' manufacturers may then outsource their production to the private sector of developing countries.[1227] For example, in 2003 the Norwegian Agency for Development Cooperation (NORAD), partnered with the Federation of Indian Chambers of Commerce and Industry (FICCI), and invested in a pilot project to train Indian grape growers about a voluntary European agricultural standard (EurepGAP).[1228] Once these grapes, which are harvested in compliance with good practices prescribed by the EurepGAP, are certified, they can gain access to the European market.[1229] Such public-private (state-to-business) technical assistance might be more effective than a public-public (state-to-state) one in that the former could cut red tape and directly benefit producers (exporters) in the developing world.[1230]

5 8 CONCLUSION

The Doha Round, the longest trade round ever, is yet another constitutional moment for the global trading system.[1231] How it ends may determine the way in which WTO members' structure trade relations between each other in the future. At the same time, however, this Round will exhaust

---

[1224] Chimni *Some Reflections on the Idea of Free Trade and Doha Round Trade Negotiations in Developing Countries In the WTO Legal System* (2009) 27–28. Governments of developing countries, such as India, are under severe political pressure against market opening from their subsistent farmers who fear the dumping of highly subsidized crops from rich countries into their markets.

[1225] Panitchpakdi "The WTO, Global Governance and Development, in The WTO and Global Governance: Future Directions" http://archive.unu.edu/unupress/sample-chapters/WTO_and_global_governance_web.pdf (Accessed on 17/06/15).

[1226] *Ibid.*

[1227] *Ibid.*

[1228] EurepGAP What Is EurepGAP, http://www.eurepgap.org/Languages/English/about.html (Accessed on 17/06/15); FICCI Quality Forum, http://www.ficci.com/fqf07/htm/europgap.htm (Accessed on 17/06/15).

[1229] The Financial Express, "European Food Safety Norms Phase II Project Likely by June", http://www.financialexpress.com/news/european-food-safety-norms-phase-ii-project-likely-byjune/70881/. (Accessed on 17/06/15).

[1230] *Ibid.*

[1231] Cho 2009.

neither development challenges nor responses thereto.[1232] It is submitted that for the Doha Round to have any meaning for the future of the WTO, it is imperative that the rhetoric of the negotiation change from a mere commercial bargain controlled by major players to a public good whose institutional success benefits developing countries, which make up more than three quarters of the WTO membership.[1233] The more WTO members subscribe to the rhetoric of commercial bargains, the further they tend to jeopardize the Doha Round itself. Although some members prefer to explore alternative avenues for allegedly equivalent commercial deals, such as RTAs,[1234] they cannot provide the same public good as the Doha Round, let alone address their high costs to the global trading system.[1235]

The lack of US leadership in the Doha Round is evidenced by both its dispassionate engagement in the negotiations[1236] and insistence on the mercantilist balance in concessions. Its trading partners, both developed and developing countries, now criticize in harmony that the United States is the "main stumbling block" to the success of the Round.[1237] US Doha leadership started with the US government's resistance to domestic lobbies from special interest groups, such as big agro-businesses and labour unions.[1238] "Free from the myopic trade policy driven by rent-seekers, the US government can re-establish its Doha goal from sealing a commercially attractive deal to helping secure a public good for the global trading system".[1239]

1232 *Ibid.*

1233 Cho "The Demise of Development in the Doha Round Negotiations" 2010, *Texas International Law Journal*.

1234 See Bridges Weekly Trade News Digest "Time for Parallel and Alternative Paths?" available at http://ictsd.org/i/news/bridges/54391/ (Accessed on 18/06/15) contending that various countries are searching for alternative venues for trade governance.

1235 See Cho "Defragmenting World Trade" http://scholarlycommons.law.northwestern.edu/njilb/vol27/iss1/6/ (Accessed on 18/06/15) arguing that the current proliferation of regional trading blocs risks fragmenting the multilateral trading system. Evenett, observing that costs of Doha failure, such as more trade disputes and trade remedies, are often underestimated. See also Gallagher "Is Development Back In The Doha Round?" http://www.southcentre.int/wp-content/uploads/2013/05/PB18_Is-development-back-in-Doha-round_EN.pdf (Accessed on 18/06/15), contending that North-South RTAs "exploit the asymmetric nature of bargaining power between developed and developing nations, divert trade away from nations with true comparative advantages, and curtail the ability of developing countries to deploy effective policies for development".

1236 See Reuters, "WTO's Lamy Says U.S. Slowing Doha Talks: Report" http://www.reuters.com/article/idUSTRE5A913T20091110 (Accessed on 19/07/15).

1237 See Bridges Weekly Trade News Digest "WTO Ministerial Lifts Hopes for Doha, But Scepticism Lingers" http://www.ictsd.org/bridges-news/bridges/issue-archive/wto-ministerial-lifts-hopes-for-doha-but-scepticism-lingers (Accessed on 19/06/15).

1238 See Buckley *The Changing Face of World Trade and the Greatest Challenge Facing the WTO and the World Today, in The WTO and The Doha Round: The Changing Face of World Trade* (2003) 5 observing that while the WTO should grant poor countries "better and fairer" access to rich countries' agricultural markets to alleviate the world's income inequality, the opposition of farmers from rich countries remains "massive and undiminished".

1239 See Cho 2009.

In terms of a strategic choice, the United States should accept the so-called 'Doha-lite', which largely reflects the current negotiation package (agriculture and NAMA) on the table.[1240] In particular, the United States must refrain from insisting on additional reductions of industrial tariffs from developing economies.[1241] Due to unilateral tariff reductions, these countries now actually apply much lower tariffs than their official bound levels.[1242] The United States argues that developing countries' tariff cut concessions in the Doha Round should be based on these applied levels, not the bound ones.[1243] However, even the mere binding of the applied tariff levels by these developing countries in the Doha Round might be adequate, if not ideal, to seal the Doha Round.

After all, what is vital for the future of the WTO is to maintain the culture of openness among WTO members, not particular numerical levels of tariff cuts which may or may not satisfy certain powerful countries' domestic constituencies.[1244] As they have done in the past, these developing countries will continue to slash their tariffs for their own economic purposes once a Doha success affirms the solemn existence of a credible multilateral trading system.[1245] This is why the United States should break from a narrow focus, defined by rent-seekers, and pursue a truly collective goal—delivering a development-friendly trade round. Concededly, it would be naïve to interpret an international negotiation like the Doha Round by a moral mandate only.[1246] As the late Tip O'Neill famously stated, all politics is local,[1247] and parochialism is often powerful enough to stall and sink international trade deals.[1248] Rightly, those impoverished foreign farmers would not cast a single vote for American politicians. After all, isn't it a democratic virtue to respond faithfully to your own local constituency?

In a nutshell, the accomplishment of the Doha Round alone can never solve all the development problems that the WTO is facing. It is however an important step towards fulfilling the WTO's of

[1240] *Ibid.*
[1241] See Cho 2010.
[1242] See Bhala "Resurrecting the Doha Round: Devilish Details, Grand Themes, and China Too" (2009) *Texas Journal of International Trade Law* 121 agreeing with United States that South-South trade must increase; poor countries must lift themselves out of poverty in part by trading more with each other.
[1243] Hohmann *Agreeing and Implementing the Doha Round of the WTO* (2008) 41-49.
[1244] *Ibid.*
[1245] Rolland "Developing Country Coalitions at the WTO: In Search of Legal Support" *Harvard International Law Journal* at 484-500.
[1246] *Ibid.*
[1247] See O'Neill *All Politics is Local, and Other Rules of the Game* (1994) (stating that politicians must understand and connect to their constituents to be successful).
[1248] *Ibid.*

WTO's sustainable development aims especially amid the previous global economic crisis.[1249] The problem, however, is that "poverty anywhere constitutes a danger to prosperity everywhere."[1250] Although the financial crisis started in the US, it now wreaks havoc on the world's poorest in a highly disproportionate manner.[1251] Poverty is one of the most horrible human agonies, and it never comes alone: it is accompanied by diseases, violence, conflicts, and wars. From the insightful perspective of "comprehensive security" posited by Robert Scalapino,[1252] "tanks and soldiers may be a necessary but insufficient condition for peace and security".[1253] Genuine peace and security derives from global citizens who have a decent amount of food to eat and decent kinds of work to do, which trade can provide. The total financial burden of concessions necessary to help deliver Doha's success would be trivial compared to astronomical military spending to keep the world safe.[1254]

[1249] *Ibid.*

[1250] Constitution of the International Labour Organization, Annex, para. I(c), available at http://www.ilo.org/ilolex/english/constq.htm (Accessed on 19/06/15).

[1251] Cho "The Demise of Development in the Doha Round Negotiations" 2010, *Texas International Law Journal.*

[1252] See Scalapino, "Regionalism in the Pacific: Prospects and Problems for the Pacific Basin," (1988) 174 discussing economic policies as a vital component of national security.

[1253] *Ibid.*

[1254] Cho 2010 54.

CHAPTER 6

Conclusions and Recommendations

6 1 INTRODUCTION

The regulation of subsidies in the World Trade Organisation (WTO) has been a highly sensitive issue. This is mainly due to the fear of compromising food security especially by developed countries. Developing countries have suffered negatively from the subsidy programmes of developed countries who continue to subsidize their agricultural sector. The Agreement on Agriculture (AoA) was adopted to eliminate the illegitimate use of trade-distorting agricultural subsidies and thereby reduce and avoid the negative effects subsidies have on global agricultural trade. However, the AoA has been fashioned in a way that is enabling developed countries to continue high levels of protectionism through subsidization, whilst many developing countries are facing severe and often damaging competition from imports artificially cheapened through subsidies.[1255]

The main objective of the AoA is to establish a fair and market-oriented trading system in agriculture, to increase market access and reduce trade-distorting agricultural subsidies.[1256] However it is argued that the agreement has not met these expectations. It has been described as flawed and highly iniquitous; and that instead of levelling the playing field in international trade in agriculture, it is strengthening the monopoly control of developed countries over global agricultural production and trade.[1257] The agreement is neither balanced nor fair as it is mainly skewed in favour of developed countries' interests.[1258] Its provisions on market access, domestic support and export subsidies basically enhance measures used by developed countries to protect their markets and agricultural sector.[1259]

1255 Martin "The WTO Agriculture Agreement: Features, Effects, Negotiations, and What is at Stake?" www.twn.org. (Accessed on 14/09/14).

1256 See the Preamble of the AoA which states that the "long-term objective as agreed at the Mid-Term Review of the Uruguay Round 'is to establish a fair and market-oriented agricultural trading system and that a reform process should be initiated through the negotiation of commitments on support and protection and through the establishment of strengthened and more operationally effective GATT rules and disciplines' …. Committed to achieving specific binding commitments in each of the following areas: market access; domestic support; export competition; and to reaching an agreement on sanitary and phytosanitary issues".

1257 Glipo "The WTO-AoA: Impact on Farmers and Rural Women in Asia" http://www.glow-boell.de/media/de/txt_rubrik_5/sus_arze_ruralwomen.pdf (Accessed on 29/06/14).

1258 Glipo "An Analysis of the WTO-AoA Review from the Perspective of Rural Women in Asia" 2003 WTO Documents at 3-7.

1259 See Glipo 2003 at 5-8.

The interpretation of provisions of the AoA and its application within the WTO impacts the economies of developing countries whose economies mainly depend on agricultural trade.[1260] This study therefore evaluates whether the AoA is facilitating global agricultural trade from a developing countries standpoint. However, it does not examine all the provisions of the AoA but it focuses on some of the problematic provisions of the agreement. It explores the potential existence of gaps and shortcomings in the regulatory framework and its implementation which could undermine its effectiveness in facilitating global agricultural trade especially for developing countries.

6 2 SUMMARY OF CHAPTERS

Chapter 1 of the study is an introductory chapter which sets out the goals and objectives. Chapter 2 provides a historical and socio-economic background of agricultural subsidies regulation on a global level. It looks into its negotiating history and it also establishes the historical origins of the AoA and of subsidies. Contentious issues that challenged the negotiations are exposed. Most of the justifications of agricultural protectionism had to do with food security.[1261] Hence negotiators of the present agriculture agreement were faced with the task of trying to strike a balance between liberalising the agricultural sector whilst ensuring food security. The chapter also explores the economic impact of agricultural subsidies on global trade. From this analysis it was revealed that the agricultural subsidy programmes of developed countries negatively affect the economies of developing countries.

The chapter further shows that the concept of free trade which underpins the trade liberalization commitments in the AoA works against the development and food security needs of developing countries.[1262] Under free trade theory, countries should produce only the goods which they can produce cheaply or on which they have comparative advantage and import those goods including

---

1260 Wayo "The Uneven Playing Field in International Trade in Developing Countries: A Critical Interjection and Review, 2014 *Journal of Applied Economics and Business Review* at 20-29.

1261 See Fernando "The Cumulative Application of the Agreement on Agriculture and the Subsidies and Countervailing Measures Agreement: An Approach to Agricultural Subsidies Based on its Effects" 2007 *International Law Journal* at 209.

1262 This is despite the commitments under the reform programme which should be made "in an equitable way among all Members, having regard to non-trade concerns, including food security and the need to protect the environment; having regard to the agreement that special and differential treatment for developing countries is an integral element of the negotiations, and taking into account the possible negative effects of the implementation of the reform programme on least-developed and net food-importing developing countries." As indicated in the preamble of the Agreement on Agriculture.

the food crops which they produce domestically, from others who can produce them cheaper and more efficiently.[1263] The implication of this is that developed countries, by virtue of their huge agricultural subsidies end up dumping food products in developing markets.[1264] Thus, developing countries in turn become more dependent on artificially cheapened imports that continue to drain their limited foreign reserves, retard the growth of their agriculture and economies and weaken their capacity to feed their own population in the long-term.[1265]

Chapter 3 of the study focused on the regulatory framework enshrined in the AoA. It examined whether the selected provisions of the AoA had any loopholes which could frustrate efforts to open up global agricultural trade for WTO members and which could be susceptible to abuse by protectionists. It was established that some of the provisions of the AoA have been manipulated by developed countries who were at the centre of the agriculture negotiations in Uruguay.[1266] The AoA seems to have been crafted to safeguard the needs and address the concerns of developed countries.[1267] Even though the AoA aims at providing for substantial progressive reductions in agricultural support and protection as well as correcting and preventing restrictions and distortions in world agricultural markets, developing countries are still experiencing a massive influx of subsidized exports and also continue to lose their share of global agricultural markets.[1268]

Chapter 4 focused on some of the cases which dealt with the selected provisions of the AoA. In that chapter the interpretations adopted by the WTO Panels and the Appellate Body were analysed in an effort to highlight the loopholes in the regulatory framework and to determine whether the

---

1263 Amadeo "Comparative Advantage" http://useconomy.about.com/od/glossary/g/comp_adv.htm (accessed on 18/09/15). David Ricardo's Theory of Comparative Advantage states that that a country that is better at producing a particular good or service will become more successful by focusing and placing much emphasis on that industry. Ricardo developed the comparative advantage theory to curb trade restrictions on wheat that England has imposed. He stressed out that it is more beneficial for England to import lower-cost, higher-quality wheat from countries that had the favourable climate and soil conditions to grow it. England could get more value by exporting products that required skilled labour and machinery, and trading that for the wheat. This theory of comparative advantage became the rationale for free trade agreements.

1264 Suparmoko "The Impact of the WTO Agreement on Agriculture in the Rice Sector" 2002 *WTO Documents*.

1265 Glipo "An Analysis of the WTO AoA Review from the Perspective of Rural Women in Asia" 2003 *WTO Documents* 5-10.

1266 Blandford "Should the Green Box be Modified?" http://www.agritrade.org/Publications/DiscussionPapers/Green_Box.pdf (accessed on 21/09/14).

1267 McMahon *Research Handbook on the WTO Agriculture Agreement: New and Emerging Issues in International Agricultural Trade Law* (2012). Also see Stevens "Agriculture in the Doha Round and EPA Negotiations: A Review of the Issues for COMESA/SADC" 2004 https://www.ids.ac.uk/files/CSAgriculture_EPANegotiations.pdf (Accessed on 02/11/15) at 1-12.

1268 *Ibid.*

interpretations adopted by the Panels and the Appellate Body are in line with the aims of the AoA and the developmental needs of developing countries. It further assesses whether the Panels and Appellate Body interpretations are opening up global trade especially for developing countries. The chapter therefore analyses the Panels and the Appellate Body's application of the AoA. It reveals the interpretations of the Agreement that favour developing countries' interests and those that undermine their interests.

Chapter 5 mainly deals with what is taking place in the proposed further negotiations. It examines the demands of both developed countries and developing countries and attempts to identify the problems affecting the negotiations. One of the main objectives of the Doha Round is to ensure that the outcome of the negotiations promote the interests of developing countries. The chapter assesses whether the interests of developing countries are being taken into consideration in the Doha Round and if there is a possibility of these interests being effectively accommodated in the eventual outcomes.

6 3 CONCLUSIONS

There is no doubt that the AoA could regulate the position of developing countries in global agricultural trade. What remains questionable is the suitability of the agreement in opening up global agricultural trade for developing countries and in turn facilitate their economic development. Developing countries need a legal framework that will reduce trade distorting subsidies and take into account their technical and resource constraints in meeting food security requirements. There is also need for developed countries to open up their markets for developing countries' exports and reduce agricultural subsidies. The agreement has to be crafted and interpreted in a manner which allows for the accommodation of developmental interests. It is submitted in this study that although the agreement puts effort into catering for developmental interests, gaps and cracks still exist thus undermining these efforts.

The problems in the regulatory framework of the AoA stem from the historical and socio-economic background of agricultural subsidies regulation on a global level. Apart from this, the AoA has loopholes/gaps. For example the agreement does not clearly provide enforcement mechanisms against member countries that continue to use trade distorting subsidies. The expiry of the Peace

Clause has also left a gap that is causing problems in global agricultural trade.[1269] The agreement provides for continuation of the reform process but the reform process has been stalled thus causing more harm. Developed countries continue to subsidize their agricultural sector at the expense of developing countries. The main problems can be classified into four. These are: the exclusion of developing countries from the negotiating process; manipulation of green box measures by developed countries; failure of the Dispute Settlement Body (DSB) and the Panels to accommodate the developmental needs of developing countries; and a lack of commitment by WTO members to complete the Doha Round agricultural negotiations.

6 3 1 Exclusion of Developing Countries from the Negotiating Process

A logical tracing of the history of the regulation of subsidies clearly depicts the political sensitivity of the area. The agriculture negotiations were dominated by the developed countries and developing countries were to some extent side-lined.[1270] The US and the EU dominate the agricultural product markets, hence their contributions to the formulation of the AoA during the Uruguay Round was fiercely respected.[1271] This obviously also had to do with their political prowess.[1272] The AoA was therefore fashioned in a way that would protect the interests of the developed world.[1273] This included continuing protection of agricultural product markets by developed countries whilst the developing countries were opening their markets.[1274]

[1269] Article 13 of the AoA termed the Peace Clause stated that "agricultural subsidies committed under the agreement cannot be challenged under other WTO agreements, in particular the Subsidies Agreement and GATT". This provision expired at the end of 2003. Basically Article 13 holds that domestic support measures and export subsidies of a WTO member that are legal under the provisions of the Agreement on Agriculture cannot be challenged by other WTO members on grounds of being illegal under the provisions of another WTO agreement. Since the Peace Clause expired, it is now possible, therefore, for developing countries and nations favouring free trade in agricultural goods, such as the Cairns Group, to use the WTO dispute settlement mechanism in order to challenge, in particular, US and EU export subsidies on agricultural products.

[1270] See Kwa "The WTO and Developing Countries: a Foreign policy in Focus Brief on WTO" http://focusweb.org/node/62 (accessed on 04-11-14). Also see Deardorff "What Should the Developing Countries Do in the Context of the Current Impasse of the Doha Round?" http://www.fordschool.umich.edu/rsie/workingpapers/wp.html (Accessed on 15-10-14).

[1271] Matthews "The Agricultural Negotiations in the Uruguay Round and the Developing Countries" 1988. http://www.trocaire.org/sites/trocaire/files/resources/policy/1988-agriculture-developing-countries-uruguay-round.pdf . (Accessed on 29/07/14).

[1272] Khor "The WTO's Doha Negotiations and Impasse: A Development Perspective" 2006.

[1273] Khor 2006 3-7. Also see WTO "The History and the Future of the World Trade Organization" 2013 *WTO Documents* generally.

[1274] *Ibid.*

6 3 2 Manipulation of Green Box measures by Developed Countries

Most of the provisions of the AoA are lenient towards the needs of developed countries at the expense of developing countries.[1275] The green box provisions which are specifically designed to regulate payments that are considered trade neutral or minimally trade distorting has grossly been manipulated by developed countries at the mercy of the AoA.[1276] It is argued that the current green box criterion allows members to enact policies that have a significant trade distorting effect.[1277] It is difficult for green box definitions to allow for the development of a full range of legitimate domestic programmes without payments being counted against domestic support limits.[1278] The green box provisions do not take into account the difficulties which developing countries are facing in providing direct payments, and underplay the desirability of payments coupled with production and price support in the context of rural development.[1279] It is not a secret that the green box measures are mostly used by developed countries, probably because of their massive financial prowess.[1280] Their widespread use by developed countries provide these countries with a massive competitive edge, even if the direct output effects are difficult to determine.[1281]

Developed countries continue to provide trade distorting subsidies under the guise of green box support.[1282] This defeats the aims and objectives of the AoA. The intended objective of the green box measures is to allow and regulate domestic support measures which have no or minimal trade distorting effects, nor positive effects on production. The output effects of these measures are difficult to determine and some argue that most of the green box measures have a positive effect on production which if true, places them in the amber category.[1283] It is therefore submitted that the green box provisions are another means of delivering income support to farmers under the

---

[1275] Khor 2006 3-7. Also see WTO "The History and the Future of the World Trade Organization" 2013 *WTO Documents* generally.
[1276] Matthews "Decoupling and the Green Box: International Dimensions of the Reinstrumentation of Agricultural Support" 2006 http://www.researchgate.net/publication/228699618_ (Accessed on 14/07/15).
[1277] *Ibid.*
[1278] Blandford "Should the Green Box be Modified?" 2007. http://www.agritrade.org/Publications/DiscussionPapers/Green_Box.pdf (accessed on 21/10/14).
[1279] Meléndez-Ortiz *Agricultural Subsidies in the WTO Green Box: Ensuring Coherence with Sustainable Development Goals*, (2009) 561-562.
[1280] *Ibid.*
[1281] Meléndez-Ortiz 2009 3-8.
[1282] Blandford "Should the Green Box be Modified?" 2007. http://www.agritrade.org/Publications/DiscussionPapers/Green_Box.pdf (accessed on 21/10/14).
[1283] See Galperín "Green box subsidies and trade-distorting support: is there a cumulative impact?" www.ictsd.org/downloads/2008/12/galperin-and-doporto.doc (Accessed on 24/09/15).

shield of the AoA. It is further submitted that the veil should be lifted where trade distorting support is being given under the guise of green box support. The WTO should review the provisions pertaining to green box measures in order to lessen the effects of these loopholes.

Several developing countries have already called for review of the green box measures. However, these efforts have faced stiff opposition from countries like US and the EU member states, who happen to be the main users of the green box subsidies which are questionable.[1284] This shows the hypocrisy of both the EU and the US. They were at the forefront of negotiating the AoA, which according to them would reduce trade distorting subsidies.[1285] Apart from the green box measures which have been used as an umbrella to shield developed countries against the disciplines of the AoA, some developed countries even continue to provide support that fall within the amber box category.[1286] However, perpetrators of these subsidies are quick to defend themselves with the green box provisions. Hence there have been a shift from the amber box to the green box and some amber box subsidies are being provided under the cover of the green box.[1287]

6 3 3 Failure of the Dispute Settlement Body and the WTO Panels to accommodate the developmental needs of developing countries

The interpretations adopted by the WTO dispute settlement forums have not met the expectations of developing countries. Of importance to developing countries are the *Cotton* decisions which have provided considerable clarity to the underhand world of WTO agricultural subsidy disciplines.[1288] As the first decisions under the relatively vague and general actionable subsidy rules of the SCM Agreement, the decisions offer the analytical and evidentiary tools for government trade officials and their counsel to assess the extent of the negative trade impact of various forms of subsidies [1289] In the case of domestic cotton subsidies, that impact is enormous at United States dollars (USD) 2.9 billion in worldwide price suppressing effects on cotton each

---

[1284] Josling "Biofuel Subsidies and the Green Box" www.ictsd.org/downloads/2008/12/josling-and-blandford.doc. (Accessed on 06/10/14).

[1285] See Mathews 2006 3-8.

[1286] Blandford "Should the Green Box be Modified?" 2007. http://www.agritrade.org/Publications/DiscussionPapers/Green_Box.pdf (accessed on 21/10/14).

[1287] *Ibid.*

[1288] Scott "Brazil's WTO Challenge to U.S. Cotton Subsidies: The Road to Effective Disciplines of Agricultural Subsidies" 2010 *Business Law Brief* at 3-8.

[1289] *Ibid.*

year.[1290] The export and local content prohibited subsidy aspects of the decision offer hope in that such highly trade distorting subsidies can be more easily identified and successfully challenged in the future or simply eliminated by WTO Members seeking to avoid a dispute settlement challenge.[1291]

The enormous trade distorting effects quantified by the *Cotton* Arbitration decisions have the additional significant benefit of supporting the Doha Round negotiating efforts by limiting the amount of trade distorting domestic support and entirely eliminating highly trade distorting export subsidies for agricultural products.[1292] These multilateral reform efforts are crucial to ensure long-lasting and comprehensive reform for the most trade distorting forms of agricultural subsidies.[1293] The *Cotton* decisions confirmed and established as a fact the wide-ranging harm inflicted on many developing countries who struggle to compete with their heavily subsidized counterparts in world markets.[1294] Based on these established wide-ranging trade distortions, the WTO Cotton decisions compel and fully support a successfully negotiated result that will alleviate the severe negative impacts of these highly trade-distorting subsidies.[1295]

Cases brought against particular types of domestic support have been sporadic.[1296] With inconclusive debates in the Committee for Agriculture and without the guidance of panel reports, countries were able largely to decide for themselves whether particular policies were consistent with the definitions of the green and blue boxes, and hence not subject to reductions.[1297] So long as countries were way below their limits on domestic support it was not a priority to challenge the notifications themselves. But the massive funding brought in by the 2002 US Farm Act caused a reconsideration of this situation, with the possibility that the limits may have been breached if

---

[1290] Schnepf "Potential Challenges to U.S. Farm Subsidies in the WTO: A Brief Overview" 2006 *Congressional Research Service* 2-7.

[1291] Josling "Unravelling the Cotton Case" 2005.

[1292] Scott 2010 2-8.

[1293] *Ibid.*

[1294] Scott "Brazil's WTO Challenge to U.S. Cotton Subsidies: The Road to Effective Disciplines of Agricultural Subsidies" 2010 Available at https://www.wcl.american.edu/blr/.../AU_BLBFall09_Anderson.pdf (Accessed on 17/10/15).

[1295] See Josling 2005 6-9. Also see Scott 2010 for more on this point.

[1296] Josling "Production and Export Subsidies in Agriculture: Lessons from GATT and WTO Disputes Involving the US and the EC" 2003 *Transatlantic Economic Disputes* at 15-20. It is submitted that the position remains the same to date possibly because it is difficult to identify when a country exceeds its commitment levels until trade distortions become apparent.

[1297] Josling 2007 5-10.

notifications had not been erroneous.[1298] The statement by the *US Cotton* panel that some of the expenditures that the US had claimed as "green" may have been mislabelled turned this possibility into a contestable proposition.[1299]

The outburst of cases on agricultural subsidies, as notified under the categories used by the AoA, illustrates that the ambiguity in the agriculture rules still exists.[1300] On the one hand, it depicts the enormous harm inflicted on many developing countries who are clearly struggling to compete with heavily subsidized developed country products in global markets.[1301] It appears as if the possibility of a change awaits the conclusion to be reached by members in the Doha Round. However, the prospect exists that the major driver of change in the agricultural policies of developed countries could be the WTO dispute settlement process, and its decisions on the classification of subsidies.[1302] So far, it is apparent that there is controversy over the role of WTO rules when they clash with powerful political interests.[1303] It is submitted that trade in agricultural products might continue to generate vexing issues for the multilateral trade system and its judicial processes until a mutually acceptable agreement is reached in the Doha Round.

6 3 4 Lack of commitment by WTO Members to complete the Doha Agricultural Negotiations

The Doha Round has become the longest trade round ever, mainly due to the selfish interest of member countries which is leading to their failure to reach common ground.[1304] When it ends this may determine the way in which WTO members structure trade relations between each other in the future.[1305] At the same time, however, this Round will exhaust neither development challenges nor responses thereto. For the Doha Round to have any meaning for the future of the WTO, it is imperative that the rhetoric of the negotiation change from a mere commercial bargain controlled

[1298] Josling 2007 5-10.
[1299] See World Trade Organization, *United States—Subsidies on Upland Cotton*, decisions in the Panel and AB reports 2005.
[1300] See Josling 2007. Also see Barton *The Evolution of the Trade Regime: Politics, Law and Economics of the GATT and WTO* (2006) 11-21.
[1301] See Steinberg "When the Peace Ends: The Vulnerability of EC and U.S. Agricultural Subsidies to WTO Legal Challenge" 2003 *Journal of International Economic Law* 2.
[1302] Josling 2007.
[1303] Barton 2006.
[1304] Meléndez-Ortiz *The Future and the WTO: Confronting the Challenges: A Collection of Short Essays* (2012) at 102-110.
[1305] Srinivasan "Doha Round of Multilateral Negotiations and Development" 2005 Available at http://web.stanford.edu/group/siepr/cgi-bin/siepr/?q=system/files/shared/pubs/papers/pdf/SCID252.pdf (Accessed on 12/10/15).

by major players to a public good whose institutional success benefits developing countries, which make up more than three quarters of its membership.[1306] The more WTO members subscribe to the rhetoric of commercial bargains, the further they tend to jeopardize the Doha Round itself.[1307] Although some members prefer to explore alternative avenues for allegedly equivalent commercial deals, such as RTAs,[1308] they could not provide the same public good as the Doha Round, let alone their high costs to the global trading system.[1309]

The lack of US leadership in the Doha Round is evidenced by both its dispassionate engagement in the negotiations[1310] and insistence on the mercantilist balance in concessions.[1311] Its trading partners, both developed and developing countries, now criticize in unison that the US is the "main stumbling block" to the success of the Round.[1312] US Doha leadership started with the US government's resistance of domestic lobbies from special interest groups, such as big agro-businesses and labour unions.[1313] "Free from the myopic trade policy driven by rent-seekers, the US government can re-establish its Doha goal from sealing a commercially attractive deal to helping secure a public good for the global trading system".[1314]

1306 Srinivasan "Doha Round of Multilateral Negotiations and Development" 2005 Available at http://web.stanford.edu/group/siepr/cgi-bin/siepr/?q=system/files/shared/pubs/papers/pdf/SCID252.pdf (Accessed on 12/10/15).

1307 *Ibid.* Also see Meléndez-Ortiz 2012 6-12.

1308 See International Centre for Trade and Sustainable Development "Time for Parallel and Alternative Paths?" at 1–2, available at http://ictsd.org/i/news/bridges/54391/ contending that various countries are searching for alternative venues for trade governance.

1309 See generally Cho "Defragmenting World Trade" 2006 Vol 27 *North Western Journal of International Law and Business* 39-40 arguing that the current proliferation of regional trading blocs risks fragmenting the multilateral trading system; also see Evenett "What Can Researchers Learn from the Suspension of the Doha Round Negotiations in 2006?" http://www.vwa.unisg.ch at 12–13 observing that costs of Doha failure, such as more trade disputes and trade remedies, are often underestimated. See also Gallagher "Is Development Back In the Doha Round?" http://www.southcentre.int/wp-content/uploads/2013/05/PB18_Is-development-back-in-Doha-round_EN.pdf at 6 contending that North-South RTAs "exploit the asymmetric nature of bargaining power between developed and developing nations, divert trade away from nations with true comparative advantages, and curtail the ability of developing countries to deploy effective policies for development".

1310 See Reuters "WTO's Lamy Says U.S. Slowing Doha Talks" http://www.reuters.com/article/idUSTRE5A913T20091110 (Accessed on 15/08/15).

1311 Cho "The Demise of Development in the Doha Round Negotiations" 2010 Vol 45 *Texas International Law Journal* at 589-599.

1312 See International Centre for Trade and Sustainable Development "WTO Ministerial Lifts Hopes for Doha, But Skepticism Lingers".

1313 See Buckly "Introduction: The Changing Face of World Trade and the Greatest Challenge Facing the WTO and the World Today in The WTO and the Doha Round: The Changing Face of World Trade" at 5 https://business.highbeam.com/437406/article-1G1-124007204/ross-p-buckley (accessed on 15/09/15) observing that while the WTO should grant poor countries "better and fairer" access to rich countries' agricultural markets to alleviate the world's income inequality, the opposition of farmers from rich countries remains "massive and undiminished".

1314 *Ibid.*

In terms of a strategic choice, the United States should accept the so-called Doha-lite, which largely reflects the current negotiation package (agriculture and NAMA) on the table. In particular, the US may need to reconsider insisting on additional reductions of industrial tariffs from emerging economies (China, India, and Brazil). Due to unilateral tariff reductions, these countries now actually apply much lower tariffs than their official bound levels.[1315] The US argues that developing countries' tariff cut concessions in the Doha Round should be based on these applied levels, not the bound ones.[1316]

However, even the mere binding of the applied tariff levels by these developing countries in the Doha Round might be adequate, if not ideal, to seal the Doha Round.[1317] After all, what is vital for the future of the WTO is to maintain the culture of openness among WTO members, not particular numerical levels of tariff cuts which may or may not satisfy certain powerful countries' domestic constituencies.[1318] As they have done in the past, these developing countries will continue to slash their tariffs for their own economic purposes once a Doha success affirms the solemn existence of a credible multilateral trading system.[1319] This is why the US should break from a narrow focus, defined by rent-seekers, and pursue a truly collective goal delivering a development friendly trade round.[1320] Concededly, it would be naive to interpret an international negotiations like the Doha Round by a moral mandate only. As the late Tip O'Neill[1321] famously stated, "all politics is local and parochialism is often powerful enough to stall and sink international trade deals".[1322]

[1315] See Bhala "Resurrecting the Doha Round: Devilish Details, Grand Themes, and China Too" 2009 Vol 45 *Texas International Law Journal* at 30-45 agreeing with United States that South-South trade must increase; poor countries must lift themselves out of poverty in part by trading more with each other.

[1316] Hohmann "Developmental Aspects of the Doha Round of Negotiations, in Agreeing and Implementing the Doha Round of the WTO" 41-49.

[1317] Cho "The Demise of Development in the Doha Round Negotiations" 2010 Vol 45 *Texas International Law Journal* at 590-598.

[1318] *Ibid.*

[1319] See Rolland "Development at the World Trade Organization" disciplinas.stoa.usp.br/.../Rolland_Development%20at%20the%20World%2 (Accessed on 21/10/15).

[1320] See Cho 2010 590-598.

[1321] See O'neill *All Politics Is Local, and Other Rules of the Game* (1994) at 19-33 stating that politicians must understand and connect to their constituents to be successful.

[1322] *Ibid.*

The problem however, is that "poverty anywhere constitutes a danger to prosperity everywhere."[1323] Although the financial crisis started in the United States, it now wreaks havoc on the world's poorest in a highly disproportionate manner.[1324] Poverty is one of the most horrible agonies, and it never comes alone: it accompanies diseases, violence, conflicts, and wars. From the insightful perspective of "comprehensive security" posited by Robert Scalapino,[1325] "tanks and soldiers may be a necessary but insufficient condition for peace and security".[1326] Genuine peace and security derives from global citizens who have a decent amount of food to eat and decent kinds of work to do, which trade can provide.[1327] The total financial burden of concessions necessary to help deliver Doha's success would be trivial compared to the astronomical military spending required to keep the world safe.[1328] The completion of the Doha Round alone could never solve all the development problems that the WTO is facing. However, it is still an important step to fulfil the WTO's ultimate aims of sustainable development especially amid the current global economic crisis.[1329]

6 4 RECOMMENDATIONS

6 4 1 Introducing proper enforcement mechanisms

The AoA is biased towards the developed countries that were at the centre stage of negotiating its provisions.[1330] It was crafted to address their problems, ensure food security and to avoid potential political instability in their countries.[1331] This appears to have been done at the expense of developing countries that have strongly adhered to the agreement in an attempt to get absorbed

1323 Constitution of the International Labour Organization, Annex, para. I(c) available at http://www.ilo.org/ilolex/english/constq.htm. (Accessed on 19/07/15).
1324 Cho 2010 at 585-599.
1325 See Scalapino "Regionalism in the Pacific: Prospects and Problems for the Pacific Basin" 1988 Vol 26 *Atlantic Community Quarterly –USA* 174 discussing economic policies as a vital component of national security.
1326 *Ibid.*
1327 Cho "The Demise of Development in the Doha Round Negotiations" 2010 *Texas International Law Journal* at 559 to 601.
1328 *Ibid.*
1329 *Ibid.*
1330 Khor "Analysis of the Doha Negotiations and The Functioning of the World Trade Organization" 2010 http://www.southcentre.int/wp-content/uploads/2013/05/RP30_Analysis-of-the-DOHA-negotiations-and-WTO_EN.pdf (Accessed on 13/10/15). Also see Clapp "Developing Countries and the WTO Agriculture Negotiations" https://www.cigionline.org/sites/default/files/Developing%20Countries%20and%20the%20WTO%20Agriculture%20Negotiations.pdf (Accessed on 04/10/15).
1331 Glipo "Agreement on Agriculture and Food Sovereignty Perspectives from Mesoamerica and Asia" https://www.boell.de/sites/default/files/assets/boell.de/images/download_de/internationalepolitik/gip3.pdf (Accessed on 10/08/15)

into the emerging global trade arena.[1332] The flaws in the negotiating process led to a lot of loopholes in the agreement which have disproportionately affected developing countries.[1333] One of the major weaknesses of the agreement is its silence on enforcement measures.[1334] It is apparent that developed countries continue to protect their agricultural sector by providing massive subsidies.[1335] However, while the AoA only prohibits trade distorting subsidies but it does not provide any clear enforcement mechanism.[1336] As a result when the dispute settlement forums make a decision, it becomes difficult to enforce such a decision. It is therefore submitted that there should be proper enforcement mechanisms to restrain countries that continue to provide trade distorting agricultural subsidies.

6 4 2 Pursuing a compromise between the demands of developed and developing countries: Need for a Doha understanding

There is need to seek a common ground between the needs of developing countries and those of developed countries. As it has been noted in the study, developing countries were left out in the previous agricultural negotiations. Many developing countries argue that the AoA is not fair in that it prohibits developing countries from using the same tools that enabled developed countries to pursue their development and food security goals in past decades.[1337] Furthermore developed countries are allowed to retain and even expand their huge agricultural subsidies whilst developing countries are prohibited from increasing their subsidies beyond the *de minimis* level.[1338] With the state of the current Doha negotiations, prospects are high that they will not be allowed to use any export subsidies in the future.[1339]

[1332] Glipo "Agreement on Agriculture and Food Sovereignty Perspectives from Mesoamerica and Asia" https://www.boell.de/sites/default/files/assets/boell.de/images/download_de/internationalepolitik/gip3.pdf (Accessed on 10/08/15).

[1333] *Ibid.*

[1334] Lal Das "Strengthening Developing Countries in the WTO" 2012 *Trade and Development Series* 8.

[1335] See Glipo for more on this.

[1336] Einarsson "The Disagreement on Agriculture" http://www.grain.org/article/entries/309-the-disagreement-on-agriculture (accessed on 04/11/14).

[1337] Arze "An Analysis of the WTO-AoA Review from the Perspective of Rural Women in Asia" 2003 *WTO Documents* 10-25.

[1338] *Ibid.*

[1339] *Ibid.*

Many important provisions in the AoA allow developed countries to evade their trade liberalization obligations thus ensuring that their agriculture remains protected.[1340] Developed countries seek to maintain their present position through the Doha Round whilst developing countries are struggling to fit into the global trading system. It is therefore submitted that developed countries should lay a fair playing ground for developing countries to be able to get into the same position as developed countries. Accordingly, there is need for more Special and Differential Treatment (SDT) provisions in favour of developing countries.

6 4 3 Need to review "Greenbox" Measures

The subsidies employed by developed countries to protect their agriculture, expand their production and gain monopoly control in the international market are accorded more protection by the exemptions introduced in the AoA's subsidy reduction provisions.[1341] The classification of subsidies into trade-distorting, which are subject to reduction discipline and non-trade distorting, which are not (green box), permits the developed countries to shift their existing massive subsidies into acceptable boxes or categories that are exempted from subsidy reduction obligations. The exemptions applying to developing countries are often of not much use, considering the long-running negative economic position of many developing countries.[1342] In the end, it can be argued that with such huge loopholes, the AoA clearly aids to legitimize and strengthen the trade-distorting practices of developed countries.[1343] There is therefore need to revise the green box provisions in the AoA to prevent them from abuse or potential abuse. It is submitted that there should be a complete oversight of all programs that are subsidized under the guise of green box.

6 4 4 Need for dispute settlement mechanisms to embrace the developmental needs of developing countries

In a few cases noted in this study, it was found that the Panel and DSB tend to adopt a strict approach in interpreting the green box and amber box provisions of the AoA. For instance, in the

---

[1340] For instance the Due Restraint Clause under Article 13 protects those subsidies that have been exempted from reduction from being challenged. The Special Safeguard provision, which applies only to those products which have been tariffed have benefited mostly developed countries.

[1341] Glipo "Agreement on Agriculture and Food Sovereignty Perspectives from Mesoamerica and Asia" 2003 Global issue Papers http://www.boell.de/sites/default/files/assets/boell.de/images/download_de/internationalepolitik/gip3.pdf (Accessed on 16-07-14).

[1342] Glipo "The WTO-AoA: Impact on Farmers and Rural Women in Asia" http://www.glow-boell.de/media/de/txt_rubrik_5/sus_arze_ruralwomen.pdf (accessed on 16-07-14).

[1343] *Ibid.*

US Upland Cotton decision, the panel ruled basically on two issues: "whether these subsidies were allowed or prohibited and whether they caused serious prejudice", even if allowed, to Brazil.[1344] It is argued that even if the "greenbox" subsidies are permitted by the AoA, they still have a trade distorting effect and continue to cause prejudice to the economies of developing countries.[1345] It is further submitted that the WTO Dispute Settlement Forums should use a flexible approach *vis a vis* a strict approach when interpreting some of the provisions of the AoA. The WTO Panels and AB should embrace the developmental needs of developing countries when making their decisions.[1346] A strict approach will only worsen the already putrefying state of the WTO agricultural trade legal framework.

[1344] See *United States-Subsidies on Upland Cotton* 2005 Reports of Panel.

[1345] See Mathews US Farm Subsidies and the Expiration of the WTO's Peace Clause. https://www.law.upenn.edu/journals/jil/articles/volume27/issue4/Porterfield27U.Pa.J.Int'lEcon.L.999(2006).pdf (Accessed on 23/09/15).

[1346] Shaffer *et al* "Towards a Development-Supportive Dispute Settlement System in the WTO" http://www.ictsd.org/downloads/2008/06/dsu_2003.pdf (Accessed on 23/09/15). Also see Shaffer "How to Make the WTO Dispute Settlement System Work for Developing Countries: Some Proactive Developing Country Strategies" For an African perspective see Mosoti "Does Africa Need the WTO Dispute Settlement System?"

7 BIBLIOGRAPHY

7 1 BOOKS

Barton *The Evolution of the Trade Regime: Politics, Law and Economics of the GATT and WTO* (2006) Princeton University Press.

Braun Joachim Von and Diaz-Bonilla Eugenio *Globalization of Food and Agriculture and the Poor* (2008) Oxford University Press.

Guzman and Sykes *Research Handbook in International Economic law* (2007) Edward Edgar Publishing Limited, UK.

Sampson and Chambers *Developing Countries and the WTO: Policy Approaches* (2008) United Nations University Press.

Hoekman and Kostecki, *The Political Economy of the World Trading System: The WTO and Beyond* (2001) Oxford University Press, United States.

Josling Timothy Stefan Tangermann TK Warley *Agriculture in the GATT* (1996) Houndmills, London, and New York.

Mandelson, *Doha a Posteriori, in Agreeing And Implementing The Doha Round Of The WTO* (2008) Cambridge University Press.

McMahon J, Desta M, *Research Handbook on the WTO Agriculture Agreement: New and Emerging Issues in International Trade Law*, (2012) Research Handbook on the WTO, Edward Elgar Publishing Ltd.

McMahon *The WTO Agreement on Agriculture: A Commentary*, (2006) Oxford Commentaries on GATT/WTO Agreements, Oxford University Press.

Meléndez-Ortiz Ricardo Christophe Bellmann and Miguel Rodriguez Mendoza *The Future and the WTO: Confronting the Challenges: A Collection of Short Essays* (2012) International Centre for Trade and Sustainable Development Publications (ICTSD).

Peter Van Den Bossche and Werner Zdouc *The Law and Policy of the World Trade Organization: Text, Cases and Materials.* Third Edition (2013) Cambridge University Press.

Thomas J Schoenbaum, *Agricultural Trade Wars: A Threat to the GATT and Global Free Trade, in GATT and Trade Liberalization in Agriculture* (1997) Ashgate Publishing.

Wilson *Standards, Regulation, and Trade: WTO Rules and Developing Country Concerns, in Development, Trade, and the WTO: A Handbook* (2002) World Bank Publications.

7 2 JOURNALS AND SCHOLARLY ARTICLES

Alan Matthews "Developing Countries' Position in WTO Agricultural Trade Negotiations" 2001 *Development Policy Review* 20 (1): 75-90.

Anderson Kym and Martin Will "Agricultural Trade Reform and the Doha Agenda" 2007 *The World Economy,* Vol 28 No9 page 263.

Babu "The Post-Bali Debacle and India's Strategy at the WTO: A Legal and Policy Perspective" 2014 *Indian Institute of Management Calcutta.*

Barichello Rick Timothy Josling and Dan Sumner "Agricultural Trade Disputes Between Canada and the United States: Costly but Diminishing, Commentary" 2007 *CD Howe Institute,* Toronto.

Bhala R "Empathizing with France and Pakistan on Agricultural Subsidy Issues in the Doha Round" 2007 *Vanderbilt Journal of Transnational Law* 40 (4):949-985.

Bhattacharya Least Developed Countries and Trade: Challenges of Implementing the Bali Package 2015 *Studies in Trade and Investment* 83.

Bridges "An ICTSD guide to the proposed Bali package" 2013 *International Centre for Trade and Sustainable Development.*

Bridges "An ICTSD guide to the proposed Bali package" 2013 *International Centre for Trade and Sustainable Development.*

Cardwell M and Rodgers C "Reforming the WTO Legal Order for Agricultural Trade: Issues for European Rural Policy in the Doha Round" 2006 *International & Comparative Law Quarterly* 55(4) 805-838.

Carmen G Gonzalez "Institutionalizing Inequality: The WTO Agreement on Agriculture, Food Security, and Developing Countries" 2002 *Columbia Journal of Environmental Law* Vol. 27 page 433.

Carol S Kramer “The Political Economy of US Agriculture, National Centre for Food and Agricultural Policy” *Resources for the Future* page 210-211.

Carolissen Lee-David *An Analysis of the Impact of the European Union's Policy of Export Subsidies has on South Africa's Agricultural Sector* (LLM Dissertation University of Western Cape South Africa 2007).

Cho “Defragmenting World Trade” 2006 *North Western Journal of International Law and Business* 39-40.

Cho “The Demise of Development in the Doha Round Negotiations” 2010 *Texas International Law Journal*.

Dasgupta “WTO and the Doha Round: An Overview” 2015

Desta M “Food Security and International Trade Law – An Appraisal of the WTO Approach” *Journal of World Trade* 2001 449-468.

Desta M “Legal Issues in International Agricultural Trade: The Evolution of the WTO Agreement on Agriculture from its Uruguay Round Origins to its Post-Hong Kong Directions” 2006 *FAO Legal Papers*.

Devereaux Charan Robert Z Lawrence and Michael D Watkins “Case Studies in US Trade Negotiation, Volume 2: Resolving Disputes” 2006 *Institute for International Economics*.

Diaz-Bonilla Eugenio & Reca Lucio "Trade and Agro-industrialization in Developing Countries: Trends and Policy Impacts," 2000 *Agricultural Economics Blackwell* vol. 23(3), pages 219-229.

Diaz-Bonilla Eugenio & Robinson Sherman & Thomas, Marcelle & Yanoma, Yukitsugu “WTO, agriculture, and developing countries," 2001 TMD discussion papers 81, *International Food Policy Research Institute* (IFPRI).

Dickinson “The Doha Development Dysfunction: Problems of the WTO Multilateral Trading System” 2013 *The Global Business Law Review Journal.*

Dube “Can the Bali Package Resolve the Doha Impasse and Secure the Future of the WTO?” 2014 *South African Institute of International Affairs*.

Dube "Can the Bali Package Resolve the Doha Impasse and Secure the Future of the WTO?" 2014 *South African Institute of International Affairs*.

Erixon "After The Bali Agreement: Lessons from the Doha Round for the WTO's Post-Bali Agenda" 2014 *European Centre for International Political Economy*.

Erixon "After The Bali Agreement: Lessons from the Doha Round for the WTO's Post-Bali Agenda" 2014 *European Centre for International Political Economy*.

Eugenio Diaz-Bonilla & David Orden & Andrzej Kwiecinski "Enabling Environment for Agricultural Growth and Competitiveness: Evaluation, Indicators and Indices," 2014 OECD *Food, Agriculture and Fisheries Papers* 67, OECD Publishing.

Food and Agricultural Organisation "The Bali Package - Implications for Trade and Food Security" 2014 *FAO Trade Policy Briefs*.

Food and Agricultural Organisation "The Bali Package - Implications for Trade and Food Security" 2014 *FAO Trade Policy Briefs*.

Fukunaga "The Road to Bali: Eria Perspectives on the WTO Ministerial and Asian Integration" 2012.

Hudec R E "Does the Agreement on Agriculture Work? Agricultural Disputes after the Uruguay Round." 1997 Paper presented at the Theme Day of the International Agricultural Trade Research Consortium.

Jensen M Jensen M, Lind K, Mortensen R, Zobbe H. Special and Differential Treatment in the WTO Agricultural Negotiations: Analysis and Policy Recommendation. June 2005; 2 (2):87-98.

Josling Timothy "The War on Terroir: Geographical Indications as a Transatlantic Trade Conflict" *Journal of Agricultural Economics*, 2006 Volume 57 Number 3 337-366.

Josling Timothy E and Timothy G Taylor "Banana Wars: The Anatomy of a Trade Dispute" 2003 *Wallingford: CABI Publishing* 169-194.

Josling Timothy, "Unravelling the Cotton Case," 2005 Bridges, April-May.

Josling Timothy, Donna Roberts, and David Orden, "Food Regulation and Trade: Toward a Safe and Open Global System" *Institute for International Economics* 2004.

Josling Timothy, Longyue Zhao, Jeronimo Carcelen and Kaush Arha, "Implications of WTO Litigation for the WTO Agricultural Negotiations" 2006 *IPC Policy Brief Kramer*.

Kanyimbo "Trade Facilitation in the Bali Package: What's in it for Africa?" 2014 *European Centre for International Political Economy*.

Kanyimbo "Trade Facilitation in the Bali Package: What's in it for Africa?" 2014 *European Centre for International Political Economy*.

Konandreas P "Trade Policy Responses to Food Price Volatility in Poor Net Food-Importing Countries" *International Centre for Trade and Sustainable Development* (ICTSD) 2012.

Kwa A "Guide to the Agreement on Agriculture: Technicalities and Trade Tricks Explained Focus on the Global South" 1997.

Lawan "The Bali Package jeopardizes our right to Food Sovereignty WTO is gambling with our future" 2013.

Mukumba "Unpacking the Bali Package A Snapshot of the Bali Ministerial Decisions of the WTO Members" 2014 *Centre for International Trade, Economics & Environment*.

Mukumba "Unpacking the Bali Package A Snapshot of the Bali Ministerial Decisions of the WTO Members" 2014 *Centre for International Trade, Economics & Environment*.

O'Connor Bernard The Law of Geographical Indications, Cameron May, London Steinberg, Richard H. and Timothy E. Josling, 2003. "When the Peace Ends: The Vulnerability of EC and US Agricultural Subsidies to WTO Legal Challenge," *Journal of International Economic Law*, 2004 Vol. 6(2), pp. 369-417.

Philippines "The Bali Package, the Trade Facilitation Agreement and the Post-Bali Work Program" 2014 *Asia Pacific Economic Cooperation*.

Philippines "The Bali Package, the Trade Facilitation Agreement and the Post-Bali Work Program" 2014 *Asia Pacific Economic Cooperation*.

Porteria "WTO on Agriculture: Over a decade of false hopes: Critique of the World Trade Organization's (WTO) Agreement on Agriculture and the 'Bali Package" 2013.

Prema-chndra Athukorala "Agricultural Trade Reforms in the Doha Round: A Developing Country Perspective" 2007 *Journal of World Trade*. 38 (5), pp.877-897.

Schnepf "Agriculture in the WTO Bali Ministerial Agreement" 2014 *Congressional Research Service.*

Schnepf "Agriculture in the WTO Bali Ministerial Agreement" 2014 *Congressional Research Service.*

Schnepf, "Potential Challenges to US Farm Subsidies in the WTO: A Brief Overview" 2006 *Congressional Research Service.*

Scott "Brazil's WTO Challenge to US Cotton Subsidies: The Road to Effective Disciplines of Agricultural Subsidies" 2010 *Business Law Brief.*

Steinberg "When the Peace Ends: The Vulnerability of EC and U.S. Agricultural Subsidies to WTO Legal Challenge," *Journal of International Economic Law,* 2003 Vol. 6(2), pp. 369-417.

Tangermann, Stefan, "Has the Uruguay Round Agreement on Agriculture Worked Well?" 2001 Paper prepared for the Theme Day of the International Agricultural Trade Research Consortium (IATRC), Washington, DC.

World Trade Organization "The Results of the Uruguay Round of Multilateral Trade Negotiations: The Legal Texts" 1995 WTO Geneva.

Young L & Wilmer F "WTO Challenges to Core Country Agricultural Policies" 2006 *A World Systems View Conference Papers International Studies Association.*

7 3 ONLINE RESOURCES/PUBLICATIONS

Allan Matthews "The Agricultural Negotiations in the Uruguay Round and the Developing Countries" Trocaire Development Review. http://www.trocaire.org/sites/trocaire/files/resources/policy/1988-agriculture-developing-countries-uruguay-round.pdf. (Accessed on 27/04/14).

Blandford "Should the Green Box be Modified?" http://www.agritrade.org/Publications/DiscussionPapers/Green_Box.pdf (Accessed on 21/09/14).

Bouët, "The Potential Cost of a Failed Doha Round" 2008, available at http://www.ifpri.org/sites/default/files/publications/ib56.pdf. (Accessed at 09/07/15).

Bridges "Kirk's Geneva Visit Signals US Engagement on Doha" 2009 available at http://www.ictsd.org/bridges-news/bridges/news/kirk%E2%80%99s-geneva-visit-signals-us-engagement-on-doha (Accessed on 16/07/15).

Business Standard "Statsguru: Making sense of the global trade debate in Bali‖" 2013 available at www.business-standard.com/content/general_pdf/120913_03.pdf .

Business Standard "Statsguru: Making sense of the global trade debate in Bali‖" 2013 available at www.business-standard.com/content/general_pdf/120913_03.pdf .

Chakravarthi Raghavan, "Agriculture: Liberalization needs to address socio-economic effects" http://www.twnside.org.sg/title/socio-cn.htm (accessed on 10-05-14).

Chatterjee "Unlocking the Doha Impasse" 2013 Available at www.cuts-citee.org/pdf/Briefing_Paper13Unlocking_the_Doha_Impasse_Imperative_of_a_Balanced_Bali_Package.pdf .

Chatterjee "Unlocking the Doha Impasse" 2013 Available at www.cuts-citee.org/pdf/Briefing_Paper13Unlocking_the_Doha_Impasse_Imperative_of_a_Balanced_Bali_Package.pdf .

Cho A Long and Winding Road: The Doha Round Negotiation in the World Trade Organization Available at http://scholarship.kentlaw.iit.edu/cgi/viewcontent.cgi?article=1161&context=fac_schol (Accessed on 25/06/15).

Clapp, Jennifer "WTO Agriculture Negotiations and the Global South" Available at http://www.yale.edu/envirocenter/clapp_paper.pdf (Accessed on 13/02/15).

Conconi "Special and Differential Treatment of Developing Countries in the WTO" http://www.ecares.org/ecare/personal/conconi$/web/S&D.pdf (Accessed on 13/06/15).

Dale Hathaway and Merlinda Ingco "Agricultural Liberalization and the Uruguay Round, in The Uruguay Round and the Developing Countries" 1 World Bank Paper No 307 http://elibrary.worldbank.org/78881611-3465-4346-A23C-5075449F48F1/FinalDownload/DownloadId-F82C89A4285339E02F5C4871F365B28C/78881611-3465-4346-A23C-5075449F48F1/doi/pdf/10.1596/0-8213-3469-7 (accessed on 27/04/14).

Doug Palmer & Darren Ennis, G-20 Leaders Pledge Quick Action on Doha Deal, 2009, http://www.reuters.com/article/idUSTRE58O5MO20090925. (Accessed on 13/06/15).

Economist "The Doha round...and round...and round" August 2, 2008. http://www.economist.com/node/1184859 (Accessed 9/05/14).

Economist, "The Doha round...and round...and round." August 2, 2008. http://www.economist.com/node/1184859 Accessed May 9, 2014.

FAO "WTO Agreement on Agriculture: The Implementation Experience: Developing Country Case Studies" Available at www.fao.org/docrep/005/y4632e/y4632e00.htm (Accessed on 10-10-14).

Glipo "Agreement on Agriculture and Food Sovereignty Perspectives from Mesoamerica and Asia" 2003 Global issue Papers. http://www.boell.de/sites/default/files/assets/boell.de/images/download_de/internationalepolitik/gip3.pdf (Accessed on 16/07/14).

Glipo "The WTO-AoA: Impact on Farmers and Rural Women in Asia Asia-Pacific Network for Food Sovereignty". http://www.glow-boell.de/media/de/txt_rubrik_5/sus_arze_ruralwomen.pdf (Accessed on 29/06/14).

Hanrahan "Agriculture in the WTO Doha Round: The Framework Agreement and Next Steps" http://nationalaglawcenter.org/wp-content/uploads/assets/crs/RS21905.pdf (accessed on 15/07/15).

Healy "The Implications of the Uruguay Round Agreement on Agriculture for Developing Countries". www.fao.org/docrep/004/w7814e/w7814e00.htm (Accessed on 28/07/14).

IMF/World Bank "Market Access for Developing Country Exports- Selected Issues" Available at www.imf.org/external/np/pdr/ma/2002/eng/092602.pdf (Accessed on 17/03/15).

Ismail "From the Hong Kong WTO Ministerial Conference to the Suspension of the Negotiations. Developing Countries Re-claim the Development Content of the WTO Doha Round" https://www.wto.org/...e/.../ismail_from_hong_kong_to_suspension.doc (Accessed on 19/06/15)

Kakabadse "The Tokyo Round and After" 1981 The World Today 305. http://www.jstor.org/action/showArticleImage?image=images%2Fpages%2Fdtc.65.tif.gif&suffix=40395495 . (Accessed on 27-05-14).

Kleen "So alike and yet so different: A comparison of the Uruguay Round and the Doha Round". http://www.ecipe.org/media/publication_pdfs/so-alike-and-yet-so-different-a-comparison-of-the-uruguay-round-and-the-doha-round.pdf (Accessed on 28-05-14).

Koo "Effects of the Canadian wheat board on the US Wheat Industry" http://www.researchgate.net/publication/23514095_effects_of_the_canadian_wheat_board_on_the_u.s._wheat_industry (Accessed on 15/06/15).

Meléndez-Ortiz "The Future and the WTO: Confronting the Challenges" http://www.ictsd.org/downloads/2012/07/the-future-and-the-wto-confronting-the-challenges.pdf (Accessed on 04-11-14).

Moon, "Is agriculture compatible with free trade? Also see Blandford, Should the Green Box be Modified?" 2007. http://www.agritrade.org/Publications/DiscussionPapers/Green_Box.pdf (Accessed on 21/9/14).

Nash 'How Freer Trade Can Help Feed the Poor", 2005, 34-36, available at http://www.imf.org/external/pubs/ft/fandd/2005/03/pdf/nash.pdf. (Accessed on 25/07/15).

Oxfam International "Rigged Rules: Dumping, from the Make Trade Fair Campaign" 2002. https://www.oxfam.org/en/campaigns (accessed on 15/07/15).

Page "Special and Differential Treatment of Developing Countries in the World Trade Organization" www.worldfuturecouncil.org/fileadmin/.../40725_Gl_Dev_Stud_2.pdf (Accessed on 22/08/15).

Patrick "Protectionism? Tariffs and other Barriers to Trade" http://www.oecd-ilibrary.org/docserver/download/0109121ec005.pdf?expires=1438165083&id=id&accname=guest&checksum=79CB8E1796A8D6BE466B12C1A02FD732 (Accessed on 16/06/15).

Puyana "The Cumulative Application of thee Agreement on Agriculture" http://www.javeriana.edu.co/juridicas/pub_rev/documents/07-JoseFernandoPlataPuyana_000.pdf (accessed on 09/09/14).

Puyana, "The Cumulative Application of thee Agreement on Agriculture" 2008. http://www.javeriana.edu.co/juridicas/pub_rev/documents/07-JoseFernandoPlataPuyana_000.pdf (accessed on 09/09/14).

Sandrey "Agriculture and the World Trade Organization – what happened since 1995?" http://paulroos.co.za/wpcontent/blogs.dir/12/files/2011/uploads/WTO_Book_Ch4_Sandrey_Decade_MBfin_20091116.pdf . (Accessed on 13/09/14).

See Kwa "The WTO and Developing Countries: a Foreign policy in Focus Brief on WTO" http://focusweb.org/node/62 (Accessed on 04-11-14).

See WTO "Agriculture: Agriculture: Explanation, Export competition/subsidies" http://www.wto.org/english/tratop_e/agric_e/ag_intro04_export_e.htm (Accessed on 22/10/14).

See WTO "Agriculture: Explanation of the Agreement on Agriculture". http://www.wto.org/english/tratop_e/agric_e/ag_intro03_domestic_e.htm (accessed on 07/08/14).

Stefan "Is the Concept of the Producer Support Estimate in need of Revision?" http://www.oecd.org%2Fdataoecd%2F6%2F49%2F35091989.pdf&ci=f2DXU6q_CYb17AaMloHYAw&usg=AFQjCNGiCpY0lec5JNgilJojcIZiZTbmrw&sig2=92xsK8gSPWsualPcOkAg-w&bvm=bv.71778758,d.ZWU (Accessed on 04 July 2014).

Team "Studies Green Box Subsidies a Theoretical and Empirical Assessment" WTO Documents 2008.
http://wtocentre.iift.ac.in/DOC/Studies_GreenBoxSubsidiesATheoreticalAndEmpericalAssessmen.pdf (Accessed on 02/08/14).

Terence P Steward "The GATT Uruguay Round: A Negotiating History" http://books.google.co.za/books?id=_zdx2wjwNeAC&lpg=PA183&ots=n5OPA_FVwd&dq=Terence%20P%20Stewart%2C%20The%20GATT%20Uruguay%20Round%3A%20A%20Negotiating%20History&pg=PA183#v=onepage&q&f=true (accessed on 08/05/14).

United Nations Conference on Trade and Development (UNCTD) "Agriculture" http://unctad.org/en/docs/edmmisc232add32_en.pdf (accessed on 15/09/14).

United Nations Conference on Trade and Development (UNCTD): Agriculture, UN 2003 http://unctad.org/en/docs/edmmisc232add32_en.pdf (accessed on 15/09/14).

Williams "Rethinking Agricultural Development: The Caribbean Challenge" http://www.ccmfuwi.org%2Ffiles%2Fpublications%2Fconference%2F1004.pdf&ei=3zDaU6_3HbOv7AbR1ID4Aw&usg=AFQjCNFJsOHkULqZXu7TMiCm0_u0u0B4qA&sig2=bymEg24pAeb1RE2ldUgvA&bvm=bv.72185853,d.ZGU&cad=rjt . (Accessed on 25 June 2013).

Wise "The Paradox of Agricultural Subsidies: Measurement Issues, Agricultural Dumping, and Policy Reform" 2004. http://ase.tufts.edu/gdae/pubs/wp/04-02agsubsidies.pdf. (Accessed on 15-07-14).

World Trade Organization "Day 9: Talks Collapse despite Progress on a List of Issues", July 29, 2008, http://www.wto.org/english/news_e/news08_e/meet08_summary_29july_e.htm (Accessed on 15/07/15).

World Trade Organization Day 9: Talks collapse despite progress on a list of issues, 2008, http://www.wto.org/english/news_e/news08_e/meet08_summary_29july_e.htm (Accessed on 11/06/15).

WTO "Agriculture Negotiations: The issues, and where we are now" https://www.wto.org/english/tratop_e/agric_e/agnegs_bkgrnd_e.doc (Accessed on12/06/15).

WTO "Agriculture: Explanation of Domestic support Measures". http://www.wto.org/english/tratop_e/agric_e/ag_intro03_domestic_e.htm . (Accessed on 23/20/14).

WTO "Agriculture: Explanation of the Agreement on Agriculture". http://www.wto.org/english/tratop_e/agric_e/ag_intro03_domestic_e.htm (accessed on 07/08/14).

WTO "Bali Ministerial Declaration and decisions" 2013 https://mc9.wto.org/draftbali-ministerial-declaration .

WTO "Bali Ministerial Declaration and decisions" 2013 https://mc9.wto.org/draftbali-ministerial-declaration .

WTO "Briefing note: Decisions for least-developed countries" 2013 available at: www.wto.org/english/thewto_e/minist_e/mc9_e/brief_ldc_e.htm .

WTO "Briefing note: Decisions for least-developed countries" 2013 available at: www.wto.org/english/thewto_e/minist_e/mc9_e/brief_ldc_e.htm .

WTO "Participation of developing countries in World Trade: Overview of major trends and underlying factors". http%3A%2F%2Fwww.wto.org%2Fenglish%2Ftratop_e%2Fdevel_e%2Fw15.htm&ei=sZDoU4fbJbKv7AarYHwDQ&usg=AFQjCNE_v0e5TNcoujjBNeai2a51I5oO0g&sig2=dtjZ9sCd68VEUBqrQtnVXw&bvm=bv.72676100,d.ZGU . (Accessed on 08/07/14).

WTO "Public Forum looks at Bali Issues" 2013 available at: www.wto.org/english/news_e/news13_e/pfor_03oct13_e.htm#ws21 .

WTO "Public Forum looks at Bali Issues" 2013 available at: www.wto.org/english/news_e/news13_e/pfor_03oct13_e.htm#ws21 .

WTO "The Doha Declaration Explained: Implementation-Related Issues and Concerns". https://www.wto.org/english/tratop_e/dda_e/dohaexplained_e.htm (accessed on 11/06/15).

WTO Agriculture: Explanation of Domestic support Measures. http://www.wto.org/english/tratop_e/agric_e/ag_intro03_domestic_e.htm (accessed on 23/20/14).

WTO Agriculture: Explanation of the Agreement on Agriculture. http://www.wto.org/english/tratop_e/agric_e/ag_intro03_domestic_e.htm (accessed on 07/08/14).

WTO Goods Schedules: Current Situation of Schedules: Current Situation of Schedules of WTO Members http://www.wto.org/english/tratop_e/schedules_e/goods_schedules_table_e.httm. (Accessed on 10-10-14).

Zepeda "The Impact of The Doha Round on Kenya" 2009 predicting that a Doha success would bring a negligible or small boost to Kenya's GDP. http://carnegieendowment.org/files/impact_doha_kenya.pdf (Accessed on 23/07/15).

7 4 WTO JURISPRUDENCE: PANEL AND APPELLATE BODY REPORTS

World Trade Organization "*European Communities - Regime for the Importation, Sale and Distribution of Bananas*" 1997 Complaint by Guatemala and Honduras, Report of the Panel, WT/DS27/R/GTM, 22 May.

World Trade Organization "European Communities - *Regime for the Importation, Sale and Distribution of Bananas*"1997 Complaint by Mexico, Report of the Panel, WT/DS27/R/MEX, 22 May.

World Trade Organization "*European Communities - Regime for the Importation, Sale and Distribution of Bananas*" 1997 Report of the Appellate Body, WT/DS27/AB/R, 9 September.

World Trade Organization "*European Communities - Regime for the Importation, Sale and Distribution of Bananas*" 1997 Complaint by the United Sates, Report of the Panel, WT/DS27/R/USA.

World Trade Organization "*European Communities - Regime for the Importation, Sale and Distribution of Bananas"* 1997 Complaint by Ecuador, Report of the Panel WT/DS27/R/ECU, 22 May.

World Trade Organization Appellate Body Report, *US - Oil Country Tubular Goods Sunset Review.*

World Trade Organization *Brazil, United States–Domestic Support and Export Credit Guarantees for Agricultural Produc*ts, WT/DS365/1 2007.

World Trade Organization *Canada, United States–Subsidies and Other Domestic Support for Corn and Other Agricultural Products,* WT/DS357/1 2007.

World Trade Organization EC – *Measures Concerning Meat and Meat Products* (Hormones), 1998 WTO/DS26 & 48/AB/R (Feb. 13).

World Trade Organization *European Communities – Export Subsidies on Sugar* 2005 Report of the Appellate Body WT/DS265/AB/R, WT/DS266/AD/R, & WT/DS283/AB/R.

World Trade Organization *European Communities – Measures Affecting the Approval and Marketing of Biotech Products* 2006 Reports of the Panel. WT/DS/291R/292R/293R.

World Trade Organization *United States – Subsidies on Upland Cotton* 2004 Report of the Panel, WT/DS267/R.

World Trade Organization *United States—Subsidies on Upland Cotton*, 2005 Reports of the Appellate Body, WT/DS265/AB/R, WT/DS266/AB/R, & WT/DS267/AB/R.

World Trade Organization, *Canada—Measures Affecting the Importation of Milk and the Exportation of Dairy Products,* 2001 Report of the Appellate Body, WT/DS103&113/AB/RW.

World Trade Organization, Canada—*Measures Affecting the Importation of Milk and the Exportation of Dairy Products,* Report of the Appellate Body, 2001 WT/DS103&113/AB/RW.

World Trade Organization, *European Communities – Export Subsidies on Sugar*, Reports of the Panels 2004 WT/DS265/R, WT/DS266/R, & WT/DS283/R.